BEHIND THE WIRE

JAMES STOUP

Copyright © 2015 James Stoup
All rights reserved
First Edition

PAGE PUBLISHING, INC.
New York, NY

First originally published by Page Publishing, Inc. 2015

ISBN 978-1-68213-108-4 (pbk)
ISBN 978-1-68213-109-1 (digital)

Printed in the United States of America

Dedication

To my dad, who was a medic with the 25th Infantry Division during WWII and who received the Purple Heart for wounds he received while treating his fellow soldiers, you not only sacrificed greatly for your country, but also for your family in everything you have done for us. Your discipline and dedication to family, community, and friends has greatly influenced my life, and you will forever be my role model and hero.

To my mom, whose love for family and friends was unconditional, thank you for your unwavering support of everything I have ever attempted or achieved in my life. And thank you for helping me set the stage for my writing career by encouraging me to take a typing class (along with the algebra class I had to repeat in summer school) after my sophomore year in high school. You are always with me, and I miss you terribly.

Preface

It's been more than fifty years since the United States began a major buildup of its forces in Vietnam. Much has been written about the war in Vietnam, and there have been many documentaries and feature films on the subject. Most of these have focused on the political and military aspects of that war and on the intense combat activity that tragically claimed the lives of over 58,000 Americans, and wounded hundreds of thousands more. But not much about this lengthy war has been portrayed in the popular culture in recent years, other than a few comparisons of its length to the war in Afghanistan. There are many today who know very little (or have forgotten) about the war in Vietnam, the circumstances surrounding it, and how the military was regarded at the time. Few are probably aware that over 2,700,000 men and women served in Vietnam, with many of them being drafted against their will. They know mostly of an all-volunteer military that is today respected and held in the highest regard... and little, if anything, of a military and a war that was reviled.

Even though much has been written about the war in Vietnam, there are still a few stories to be told, and mine is one of them. It's a story about my experiences and perspectives on that war, having spent "a year in the Nam," as it was known by those who served there. It's a story about life in the rear, behind the barbed wire that surrounded all military base camps, rather than life in the field. It's a story that takes place during a period of peak troop strength (nearly 500,000 troops in-country when I arrived) and minimal combat activity. And it's a story about the large "subculture" of antimilitary/antiwar/anti-establishment troops, many of whom were drafted into service, and how they lived and experienced their year in the Nam. Although glimpses of this subculture have been portrayed in the media, very few have focused entirely on this group. And few, if any, have told a complete "arrival to departure" story that depicts the mandated, to the day, one year of service that was unique, not only to this war, but in the entire history of the U.S. military as well.

But this book does just that. It chronicles what I experienced not only as a REMF (rear echelon motherfucker), but also as an army journalist during my yearlong tour of duty in Vietnam. But it's not just my story. It's also a collective story that will be familiar, in many of its aspects, to tens if not hundreds of thousands of troops who served during the Vietnam War. A first draft of my story was completed in 1994, but there seemed to be little interest in Vietnam stories in the roaring '90s. So I let it sit on a shelf until I picked it up again in 2014 and began a rewrite. And now, almost forty years after the end of "the war we lost" (although some military and history revisionists will claim that it was South Vietnam that lost the war, not the United States), I felt it was time for my story to finally be told.

Behind the Wire describes my exploits and experiences as part of a subculture that existed in the army and elsewhere in the military throughout the ten-year period of the Vietnam War. It became dominant, however, in the latter years of the war. There are those in military and political circles who will deny that this subculture existed in Vietnam…or at least will claim that it merely paralleled what was going on in American society at the time (which is true, to an extent, as I briefly point out in the first chapter of the book). But regardless of what is claimed, this subculture, not to mention an entire "lifestyle" that evolved in all ranks of the military as the war in Vietnam progressed, not only existed, but also dramatically impacted the effectiveness of the military and its mission in Vietnam. Just as the protesters back home were changing the country's view of and support for the war, so too were many of the troops in Vietnam protesting the war in their own way. And with the army and war effort in disarray in those latter years, all of this had a definite impact on the face of the war.

BEHIND THE WIRE

Throughout history, there have been many interesting, unique, frightening, and sad stories written about the way we have fought and lived our wars. Untold numbers of stories have been written in the literature and illustrated in the media on this subject. In addition to the myriad of combat stories, many behind-the-scenes stories have also been portrayed—from the unordinary and unorthodox to the humorous and sometimes absurd aspects of our war efforts in the course of our history. Many have been based on facts and actual events while others have been fictional depictions. *Behind the Wire* is another one of these stories—a sometimes hard-to-believe true story that chronicles my actual experiences during my year in the Nam.

CHAPTER 1

How I Got There

Stop the Bombing

I am terrified of bombs,
of cold wet leaves and bamboo splinters
in my feet, of a bullet cracking through
the trees, across the world, killing me –
there is a bullet in my brain,
behind my eyes, so that all I see is pain.

I am in Vietnam
who will console me?

From the six o'clock news,
from the headlines lurking on the street,
between the angry love songs on the radio,
from the frightened hawks
and angry doves I meet
a war I will not fight is killing me –

I am in Vietnam
who will console me?

I am in Vietnam
who will console me?

(Corita Kent, artist [1918–1986], from her
screen print, 1967)

March 23, 2013

As a result of my annual eye exam at the Miami VA, I was prescribed a new pair of glasses. So I made my way to an optical store in Broward County where veterans can pick up their free pair of glasses. While browsing over the (limited for veterans) frame choices, I overheard a conversation another veteran was having with a store employee about his experiences in Vietnam and her experiences as an air force wife living in Okinawa during the war. She was relating a story about how they discovered a dead marine near her apartment on the base one morning and that he had died as a result of a heroin overdose and how drug use was becoming a problem over there at that point in time. The veteran, who it turns out was also a marine, related that drugs had not yet reared its head when he served in Vietnam from 1965 to 1966—other than a little pot smoking early on in the war. Upon hearing this, I blurted out loudly, "I was in Vietnam during the marijuana period," and at that point joined the conversation about the war and drugs and other interesting anecdotes. The veteran's wife, of Southeast Asian descent (I don't think she was Vietnamese), sat quietly in the back of the store listening intently to our stories.

The ex-marine and I began exchanging war stories. I surmised he was a few years younger than me and, by his age, figured he had either been drafted or enlisted around the age of eighteen. But it became readily apparent that our stories were very different. I mentioned that there weren't a lot of battles raging when I was there in 1970–1971 and that I had managed to avoid any combat activity during my tour. He related, on the other hand, how horrible the war was in the early years, and that he had served in I Corps (South Vietnam was divided into four Corps Tactical Zones, from I to IV), with I Corps being the farthest north and the most notorious for vicious battles. He said that unlike the current Afghanistan war where a soldier could get into major trouble for posing with a dead enemy combatant—and certainly for urinating on a corpse—what they got away with was unbelievable. He said there were no rules in those early days and the military at the time was obsessed with "body counts" (body counts were always important throughout the war, as the military used them to justify the need for more troops and material support). He related how his captain wanted proof of the number of enemy killed and that bringing back an ear from each enemy killed wasn't good enough. "Every man has two ears, two hands and two feet," the captain told them. So he instructed them to bring back the penis of every man killed "instead of the more traditional ear." This probably wasn't a common practice, but I didn't doubt that what he was telling was true.

After hearing this, I was not about to tell him any more about my cushy assignments in the south during the 1970–1971 period of the war. I was saved when his wife motioned to him that they had to go, at which point he shook my hand and thanked me for my service. I was stunned. For after hearing a little of what he had experienced and knowing the horrors of the war that many GIs had experienced, I felt somewhat embarrassed about my service by comparison. I reacted by saying, while still holding his hand, "No, thank you for your service."

I had almost the opposite experience during my yearlong tour of duty in Vietnam. My time was spent in the rear rather than on the front lines. It was during the beginning of the troop withdrawal phase of the war (there were nearly 500,000 troops in Vietnam when I first arrived). Rather than being terrible, my year in the Nam was actually exciting, exotic, and often fascinating for a number of reasons. I've seen a lot of movies and documentaries and have read a lot of compelling books and stories about the Vietnam War. But the story I'm about to present shines a somewhat different light on the Vietnam experience. It describes what went on behind the scenes and what happened to the war effort when the military began to lose the support of the nation, and eventually control of itself. It's a story that tens if not hundreds of thousands of men who served in the rear can relate to, as it captures many of their experiences as well.

May 13, 1970

The bus picked us up at the holding barracks at Fort Dix, New Jersey, at 0400 hours, to transport us to McGuire Air Force Base, a short twenty-minute ride away. It was one of those OD green buses with the mesh screens covering the windows—to prevent anyone from escaping, I suppose. We'd packed our duffel bags the night before in preparation for our early departure. We didn't take a lot of stuff, just one additional uniform, our shaving kits, our orders and travel documents, and a few personal items. We'd get outfitted with all our jungle attire when we arrive "in-country."

We filed onto the bus with our bags in hand and took our seats without a word being spoken by anyone. It was a cool late-spring morning, still pitch-black, and the silence was deafening. We were wearing summer khakis with short sleeves, earlier than the official season for this uniform I guess because we were heading to the tropics. So it was chilly and I had goose bumps, and I was shaking a little. As the bus pulled away from the barracks, the driver turned on the heat and my goose bumps disappeared. I still wasn't completely awake at this point, and my thoughts seemed almost dreamlike. Like so many guys who went before me, I couldn't believe it was happening to me. In my wildest dreams, I never thought I'd be going off to war…to Vietnam…halfway around the world.

As the bus pulled up to the passenger terminal at McGuire, we grabbed our bags and stood in the aisle waiting for the door to open. The silence that had accompanied us for the entire ride was finally broken when someone cut a fart, which also cut the tension that had filled the air. We all laughed, and as if someone had turned on a switch, we all started talking and joking, releasing a whole lot of tension that each of us had been holding inside. All of a sudden, I was wide awake and realized that nothing seemed normal, at least not by my previous army training and travel experiences. There was no officer or NCO barking orders at us. The sergeant in charge of our transport was calm and supportive. He knew that most of us were scared shitless, and he also knew the horrors that some of us would be facing and that some of us probably would not be returning alive. You could tell that he wanted this time to be as easy for us as possible.

We shuffled single file through the main doors into a room that was not unlike a small-city airport terminal. We were processed at check-in counters, our bags were tagged and put on a conveyor belt, and we were handed our tickets. After that, we were on our own to find a place to sit or lie down if we could find a spot and wait for our flight to be called. The room was lined with wooden benches, like the kind you'd find at a train station. There were vending machines and a coffee station, but no restaurant or snack bar. It was now close to 0600 hours, and daylight was starting to creep in through the terminal windows.

I was staring into space, lost in a myriad of thoughts and emotions, when I suddenly became aware of the song playing on the PA system. It was Peter, Paul and Mary's "Leaving on a Jet Plane": "Don't know when I'll be back again…" Listening to the song immediately threw me into a state of melancholy, but only for a few seconds, as the sound of music was broken by a loud voice announcing the departure of MAC Flight 717. With that, an NCO barked out orders for us to get off our asses and head single file for the tarmac. The peaceful lull was over, the time had come to face the music rather than listen to it, and my stomach started churning with anxiety.

The plane was a stretch DC-8, retrofitted to carry a maximum number of passengers in a minimum amount of comfort. Upon boarding the plane and looking down the aisle, it seemed like the rows of seats were endless. As soon as we had all taken our seats and were buckled in, the plane taxied toward the main runway. We were on a Seaboard World Airlines charter, one of the many charter and commercial airlines used by the military to ferry GIs to and from Vietnam. It hit full throttle as it turned onto the main runway, thundering loudly, and so loaded with GIs and their gear that it barely cleared the fence at the end of the runway. It nearly scared the shit out of me, and I figured that it was just the first of many scary moments that I was about to experience.

As we reached our cruising altitude, I noticed that an uneasy calm had taken hold over the seemingly endless cabin. I imagined that just about everyone, with the possible exception of the GIs returning for their second or even third tours (repeat tours occurred more often than one would imagine for, unbeknownst to me at this time, a lot of Vietnam duty had become very cushy and rewarding), was thinking the same thing: *Why the hell am I on this airplane?… Am I going to make it back in one piece?…Am I going to die?…* I know I asked myself those questions. Why was I going off to a war that I considered both illegal and immoral and wanted no part of? Why hadn't I gone to Canada or risked going to prison for refusing the draft? A friend, jokingly I think, offered to puncture my eardrum. Another said he knew an antiwar psychiatrist in New York City who would document that I was a homosexual. But these alternatives seemed severe and not very appealing. The truth of the matter is, I just hadn't prepared a good out. Unlike Dick Cheney, I wasn't going to take the graduate school deferment route. And unlike George W. Bush, my dad wasn't connected and couldn't get me into the Reserves or the National Guard. So there I was, jetting off to Southeast Asia. And unbeknownst to me, heading off to the most memorable adventure of my life.

An hour after departing McGuire, we were served our first meal, which actually wasn't bad by military and charter airline standards. We were served by a crew of "mature" female flight attendants (known as stewardesses back then), who were very cordial and professional. Those were the days when commercial airlines had very attractive and young flight attendants, with strictly enforced height and weight requirements. But I guess they didn't want to tempt us with attractive women on this long flight. And alcohol, of course, was out of the question. After the meal, which was accompanied by somewhat lively conversation in the cabin, we all settled back down into a quiet mode as we sped toward our first refueling stop in Anchorage, Alaska. One can only imagine what was going through everyone's mind at this stage of the trip.

The first thing that entered my mind was an experience I had just two short weeks ago. My orders for Vietnam included a thirty-day leave, so I headed home from Fort Benning to psychologically prepare myself for going to war. I spent most of the time with my family and with my girlfriend Paula, who was just about to complete her first year of teaching high school English in Lancaster, Pennsylvania. On my last weekend of leave, Paula and I joined her roommate from college, Marie, on a trip to visit her boyfriend Bobby, who was a student at the University of Maryland in College Park. While walking from his apartment to the campus on Sunday morning, we noticed that the streets were lined for blocks with National Guard troops. They were fully armed and equipped with gas masks. We quickly learned that there was a big antiwar demonstration planned for that morning, so we decided to hang around and watch. Small crowds of students and locals were gathered throughout the campus, seemingly unorganized. But their numbers were growing, and it appeared as if they were waiting for some kind of call to arms. Occasionally, they would taunt the troops with antiwar chants and slogans, but otherwise they were passive.

Before any kind of movement from the students began, the Guard apparently got the signal to move in and the troops started crossing the street and entering the campus grounds. As they approached the clusters of students, they donned their gas masks and started firing tear gas grenades into the crowd. At that point, people started screaming and running in every direction. As we began our own retreat, a tear gas grenade exploded near my feet, and it became readily apparent that we had better get the hell out of there. So we joined the frenzied exodus and made it off campus and to our car without serious incident. Two weeks later, I was on an airplane headed for Vietnam.

1968–1969

Protesting the war—I hadn't done much of that on the small campus in Rensselaer, Indiana, where I attended college from 1965 to 1969. As a political science major, I was well aware of the issues and politics surrounding the Vietnam War. But unlike the larger urban and university campuses where antiwar sentiment started early on, it took a little longer to reach our rural, conservative campus. When I began my studies, Lyndon Johnson was president and much of the country still possessed a "my country right or wrong" mentality. But support for the war was beginning to wane as the credibility of information on the Gulf of Tonkin Incident and other justifications for our involvement began to surface and as more and more men were dying for an increasingly questionable cause. It was now 1967, and our involvement in Vietnam was increasing at an alarming rate, with the draft pulling tens of thousands of young men into the war every month. The national political scene was changing just as rapidly. Eugene McCarthy mounted a campaign to challenge Johnson, which prompted me to get very active in both campus and national politics. I campaigned for "Clean Gene" in both Indiana and Wisconsin, joining the grassroots effort to unseat the president and end the war.

Vietnam. What was happening over there? All I knew was that I was being increasingly surrounded by it—between the growing antiwar sentiment, the tumultuous political process pushing this sentiment, the expanding media coverage of the war, and the draft that was hanging over our heads (if we didn't maintain a C average, we'd lose our student deferments). It was impossible to avoid the Vietnam War.

In the spring of 1968, I was elected to serve as president of the student body at Saint Joseph's College in my senior year. My term in office, representing the student body as a member of the college administration, would be during the amazing academic year of 1968–1969, a time of great political, social, and cultural change in the country. During the summer, I continued to support McCarthy's campaign, but then Bobby Kennedy entered the primaries and I was torn as to who to support, based on their potential electability. Then Kennedy was assassinated, bringing sadness and turmoil into an already volatile electoral process. Before returning to college for my senior year, I attended the Democratic National Convention in Chicago as an "outside the convention hall" observer and witnessed the chaos and bloodshed that ensued. Discouraged by the Hubert Humphrey nomination and fearing a Nixon presidency, I returned to campus a few days after the convention not knowing what my final year at college would be like or what the future would bring.

I was now well into the 1968–1969 school year, and change was sweeping the country (and our campus) in so many ways. And a lot happened that year. Martin Luther King, Jr., was assassinated, and racial politics in the nation and on college campuses became a sister issue to the Vietnam War. I formed the first Black Student Union on campus even though we only had about ten black students, and this didn't sit well in the community (Saint Joe's was located in a very conservative rural community in the northwest corner of Indiana). Lyndon Johnson was replaced by Richard Nixon, and the war effort continued to escalate despite a growing national outcry. And outside of the political arena, social and cultural changes were sweeping the country. In that academic year alone, there was Woodstock; the "summer of love" in San Francisco; the free-love movement and sexual revolution; an increased national focus on marijuana, LSD, and the emerging drug culture; and the Stonewall revolt and the resulting gay revolution. "Sex, drugs, and rock & roll" had become the background palette to the rapidly changing national picture.

I was so distracted with everything that was happening nationally and on campus that I failed to adequately plan what might happen to me after graduation. Oh sure, I thought about everything from law school (even took the LSATs and applied to a couple of schools) to finding a job (doing what I had no idea). But the one thing I hadn't planned on was what to do about the draft should I get a "greetings" from Uncle Sam after graduation. Then I remembered something about the draft that suddenly popped into my head. One of my best friends who graduated in 1968, a fellow political science major who was in some of my classes, gave me an article about the draft and asked me to read it. I had forgotten about that article, but knew I had torn it out of the newspaper and placed it in one of my pol sci textbooks. I looked through my books and found the clipping. It was from the *Chicago Sun Times*, dated Saturday, March 2, 1968:

MOSTLY COLLEGE GRADUATE DRAFTEES SEEN FOR 1969

> *Washington (UPI)—A congressional committee was told Friday that almost all of next year's draftees are likely to be college graduates as a result of an administration decision denying deferments to graduate students.*
>
> *Rep. Frank Thompson Jr. (D-N.J.) said the consequences of that decision and another to continue calling up older men first would be to create "a vast number of college-graduate buck privates."*
>
> *Mrs. Betty Vetter, director of the nonprofit Scientific Manpower Commission, told the special House subcommittee on education that the draft of 240,000 men in the year starting June 1 would come*

almost entirely out of the graduate schools because the end of deferments of graduate students suddenly made 280,000 young men eligible for the draft.

Lt. Gen. Lewis B. Hershey, the Selective Service director, said that it was up to the secretary of defense to change the order so a mixture of 19-year-olds and college graduates could be drafted. "I'm just a broker," Hershey said. "I depend on the call from the secretary of defense."

Two educators—Kingman Brewster, president of Yale University, and Fred H. Harrington, president of the University of Wisconsin—said exposing graduate students to a mass sudden induction would not be in the interests of the nation, the colleges or the students.

Such a possibility arose Feb. 15 when the National Security Council decided to end graduate deferments and retain the oldest-first order of call. "If all are called it would be disastrous and put a heavy burden on colleges at a time when we are expected, in the national interest, to turn out teachers and scientists," Harrington said.

"I would favor abolition of all student deferments, including undergraduates," said Brewster. He said it would at least result in a stable policy, "but under the confusion that exists with the present policy neither schools nor students can count on being able to complete a course once it is started."

My daydreaming was interrupted by a stewardess who asked me if I wanted something to drink. I was on the aisle, and the two guys next to me were sleeping. I ordered a Coke, and she returned with the drink and handed it to me with a knowing smile. I took a couple of sips, then closed my eyes and drifted back to 1968.

My administration instituted a first-ever student-sponsored concert and lecture series that year. Concerts we produced included performances by Bobby Vinton, Gary Puckett and the Union Gap, and Neil Diamond—not bad for a college with only 1,200 students. But my baby was the lecture series, with the first program being a "teach-in" on Vietnam (teach-ins had become a very popular genre on college campuses in those years). Unfortunately, hardly anyone attended the lecture from our mostly apathetic student body. So I decided to crank things up a bit and turned to a "big name" for our next lecture—Abbie Hoffman. Suddenly, we got the attention of not only the student body, but the college administration and the local community as well. For starters, I almost got kicked out of school for not following the college's speaker policy by booking Abbie without getting the necessary approvals. (I intentionally circumvented the policy knowing he would be rejected for being "too controversial.") After threatening to cancel the already-announced appearance by Hoffman, I convinced them to approve the event by telling them that they ran the risk of creating a "riot" on campus if they canceled. They agreed only after I promised to bring in a speaker from "the other side" of the political spectrum for the next lecture. So I booked the national secretary of the John Birch Society for the next event in the lecture series.

As if dealing with the college administration wasn't enough, I was contacted by the FBI shortly after the booking announcement was made. I was "asked" to come to the FBI's state headquarters in Indianapolis for an interview. Two of my fellow student officers accompanied me. They wanted to know why we were bringing Hoffman to our campus and if we believed in his cause and his movement (the Yippies, for Christ's sake). Abbie was out on bail at the time awaiting the "Chicago 7" trial, and he needed FBI permission to travel out of state. I fed them the "academic freedom" line, and they sent us on our way as they had no grounds to deny the event from happening. *Note: In the decades to follow, the government, via freedom of information acts, opened up many FBI files from the Nixon era, including his "enemies list" files on war protestors and social misfits. Even though I never looked into it, I'm sure the FBI had a file on me.* Hoffman flew into Indianapolis a few days later, and a couple of friends and I went to pick him up. On the approximate one-hour drive back to Rensselaer from the airport, we were tailed by the FBI.

We saw men in gray suits and dark glasses positioned on street corners in almost every little town we passed through along the way. It was hilarious.

The lecture came off without a hitch, but what was supposed to have been a speech to Saint Joe students came off as probably the biggest event the local community had ever seen: FBI agents, the state police, local cops, campus security, roadblocks. The campus jocks, adorned in their red blazers, ringed the front of the arena to prevent the attendees from rushing the stage. Originally scheduled to be held in the student dining hall, which was usually ample for the few students that showed up for these lectures, the event was moved to the field house, which was packed with thousands of people. As word and publicity got out that Abbie Hoffman was appearing, people came from cities and university campuses throughout a three-state area, many of them from Chicago.

After ten minutes of the crowd chanting "we love Daley" (almost two-thirds of our student body was from the Chicago area), Abbie appeared onstage, wearing a Chicago Police Department shirt. The crowd went wild. Despite initial jeers and taunts, he somehow managed to quiet the crowd, and what was to follow was truly amazing. He so captivated the audience with his stories, antics, and colorful language that for the rest of the lecture, you could almost hear a pin drop in the arena. At the conclusion of his speech, which centered on what was wrong with America, including a reference to its leaders (including the trustees of our college) as old motherfuckers, he fielded questions from the audience. One question came from a member of the college's Young Republican Club (in those days, the term "young Republican" was considered an oxymoron, and it's amazing how that still rings true almost forty-five years later). He challenged Hoffman's contention that we should withdraw totally and immediately from Vietnam. He said he believed Richard Nixon would end the war honorably. And besides that, what we were doing for the people over there was just and necessary, he continued. So Abbie invited him to go to Vietnam if he felt that way. "And from what I've heard," he quipped, "there's a lot of good grass over there…

You'll like it!" Little did I know how much that statement would ring true for me.

As his speech ended to thunderous applause, we whisked Abbie out a side door and into my buddy Michael's waiting car, along with the quite attractive editor of the Purdue University student newspaper, who had been begging me for days (ever since she learned about his appearance) to go along so she could interview him. She was so charming and persistent—how could I refuse? So with lights flashing, a state police escort led us off campus to the town limits. We drove him to the New Hyde Park section of Chicago and dropped him off at Jerry Rubin's apartment—truly a moment in history that was indicative of those incredible times!

We were now over western Canada and beginning our descent for our first refueling stop in Anchorage. As I sat seemingly glued to my seat, staring straight ahead into the eerie silence that had a hold over the plane's 220 passengers, an Arlo Guthrie song that we sang so often in college protest days kept coming into my head:

> And it's one, two, three
> what are we fighting for?
> Don't ask me I don't give a damn,
> next stop is Viet Nam.
> And it's five, six, seven
> Open up the pearly gates.
> There ain't no time to wonder why,
> Whoopee, we're all gonna die…

And then something really strange happened. As if out of nowhere, the faint sounds of the very song that had been playing in my head began to be heard from the front of the plane. A couple of guys began singing the tune, and gradually, more and more joined in. "And it's one, two, three what are we fighting for…don't ask me I don't give a damn…next stop is Viet Nam…" It blew my mind! Things were already getting surreal, and I hadn't even completed the first leg of the journey.

After a brief refueling and refreshment stop where we gobbled up Eskimo Pies and Eskimo souvenirs, we took off for the long ride across the Pacific, passing over amazing fields of Alaskan glaciers before we disappeared into the clouds. Before long, I settled back into the frozen silence of my uncomfortable surroundings, my thoughts again drifting back to the events that led me to this moment in time. This time, my entire army experience to date flashed before me in full military review.

It was early July 1969, not quite two months since graduation, when I received the anticipated "greetings" from Uncle Sam in the mail and was told to report to 401 North Broad Street in Philadelphia to take the required physical exam. I successfully completed the exam and was declared a perfect physical specimen. At that point, I was reclassified 1A and was told to expect my draft notice within a few weeks. I panicked. I was being drafted and would probably end up in Vietnam. The inevitable that I had thought about and feared for so long was finally here. I had already ruled out graduate school (which was no longer an option, anyway) and the more drastic alternatives of prison, harming myself, or leaving the country. So now what was I going to do. I sought the counsel of others and tried to pursue a rational and logical course of thought and action. "I do have a college degree," I said to myself. "And military service on my résumé would look good in some circles, especially political circles, and especially if I was an officer. Maybe I should enlist and get something out of this." I really wasn't enthusiastic about this course of action, but I pursued it nonetheless.

Right off the bat, I ruled out the air force and the navy, as they were four-year enlistments (as opposed to three years for the army), and they both had long waiting lists for enlistments anyway. The marines weren't even within the realm of consideration although I learned I could have been drafted into that elite corps if they hadn't met their recruiting goals. And forget about the National Guard, the Reserves, and the coast guard—their waiting lists were even longer. So that left the U.S. Army.

I'd like to point out here that a number of our national leaders somehow managed to get into the National Guard and the Reserves despite their long waiting lists, like my contemporary Vice President Dan Quayle, who got into the National Guard at the eleventh hour (thanks, senator from Indiana dad). And President George W. Bush, who "served his country" in the Texas Reserves (thanks, U.S. Congressman from Texas dad). Yet somehow Bush managed to campaign for his father's bid for the presidency in Alabama while supposedly on duty in Texas—an "unsubstantiated" claim made by Dan Rather in a news report during the Bush II campaign that cost him his job at CBS News. Somehow, the documents proving the claim mysteriously disappeared from Reserve files. To this day, it pisses me off that Bush, along with college deferment king Dick Cheney (and other senior members of that administration), avoided the Vietnam War by any means possible. None of these men tasted war, yet they had no problem sending our young men and women into the illegal Iraq War and into the Afghanistan War, which has now surpassed Vietnam as the longest war in this country's history.

So off I went to the army recruiting station in Upper Darby, Pennsylvania. After hearing their pitch about officers candidate school and giving it a few days of consideration, I made the decision to enlist for OCS, which added a third-year commitment to the two years I would have served under the draft. After signing the papers, it was "dream sheet" time, where you could select three choices from the various officer corps for your ultimate commission. One caveat, however. One of the choices had to be in a combat arms—either armor, artillery, or infantry. So I chose the adjutant general's corps (paper pushers), transportation, and armor (always wanted to drive a tank). There were three officer candidate schools at the time: Fort Sill, Oklahoma, which commissioned artillery officers; Fort Benning, Georgia, which commissioned infantry officers; and Fort Belvoir, Virginia, which commissioned all others. Take a guess where I ended up.

We were now somewhere over the great blue ocean, our trajectory arching high as we made our way to our next refueling stop in Okinawa, Japan. I had to use the lavatory, so I unbuckled my seat belt and prepared to make my way to the bathroom. As I stood up, the guy next to me, an eighteen-year-old from Little Rock, opened his eyes and looked up at me. I could sense his uneasiness and see the fear in his eyes.

He gave me a halfhearted smile before closing his eyes again and turning his head toward the window. As I made my way down the aisle, I looked from side to side at my fellow travelers. Most of them were sleeping; a few were reading. Most of the window shades had been pulled down, so the cabin was somewhat dark, with just a few glimmers of light streaming from the bottom of the shades that weren't fully closed. Most of the guys who were awake were staring straight ahead, as if in a trance. Suddenly, I had the feeling of otherworldliness. I felt like I was walking on air rather than on a solid surface. I was floating above a great ocean of tears—an ocean of tears that had been shed by the countless numbers of American and Vietnamese families mourning their dead, tears that didn't wash away the sadness and the tragedy that this war had brought them. I was jolted out of my reverie by an announcement over the PA system from one of the flight attendants that a meal was about to be served. With that, the cabin lights came on and I proceeded to the lavatory.

In late August, I finally got my orders to report for duty; and as luck would have it, my orders called for basic training at Fort Dix, New Jersey, one of the cushiest training bases at the time. I didn't have to report for duty until late September, and it was practically commuting distance from Philadelphia where my family lived (and from Lancaster where my girlfriend lived). During my weeks of training, I got lots of visitors and even made it home twice on weekend passes. The training itself, while not a piece of cake, wasn't as bad as I had imagined. We had beautiful early fall temperatures, unlike the heat, humidity, and mosquitos at Fort Polk, Louisiana (little Vietnam, as it was known), or at lifer land, Fort Benning, Georgia, as I had heard from those who suffered at those bases. No, at Fort Dix, we did things like sneak off the base during compass training to enjoy candy bars at a local convenience store, flash peace signs at passing motorists while on guard duty, and most bizarre of all, guard the field house on weekends during antiwar protests that occasionally took place on the base. I guess they wanted to make sure the hippies didn't break into the facility to take showers or something. Needless to say, I lucked out on this first assignment.

But it wasn't all roses. I was still in a mild state of shock that this recent college graduate was running around a military training base with a bunch of primarily eighteen-year-olds learning how to kill with rifles, bayonets, and other such devices. The threat of Vietnam was now hanging even greater over my head. I hated the war and began feeling guilty for enlisting to be an officer in an organization that I had little respect for. A memory that still stands out in my mind was being in the pine barrens of New Jersey on a map training exercise. We were all sent off alone to find our way to a designated point using only a compass and a topographic map. Of course, I got lost along the way and couldn't figure out where I was going (can you even imagine if I would have to do that for real in Vietnam?), when I came upon a civilian highway on the edge of the base. Cars were streaming by, and there was no fence keeping me in. For a brief moment, the thought actually entered my mind that this would be an opportunity to bolt if I wanted to go AWOL—or even desert. The outside world was right there. It was at that moment that it fully dawned on me that I was no longer a free agent. My freedom had been taken away from me by the draft, and I suddenly related to people who were in prison, stripped of their freedom for a crime they did (or didn't) commit. But here there were no walls, or fences, or barbed wire—just a military entity that controlled my every move. The daydream ended when one of my fellow trainees came down the path, and fortunately he knew where he was going and led me to my destination. Another successful training exercise! At the end of eight weeks, basic training was behind me. So far so good.

During the last week of basic, we received our orders for AIT—advanced individual training. I wasn't quite as anxious this time, as there were so many half-decent possibilities. One's AIT selection usually determined one's MOS (military occupational specialty or job), unless further training in a really specialized area, like language school or OCS, was to follow. But then again, the army in those days still had the reputation for making cooks out of mechanics, and mechanics out of cooks. So who knew? Our orders were read aloud in our final formation before graduation: "Stoup...Fort Leonard Wood, Missouri...combat engineering." Of course, the first word I heard was "combat." I had no idea what a combat engineer did. At first glance, I found it somewhat strange that they were sending a left-brained guy with no science or math aptitude to engineering school. But I quickly learned that combat engineers used heavy equipment for construction of roads and structures, cleared jungle for base camps, blew up things, and built bridges. Not a lot of engineering skill required. What might be good about this assignment, I thought, was that engineering officers were commissioned out of Fort Belvoir, Virginia, as was AG and all other noncombat disciplines. On the downside, Fort Leonard Wood was located high in the Ozark Mountains of Missouri, and all the training took place out of doors—in the middle of winter. But if there was any hope that this meant I might get to Fort Belvoir for OCS rather than Fort Benning for infantry, I'd put up with anything.

The training at Leonard Wood wasn't too bad, and thanks to the companionship of a lot of guys who shared my opinion of the military, we managed to laugh our way through the experience. In fact, laughter—at the situations we all found ourselves in and at the characters the career army seemed to have in such ample supply—really helped us all get by. For example, one day, our training called for us to build a floating Bailey bridge over the Ozark River, which didn't happen because the river was frozen. So we stood around fifty-gallon fire barrels all day "smokin' and jokin'" instead. As for characters, our platoon leader, a staff sergeant with twenty years under his belt, was one of them. He was a pudgy, somewhat pathetic little man, at least from a career military standpoint. But under his attempted gruff platoon sergeant exterior was a really nice man. I could imagine him being a great father to his children.

The best story of the whole eight-week experience was this. One morning, Sarge decided to "march" us to training rather than let us walk there (a remnant of his drill sergeant days, I suppose). The only problem with this was that the company streets were covered with snow and ice. To fully appreciate this story, you have to visualize how they had us dress for training in the dead of winter. To stay warm for outdoor training, we wore two layers of long underwear, double socks, fatigues, jacket liners, coats, hats, gloves, boots, etc. In our OD green (often used) winter uniforms, we all looked like Depression-era children in snowsuits. With all this bulky attire on our bodies, we were barely able to walk, much less march. We lined up in formation outside the barracks, and then Sarge began to march us to training, singing a familiar cadence. Only leather-bottom boots and ice didn't work well together, and we all started falling onto the street, with the guys in the front rows falling back on the guys behind them and so on. This infuriated Sarge, who thought we were doing it on purpose. He yelled at us to get up off our asses and get back in formation. Then he started marching us again—and we kept falling. Now you also have to appreciate how cold it was at 0600 hours and how funny this whole scene had become.

Needless to say, we became hysterical, and the more we laughed the more we cried—with white smoke pouring out of our mouths. And it was so cold that our eyelids froze shut from the tears. Meanwhile, Sarge kept screaming for us to get up and march. Ah, Fort Leonard Wood!

After eight weeks of combat engineering training, and a lot of funny "winter in the Ozarks" experiences, it was time to get our orders. With great anticipation, we all gathered at company headquarters the day our orders were to be read. For the guys not going to OCS, it was D-day—the day they learned if they were staying in the States…going to Germany or Korea…or going to Vietnam. For those of us awaiting orders for OCS, it was which circle of hell we would be banished to. As my name was read, I closed my eyes and crossed my fingers. And then I heard it: "Stoup…Fort Benning, Georgia… Infantry." My heart sank into my stomach. They were sending me to infantry officer candidate school, where after successfully completing the training, I would be commissioned a second lieutenant and sent to Vietnam to lead a platoon of eighteen-year-old grunts to their slaughter. Now what the hell was I going to do?

The cabin lights came on, and the refreshment cart came rolling down the aisle. I wasn't thirsty, but I did have to use the john, so I bolted out of my seat and made my way to the lavatory before I got trapped by the cart. When I returned, I settled in and reclined my seat. I was really tired for some reason, probably because I was mentally spent and the day had been so long. I closed my eyes, and my recollection dreaming of how I got here picked up right where it had left off.

After two not-so-bad army training experiences, I was about to undergo something that Dante certainly would have written about if he had been subjected to it. I'll spare you the training horror stories of abuse and degradation and all the ways that we learned to survive and kill. But if you have seen any of the Vietnam movies (like *Platoon* or *Full Metal Jacket*) or read any number of books on the subject, you get the picture. And in addition to all the bullshit and rigorous training, I also had to deal with being in a constant state of depression, anxiety, and feelings of guilt. It was one thing to be sent to Vietnam as an infantry officer and have to be responsive to the military command and the war. But it was another to be responsible for the lives of young men drafted into the army from the ghetto and the cornfields and the small towns of America. This played heavily on my mind during those early weeks of training. To make what could be a long story short, I resigned from OCS at the earliest possible point that I could, which was eight weeks into the twenty-four-week training program. Of course, the first eight weeks of the program were physically and mentally the toughest. But yes, believe it or not, you could resign from the program—but not without paying a price.

When you're in officer candidate school, you are bumped up to an E-5 pay grade, which is equivalent to a sergeant, and have a certain amount of "respect" compared to the lower enlisted ranks. However, as soon as you leave the program, you are demoted back to E-1, a buck private, and placed in a holding company to await your orders, which usually took about thirty days. So my fellow dropouts and miscellaneous others awaiting orders just hung around our barracks. We played a lot of cards, tried to avoid details, headed to the beaches of the Florida Panhandle on the weekends, and hoped that "luck would be a lady" when it came to our orders. Just a day shy of thirty they arrived. I was being sent to Vietnam as an E-1 private in my AIT MOS—combat engineer.

I awoke from my nightmare not realizing how much time had passed. The guy sitting next to me nudged my arm and told me to look out the window. In the distance was Mount Fuji, with its hauntingly beautiful snow-covered peak reaching high above the clouds. I was transfixed on the majestic image and suddenly realized that I wasn't in Kansas anymore.

We landed at our final refueling stop in Okinawa and had about an hour to see as much as we could see. I spent most of it trying to absorb the fact that I was in Japan, even though we were on an American military base. But as soon as we left Okinawa, the sightseeing was over; and in a little less than three hours, we were making our descent into South Vietnam. As the ground came into view, I noticed a number of large craters pockmarking the landscape—obviously the result of our massive B-52 bombing campaigns.

Our final destination was Bien Hoa Air Force Base, just outside of Saigon. Even though I wasn't a seasoned air traveler in those days, I noticed that our descent and approach pattern seemed a bit erratic. Then I overheard a guy in the row behind us telling his seatmate that the pilot was taking evasive tactics necessary when landing in a combat zone. I didn't know if that was true or just one of the many "war stories" that returning GIs seemed to love telling us turtles (new guys). We even heard that "Freedom Birds" (the name given to the commercial and charter airlines that ferried GIs to and from Vietnam) had been shot down once or twice. In fact, during training, we heard a lot of stories about the Nam.

As we touched down, one of the songs that the drill sergeants used to sing while we were marching popped into my head:

> Viet nam…Viet nam…
> Late at night while you're sleeping
> Charlie Cong comes a creeping
> a-l-o-n-g
> Viet nam

CHAPTER 2

In-Country Orientation

The DC8 touched down onto a very wide and modern runway and then taxied past a number of large structures before stopping in front of what appeared to be the main terminal building. It was May 15, 1970 (we lost a day when we crossed the international date line). One by one, in silence, we got up, grabbed our personal effects, and made our way to the nearest exit. As I neared the aircraft door, I felt the Vietnam atmosphere for the first time as a blast of hot air hit me in the face. Even before I could fully absorb the dramatic change in temperature and humidity, my senses were again assaulted—this time by a distinct odor that permeated the air. It was the mixture of kerosene and waste matter…burning shit…a smell that would become all-too familiar to us during our year in the Nam. For sanitation purposes, waste matter was burned rather than buried, and it was usually the older papa sans who had the chore of cleaning the latrines—except on rare occasion in the field when some poor soldier would pull that detail.

Once inside the terminal building, an orderly sense of military chaos ensued…just like stateside. I was about to be processed "in country," an ordeal that would take the better part of three days to complete. Arriving in South Vietnam at Bien Hoa, rather than Cam Ranh Bay, meant I had a good chance of remaining in the southern part of the country. But I'd have to wait a few days for my orders before I would know where they were going to send me. After our IDs and papers were stamped, they herded us onto OD green buses for the short fifteen-minute ride to the 90th Replacement Battalion at the largest of all Vietnam base camps—Long Bien. The ride on a wide, well-paved highway took us past impressive-looking military installations, as well as through small villages that were crowded one on top of the other. The road was clogged with military traffic, odd-looking Vietnamese vehicles, motor scooters and bicycles, as well as animals and foot traffic—but very few cars. The whole scene reminded me of a Bob Hope road movie.

As we approached the Long Bien base camp, I couldn't believe my eyes. If one needed evidence of the extent of our military and economic investment in Vietnam, it lay before me in one large modern mini city. We passed through the main gate and continued driving on wide, smooth pavement that was bordered on either side with curbs and sidewalks. We drove past swimming pools; officer, NCO, and enlisted men's clubs; and even a Chinese restaurant or two—all interspersed with barracks buildings that looked like apartment complexes. I was totally amazed. The place must have cost hundreds of millions to construct.

Upon arriving at the reception station, we were directed to the processing building where we were given a handful of pamphlets to read and more paperwork to fill out. At this point, we also had to turn in our U.S. currency, which was exchanged for MPC (military paper currency). This was done to prevent greenbacks from getting into the hands of the enemy. It seems there was a huge black market for U.S. dollars in Vietnam—and as it turned out, for MPC as well. MPC was much smaller in size than dollars, and even nickels, dimes, and quarters were issued in paper. The highest denomination was $20. The currency also came in different colors and featured images of tanks, military aircraft, and figures from U.S. history. It looked like play money.

After our initial processing, we were given bed linens and assigned to a "hootch" in a barracks-style complex in an older section of the base camp. Hootches would become my home during my year in the Nam, and the fine art of living in and accessorizing them will be described as this story continues. As I approached my assigned hootch, I noticed the ammunition boxes filled with sand that formed a wall around the structure. Looking at the safety wall that surrounded the hootch reminded me that I was in a combat zone—a thought that had eluded me up until now in the secure surroundings of the Long Bien base camp.

There wasn't much to do for the rest of the day, except ducking details—a skill I had perfected during my training days. In fact, I was so good at it in OCS that I was given the nickname "the phantom," a label I'm proud of even to this day. One of the guys who arrived with me, and was assigned to the same hootch, came up to me as I was making my bed and said he had heard of a surefire way to get out of a potential detail—like KP. I was all ears and asked him what it was. He said, "Let's go swimming at the big Long Binh pool." "Are you crazy?" I responded. "No," he said, and explained that one of the guys at the arrival center had told him that it was a well-known secret passed along to the new guys. He said that a personnel roster had yet to be developed, and they'd never know we were gone. "But I didn't bring a swimming suit," I continued, naively, and still in disbelief at the offer. "No one wears swimming suits here," he responded, which was a bit of a stretch of the truth. "The guys just wear their boxer shorts," he continued. So without giving it a lot of thought, I said, "What the hell," and the two of us slipped out and made our way to the base pool. We spent the afternoon there and came back just in time for dinner at the mess hall with, like he said, no one knowing that we had been gone. It was the first of the many bold moves that I'd make during my tour of duty in Vietnam.

As night rolled in, I settled into my temporary quarters and began writing the first of almost daily letters home and to my girlfriend, letting them know that I had arrived safely. In the background, Santana's *Abraxas* was playing on someone's radio. As I listened, I was introduced to another Vietnam phenomenon—AFVN radio. The station's format was so similar to stateside programming that for a moment, I almost forgot where I was. More on this later. I wanted to go over and introduce myself to the guy with the radio, for he was a spec 4 (specialist fourth class) and looked like he'd been here before. I was dying to know more about the Nam—what it was like, and what I could expect. But he, and the few other guys in the hootch, was keeping pretty much to himself, and I sensed that he wanted to be alone with his thoughts. I guess everyone was dealing with being here in their own way, not to mention the fact that we were all zombies as a result of just having traveled halfway around the world.

Even though I was dead tired, I couldn't sleep. As midnight approached, things got really quiet. I lay in bed waiting to hear the sounds of the war…or at least what I imagined them to be. On occasion, the distant sound of a helicopter swept through the air—a sound that would be a constant that year, especially in the latter months of my tour. And every now and then, I heard explosions in the distance that sounded like fireworks going off. But fatigue gradually took hold of me and I fell asleep, ending my first day in Vietnam.

We were awakened at 0600 hours the next morning by the NCO on duty. His "wake-up call" wasn't harsh like it had been during training. But it was still an army "get your sorry asses out of bed" wake-up call. As I sat up, the guy two bunks down from me who hadn't said a word to me up until now looked me straight in the eye and said, "364 and a wake-up!" The countdown to going home had begun, and the characters and the lingo of the Nam were beginning to emerge.

The next couple of days were spent at an in-country orientation center on the Long Bien base. It was a mini training compound that consisted of classroom buildings and a large outdoor demonstration area. The demonstration area was lined on one side with bleachers that were covered with a makeshift canopy to protect our yet-to-be-tanned skin from the strong Vietnam sun—and to keep us from getting wet during the rainy season, I would imagine. It was here that we learned the "do's and don'ts" of the Nam from lifers who obviously relished trying to impress us with their Vietnam experiences. Like standup comics at a marathon performance, each instructor tried to outdo the other, telling us war story after war story about the way it was and the way it will be for us.

Note: I should point out here that the term "lifer" refers to any career military personnel and was used heavily during the Vietnam War. The term was not one of endearment and was used primarily by disgruntled

GIs who resented the NCOs and officers who often harassed them for not sharing their love of the army or the Vietnam War. (But there were also a lot of "good" lifers—career military professionals who took their jobs seriously, but also respected the troops and treated them well). This lack of respect for the career military also became prevalent in the civilian population as well, due to a growing hatred of the Vietnam War. Unfortunately, this lack of respect, and gratitude, for the military was taken out on everyone when they returned home, even on the troops who didn't want to be there.

We were instructed in everything from how to dress to what water we could drink. We were told about everyday precautions we should take, like shaking out our boots before putting them on to make sure they hadn't become the resting place for spiders or scorpions. And they highly recommended that we take the giant mothball-looking orange malaria pills that had been issued to us, even though many guys ignored this advice because a common side effect of the pills was diarrhea. We were given a short briefing on the culture and some of the customs of the Vietnamese people, as well as some of the taboos—like not touching them on the top of their heads, an area they considered sacred. But cultural appreciation wasn't taken very seriously, as ethnic bias and even racism was prevalent in the military in Vietnam, just as it was in just about every war that we've fought throughout the world. Many of the troops called the Vietnamese "gooks," and as such they were regarded, shall we say, as lesser human beings. We were told not to trust any of them, "for you couldn't tell the civilians from the Viet Cong, and therefore you never knew who the enemy was." There was an element of truth to that—innocent villagers by day, Viet Cong by night.

We were warned about booby traps and were shown samples and given demonstrations of some of the devices that we might encounter. Sharpened bamboo sticks, in a variety of forms, seemed to be the most commonly used devices, whether swinging down from trees or lined on the bottom of pits that had been covered with foliage. We had heard a lot about these things in training as well. But to listen to these guys talk, you'd think everything in Vietnam was booby-trapped. For instance, they told us not to drink the local beer, as it was occasionally laced with broken glass fragments. And of course, we were advised not to eat the local food, as the Vietnamese cooked cats, dogs, rats, snakes, and who knows what else. That was one suggestion that I rarely heeded, as I learned to love Vietnamese food. But as much as I enjoyed it, I'll have to admit that I seldom asked what went into the dishes prepared for me. I figured what I didn't know wouldn't hurt me—and fortunately, it never did.

In between orientation sessions, we continued our in-country processing, which included more paperwork, more shots, and being issued the latest in jungle wear—fatigues, boots, hats, T-shirts, boxers, socks, all in olive drab. Being "green" took on a whole new meaning once arriving in Vietnam, as it was hard to hide the fact that you were the new guy on the block. For starters, your new fatigues and boots were bright green, and it took weeks, if not months, for the more seasoned "faded" look to set in. And the amount of time you'd been in-country definitely carried status in the Nam. The longer you were there, the "shorter" you became, and short-timers were treated with special favor and great respect.

The power of short-timers and their effect on the war will be examined in greater detail as this story continues.

Turtles (the name given to new arrivals), on the other hand, were usually treated skeptically, especially by the infantry and grunts in the field. We were considered dangerous because we hadn't yet learned the ways of the Nam. Turtles could make mistakes that could potentially spell disaster and cost someone their life. So other than the novelty of breaking us in and showing us the ropes, we were generally treated with suspicion by the more seasoned troops.

Two other characteristics that labeled us as new guys were our short haircuts that had yet to grow out from our training days and our white untanned skin (blacks and Latinos had an advantage here). So needless to say, we turtles did all we could to accelerate the process of being accepted. Like in any caste system, and there was definitely a caste system among the troops in Vietnam, status and acceptance was very important. We couldn't wait for our hair to grow out, we'd lay in the sun as much as possible in those first days, and we'd wash those new fatigues as often as possible to break them in.

Evenings at the replacement station were spent listening to the radio, writing letters, and exchanging "where we're from and how we got here" stories with each other. Occasionally, someone returning for their second tour of duty would entertain us with Vietnam stories that were a lot more enlightening than those heard in orientation. We heard incredible tales about life in the "bush" and equally amazing stories about life in the rear. These stories verified everything we'd heard in training about the women and the dope that were so readily available. Listening to these guys also gave us our first real exposure to the jargon that had become synonymous with serving in Vietnam. For example, "back in the world" referred to back home, the States, or any place other than Vietnam. Being "turtles," getting "short," "fragging the lifers," riding in "Hueys (UH1) and shithooks (Chinook) helicopters," "gooks," and "hootches" were just a few of the many code words and expressions that were the unofficial language of the Nam.

On my third evening in Long Bien, I went shopping for personal supplies at the massive base PX. While in the checkout line, the guy behind me struck up a conversation, asking me where I was from. As it turned out, he was an officer (a captain) and a lawyer returning from emergency leave back in the world. I found it a little disconcerting that he was so friendly toward me, a lowly private, as there was a code of conduct in the military that generally prevented officers from fraternizing with enlisted personnel (and vice versa). But then again, it was just a chat in a checkout line at the PX. He asked me if I wanted to go have a Coke, and I said sure.

It wasn't long before we had established that we had something in common—a strong distrust of the military and a hatred for the war (sentiments, as I would soon learn, that were shared by the majority of the troops serving in Vietnam). He must have sensed that I was a little older than the average eighteen-year-old recruit, and when he learned that I had a degree in political science, the pace of our conversation quickened. He told me that he too had been drafted as soon as he got out of law school, and how he had lucked out by getting a commission without having to go through the bullshit of ROTC or OCS, because the army was shorthanded and needed lawyers. We talked about our antiwar activity while in college and which politicians and organizations we had supported. And then he pulled something out of his wallet to show me. It was a piece of paper with a paragraph of copy typed on it with the title: Article 138, UCMJ (Uniform Code of Military Justice). He read it to me then explained what it meant. It was sort of an escape clause, a catch-22 if you will, in the military code of justice that he said might be useful to me someday. Essentially, it says that if you submit a grievance to your commanding officer, and if that officer fails to respond or act on that grievance, the person submitting the complaint has the right to resubmit the grievance to the commanding officer exercising general court-martial jurisdiction. In other words, you can go over the head of your commanding officer and go directly to the unit's senior officer, which could be as high as a colonel. This would get him into a lot of trouble, while ensuring action and protecting you from any (official) repercussions. I didn't fully comprehend at the time what he had just read or why he had given it to me. But I thanked him just the same and slipped the piece of paper into my wallet. Little did I realize how important it would be to me later in my tour of duty.

As I was leaving the PX, I couldn't believe my eyes. There before me stood Dennis Buckman, one of my best buddies in both basic training and AIT. We went back inside and right to the snack bar so he could fill me in on his trip over. As it turns out, his plane broke down twice and it took him two-and-a-half days to get here. But on the upside, he said they put the guys up in first class hotels in both Anchorage and Tokyo. Even though we would be assigned to different units, I'd run into and spend many a drunken night with Dennis while in the Nam.

Other than "rapping," listening to music, and writing letters home, the big three pastimes in the Nam (smoking dope would become the fourth), there was little else to do in our intentionally secure confines other than wonder what Vietnam was really like and what our destinies would be. Fortunately, the days spent with our seasoned trainers who tried to scare the shit out of us with their war stories and impress us with their heroics passed quickly. We couldn't wait to get out of there, as the accommodations sucked as well. There was no hot water in the showers, and the cold water often ran out as well. We could hear rats scampering under the hootches at night, and the mosquitos were rampant—I was getting eaten alive (apparently the priority was for spraying Agent Orange to defoliate the countryside, as opposed to spraying for mosquitos at the base camps).

At the end of the third day, it was time to finally receive our orders. The moment came without fanfare as my name was called and I was handed a piece of paper that would tell me where my first adventure would take place. Even though it meant nothing to me when I read it, there it was, my first assignment—Company C, 65th Engineer Battalion, 25th Infantry Division. I was headed to the "Tropic Lightning" Division, headquartered in Cu Chi, just a short twenty miles or so up Highway 1 from Long Bien. The next morning, I'd be boarding a bus and heading to my first duty station in the Nam.

CHAPTER 3

Welcome to Cu Chi

I woke up early the next morning and was dressed by the time they turned the lights on in the hootch. Turning on all the lights at once with an accompanying friendly shout of "Get your lazy asses out of bed" was a favorite wake-up call of lifers everywhere. But this morning, I had beaten them to the punch. I couldn't wait to get out of there and begin my adventure, so with duffel bag and paperwork in hand, I was the first one in line when the bus pulled up to take us to our various destinations.

Even though the ride to Cu Chi was relatively short, about twenty miles, I did my best to drink in everything along the way. I marveled once again at the size of the Long Binh base camp as we made our way to the main gate. Not too far down the road, I was again reminded of our commanding presence in Vietnam as we drove past the MACV (Military Assistance Command Vietnam) complex of large high-rise buildings. This was headquarters, HQ, for all military operations in Vietnam. I'd have the opportunity to witness this "Pentagon East" up close and personal in the months to come.

As we left the military command area, the landscape finally began to look Asian. The wide, paved highways leading to and from Long Binh narrowed to a rutty two-lane road as we drove through countryside that was spotted with small houses, churches, and farm fields. A lot of the buildings were constructed of concrete, with either smooth or stucco-like finishes. Houses of the apparently more well-to-do were faced in the front or decorated with colorful ceramic tile and were occasionally surrounded with walls. Graveyards also spotted the landscape and were very different from graveyards back home. Because of the monsoon rains and low-lying terrain, above-ground crypts were the norm, and most of them were very ornate, colorful, and "Oriental" looking.

The farther away from metro Saigon we got, the poorer the landscape and structures became. Houses, or huts, were now constructed of just about anything—stone, wood, bamboo, straw, and often featured metal roofs and siding that were made from flattened-out beer and soda cans discarded by the GIs. As I was to observe throughout my travels in the Nam, scavenging in the dumps of American base camps and outposts was a very common, and often lucrative, practice among the Vietnamese. Large groups of locals usually waited in anticipation for our trucks to arrive at the dumps, and the frenzy to grab our discarded trash often caused near-riot situations.

We passed through many small villages along the way, often slowing down due to the congestion that always seemed to clog the local roadways. "Damn gooks," the guy sitting next to me at the window blurted out. He was wearing sergeant stripes, so I figured he was heading to Cu Chi for his second tour of duty. "Did you know the 25th has 188,000 VC and NVA kills to their credit?" he asked me.

"No, I didn't," I replied. Without saying anything else, he turned his head and continued staring out the window.

These villages were hubs of commercial activity, selling everything from local produce, prepared food, and animals to clothing, building materials, and a variety of "black market" goods. The smells were pervasive and ranged from tantalizing to repulsive. Along the main road, scores of Vietnamese either walked, rode bikes, traveled in oxcarts, or were stuffed into Lambrettas, minivans/trucks designed to carry either people or goods. Every now and then, an old beat-up bus would roll by, so loaded with passengers and rooftop cargo, which often included chickens and other live animals, that it was barely able to stay its course. The roads weren't designed to carry this kind of traffic, and during monsoon season, the problem was even worse.

Occasionally, the scene was picturesque, reminding me of travelogues or postcards of the Orient. Vistas of rice fields with their levees, with palm and banana trees swaying in the background, captured me in its simplicity and beauty. Vietnamese women, dressed in the traditional *ao dai*, were captivating, with many balancing heavy loads of water or firewood on their backs as they made their way along the road. Men and children worked the fields, often riding on the backs of oxen or water buffalo. It was a beautiful sight, and deceptively serene.

Without warning, my feeling of serenity changed to a sense of nervous anxiety. I knew we had to be getting close to our destination, and it suddenly hit me that I was about to join an infantry division as a combat engineer. Even though I had received some training for the position, it was definitely not a job that I wanted to do. So I started scheming in my head the course of action I would take when I got to my unit. (Actually, I had come up with this plan before I arrived in Vietnam, having been given some advice by a couple of guys who had "been there, done that.") I'd proceed immediately to headquarters and see if I could get a desk job. After all, I could type ninety words per minute—and I could write. Maybe I could get a job with the division newspaper. At any rate, I'd give it a try.

My focus turned back to the landscape as we gradually approached another village, this one much larger than any we'd passed through since leaving Long Binh. It was Cu Chi village. Like the others, it was teeming with activity. But unlike the others, it had a more organized small-town feel to it. This was due to the amount of commerce and government activity that was based in this provincial center. And as we would learn much later in the war, it was also due to the fact that Cu Chi housed a major base camp for the Viet Cong—in an incredible complex of underground tunnels that stretched for miles in all directions. A division of troops, a hospital, and a major supply center were "under" the village—and under the 25th Infantry Division's base camp.

After passing through the village, the land became increasingly barren. In stark contrast to the lush countryside I'd seen so far, the land was now stripped of vegetation and structures of any kind. It seemed almost unnatural—and it was. In the distance, a small "city" became visible, surrounded by layers of barbed wire and dotted with guard towers rising far above the ground. We were approaching

Cu Chi Base Camp, headquarters of the U.S. Army's 25th "Tropic Lightning" Infantry Division.

We drove through the main gates of the base camp after the driver showed his pass to the MPs guarding the entrance. Again, we were greeted with paved highway and structures that comprised this small city. But this time it looked more like an army base, with a certain frontier sense about it. We passed a striking modern chapel and a number of office-type buildings before coming to a plaza located in the center of the base. A large rustic, yet modern wooden structure with a series of large flagpoles in the foreground anchored the plaza. Air conditioners were evident in most of the building's windows. It was division headquarters. Wide, paved roads surrounded the complex, and as I was to soon learn, they also served as parade grounds for the occasional ceremonies the division would put us through. In front of the headquarters building, there was a large area of well-manicured lawn, and right smack in the middle was a huge concrete "electric strawberry" (as the division insignia was known) painted in the bright red and yellow colors of the division insignia. The 25th Infantry Division insignia consisted of a red strawberry-looking shape (probably representing some Hawaiian fruit, as the division was based at Schofield Barracks in Hawaii), with a yellow lightning bolt running through it. It must have been fifty feet long and twenty feet wide. In my estimation, the visual of the huge insignia in the middle of the lawn seemed a bit "overstated." But as I was to learn, the unusual and the unexpected was the norm in Vietnam—an aspect of a "new reality" that would follow me throughout my year in the Nam.

Much to my dismay, after venturing a little farther down the road, the bus pulled into the "Tropic Lightning Reception Station." All I could think of was being subjected to another couple of days of processing bullshit. But after only a few hours of paperwork and orientation, a small truck took me to the opposite end of the base and to my new unit—the 65th Engineer Battalion. Next to the entrance of the battalion was a fairly large building with a sign over the entrance that read, Sauna Bath. It seemed out of place for this "oasis" to be located in a somewhat remote part of the base camp, not to mention being located on the base camp at all, rather than on its outskirts. Little did I realize what an oasis this place would turn out to be—affectionately known by the troops as the "steam and cream."

We drove into the battalion area under an arch made from utility poles. Across the top of the arch was a banner featuring the insignia and slogan of the 65th Engineers: First In—Last Out. A comforting message! I was dropped off in front of the battalion headquarters building, a fairly modest structure with air conditioners sticking out of its two windows. The battalion insignia hung over the door, and two small banana trees stood in an otherwise barren front yard on either side of the entrance. The whole area was a lot more worn than Long Binh, with the streets only partially paved and the sidewalks cracked and fragmented. The hootches looked more like Depression-era dwellings than barracks. Laundry hung from clotheslines behind some of the structures, and latrines dotted the area. A trace of the now-familiar fragrance of burning shit hung in the air. A couple of guys walked by and gave me a knowing look. They were wearing faded fatigues and jungle hats adorned with unit pins and colorful headbands. They were also wearing John Lennon–style sunglasses. As they passed, one of them flashed me the peace sign. It was now late afternoon.

I entered the battalion headquarters building and was greeted by a clerk who welcomed me to the Nam with a big grin. He introduced himself as Ed Mack, "but you can call me Mackie," he said. He led me down a hallway to a room furnished with a couple of tables and chairs and gave me more forms to fill out. Before I was finished, the S-2 (battalion intelligence) NCO in charge, Sergeant First Class Martinez, entered the room. He shook my hand and welcomed me to the 65th Engineers. I handed him my orders and personnel file, which you always carried with you when traveling to and from assignments. He quickly reviewed my documents and started asking me questions about my background and training. "I see you're a college man," he remarked. That was my cue. Before he could get another word out of his mouth, I proceeded to tell him that not only was I a college man, but I could write and type ninety words per minute. I asked him if there were any clerk or writing positions open, if they had a battalion newspaper, and if the division might need a writer. He looked up at me, then back down at my records.

I suddenly felt a bit self-conscious and realized that I had been talking a mile a minute. I pulled back, not wanting to appear desperate. He hesitated, rubbed his lips with one hand, and said, "The CO's been talking about starting up a battalion newsletter, and I could use some help with my paperwork. There's a slot in S-2 I think I could put you in. I'll talk to the CO and see what he thinks. Come back and see me at 0800 hours in the morning."

I couldn't believe it. I just might actually get out of being a combat engineer after all. I had heard, and to a certain extent at this point in my service experience observed, that playing the system and "getting over" was a way of life in the military, but I hadn't really had a chance to participate in this game until now. My heart was pounding, but I didn't want to appear too excited. Mackie reentered the room, and SFC Martinez told him to assign me to the S-2 hootch. "Specialist Mack will take care of everything you need," he added as he left the room.

Mackie walked me to the supply building where I would get my bedding and a few other essential items. "You trade in your sheets for clean ones every Monday morning," he said. "Just bring them back here to supply. You're on your own as far as laundering your towels and clothes. There's a base laundry, or you can get your hootch maid to do your laundry for about $5 a week," he added.

"What's a hootch maid?" I asked him. He proceeded to explain that hootch maids were Vietnamese women that came on base daily to work for the troops. They did your laundry, polished your boots, did basic hootch cleaning, and could bring in certain "items" and supply other "favors," as I'd learn a little later.

As we walked toward the S-2 hootch, he pointed out the mess hall. "Food's not bad most of the time. And there's always the PX and the EM club for snacks if you can't stand the stuff," he added.

"What about Vietnamese food?" I asked. Rather than answering, he just looked at me like I was crazy. Ed Mack turned out to be a real pleasant guy with a mild disposition—a "brother" from

Baltimore. He'd been in country for about three months and told me he'd show me the ropes at HQ if I got the job in S-2.

We turned down a dilapidated concrete walkway that was lined with hootches on both sides. They were wooden structures, with angled roofs that extended out over the windows, which kept the runoff from the monsoon rains from getting into the buildings. The windows were covered with screens to let in air and keep out insects. Each hootch was surrounded with protective walls, most of them made from ammunition boxes filled with sand halfway up then OD-colored sandbags up to the windows. As we entered the hootch, Mackie led me to a bed in an empty space in the middle of the large open room.

The inside of the hootch, though, had been divided into semi-private rooms for the seven (now eight) occupants by a variety of partitions and room dividers. The dividers were made with things like plywood, blankets, mosquito nets, poncho liners, and other more creative items. Decorating your space was a very big part of the Vietnam experience, especially for the troops in the rear. But even the grunts in the field went to incredible lengths to bring creature comforts to their frontline abodes.

By now, it was well into the dinner hour, and Mackie asked me if I wanted to join him for some chow. I thanked him for the offer, but decided to unpack and get settled instead. With all the excitement and tensions of the day, I didn't have much of an appetite anyway. "And if I get hungry later, there's always the EM club, right, Mackie?" I said, quoting him as he made his way out the door. As I unpacked my duffel bag and made my bed, a sense of loneliness and mild depression came over me. I'd get this feeling more than once in the coming year, especially when I would change units and have to leave my friends behind. Besides, I'd been in Vietnam for almost a week now without really getting to know anyone and with no opportunities for calls or letters from home.

Just as I was about finished unpacking, the door to the hootch swung open and two guys walked in. They didn't notice me at first as they were arguing over the merits and features of Pioneer versus TEAC audio tape decks. At a pause in the conversation, one of them looked up and noticed me. He had a slight build, blond hair, a pronounced moustache, and wore wire-rimmed glasses. "Hey, Tom, look what we have here…a turtle fresh in from the world." They both headed my way with hands extended. "Welcome to the Nam," said the blond guy with the wire-rimmed glasses. "I'm Doc Gilroy, and this is Tom Reese." I put out my hand expecting a traditional handshake, but Doc slid the palm of his hand around mine and grasped my thumb in the 1960s handshake of brotherhood. As I was to learn, this was the preferred handshake among the (nonblack) troops in the Nam. The brothers had a much more elaborate greeting for each other (and for all nonbrothers who could master it) that bordered on ritual.

For at least the next two hours, we sat around the hootch rapping and listening to music. In fact, rapping and music were the two main pastimes of life in the Nam, as well as a variety of "refreshments and diversions" that would soon become readily evident. As I became more comfortable with my new environment, I began to notice things in much greater detail, like how elaborately each guy had their area fixed up. Trunks were used as coffee tables; there were armchairs and lamps, posters and a variety of artwork, furnishings that changed the look of the place from barracks to, well, home. Just about everyone in the hootch had some kind of stereo system, with Tom's full-blown component system (gigantic speakers, amp, and reel-to-reel tape deck) by far the most impressive. Everyone also had a fan, and two guys even had little refrigerators. Three of the guys had TVs. The place was a virtual marketplace of appliances and electronics. And as I was to learn, as guys were leaving at the end of their tours, they either sold what they could, or just passed along their gear and goods to new arrivals in an almost ceremonial gesture of goodwill that was indicative of the Vietnam culture. As I traveled around the country during my year in the Nam, it never ceased to amaze me just how elaborate and ingenious the troops were when it came to fixing up their own little parts of the world.

It was now approaching 2100 hours, and Doc seemed to be a little anxious. He would start to ask me a question, then pause, look me in the eye, then change the subject. After two or three false starts, he finally came out with it. "Do you like to smoke pot," he asked. Finally, my curiosity about everything I'd heard about pot and Vietnam was about to be answered. I wanted to respond by saying, "I thought you'd never ask!" But instead, I told him: "I've tried it once or twice." His face lit up, and he turned to Tom and said, "I think it's time to initiate our new friend here to the ways of the Nam."

With that, Doc said, "Let's take a little walk," and he led us out of the hootch for a three-block walk to a hootch occupied by a group of combat engineers. Along the way, he explained to me that the residential compound in the battalion area was divided into three sections. The officers had their slightly more upscale hootches in the section closest to headquarters and the officers club. The NCOs resided in the section closest to the NCO club and the mess hall. And the troops had the largest section closest to the perimeter. It seemed to make sense. The officers, headquarters, officers club. The NCOs, NCO club, mess hall. The troops, perimeter, and the closest proximity to danger. "But fuck it," as Doc would say. "The farther away from the lifers, the better."

As we walked through the company area toward our destination, my briefing continued. Doc told me, with Tom nodding in agreement, that there was sort of an unwritten code that the officers and NCOs didn't come into our area at night unless there was a good reason for it. In other words, they didn't interfere with the after-hours "activity" that took place in the hootches and the bunkers. There were bunkers scattered throughout the living and working areas of the base camp, generally single-room fortresses constructed of heavy timber and sandbags. They were safe havens where everyone took shelter in the event of an incoming rocket or mortar attack. But at night, the bunkers also served as party places, both on the inside and on the roofs. Guys would often climb up on top of the bunkers and sit on beach chairs or poncho liners, get stoned, and observe the light show of the war that was often visible in the distance.

As we entered the hootch Doc had led us to, I noticed an immediate difference between this abode and the one we were living in. It was a lot less "fixed up," with equipment and personal belongings scattered all over the place. There were also a lot of weapons lying around—M-16 rifles, grenade launchers, helmets, flak jackets, and the like. And to my surprise, ammunition, including grenades, were also scattered all over the place. Tom picked up on my apprehension as I carefully avoided stepping on a grenade and said, "Don't worry... it takes a lot to get those things to blow." These guys apparently didn't care much about housekeeping. After spending their days in the field risking their lives doing the kind of work they did as combat engineers, I guess neatness and order really didn't matter much. Shelter from the elements, insects, and a dry bed was all they really cared about. They also partied hard, as I was about to find out.

Doc introduced me to the guys, a real seasoned bunch with deeply tanned skin, hair bleached out from the sun, and most with long, bushy mustaches. He informed them that he and Tom had brought me over "to be initiated into the brotherhood of the Nam." As had happened with Doc, smiles came across all of their faces. It was like they all knew something that I didn't know. And they did. These guys, like everyone else I had met so far, were very friendly. Some of them were dressed in fatigue trousers (I learned the hard way in basic training that they were called trousers, not pants, in the military) with no shirts, while others were wearing OD boxer shorts and T-shirts. Some were still wearing their jungle boots, while others were wearing flip-flops. I felt a little out of place, as I was still wearing my fatigue trousers and shirt, and they were very green. I learned that evening that practically no one wore underwear in Vietnam. The guys said it was "too hot to wear 'em" and that underwear just made you sweat. It seems jungle rot and rashes were a big problem in the Nam, and you did whatever you could to prevent this stuff from making your life (more) miserable.

As I sat down on the edge of one of the bunks, one of the guys pulled a large paper bag out of his trunk. Two other guys pulled ornate pipes out of their fatigue pockets. Another pulled out a pack of rolling papers. The guy holding the bag dipped his hand in and pulled out a fistful of marijuana. Before long, one of the pipes was passed my way and I took a big hit. I drew in too much smoke and started coughing and hacking. As if in chorus, the engineers, as well as Doc and Tom, laughed in delight at my suffering. After a few more passes of the pipe, the group settled down and then the war stories began.

With each guy adding an aspect or little twist to the tales, they proceeded to tell me how abundant pot was in the Nam and how cheap it was. They said it helped them relax and get their minds off the war, and that if it wasn't around, they didn't know how they'd get by. For the most part, they said they didn't smoke the stuff while on duty, especially hazardous duty. But otherwise, they were pretty much stoned all the time. The pipe came around again, and I took another hit. It was followed closely by a joint. I asked the guys their opinion as to how many of the troops they thought got high. The most seasoned of the group, a guy named Alex who had the longest mustache and the most time in country, ten months, replied with a smile of knowing confidence. "I'd say somewhere around 65 percent of the troops get high, at least occasionally. Another 25 percent are 'juicers' who drink a lot of alcohol to get their buzz. And then there's the other 10 percent or so that are either totally straight, super religious, or whatever." As my tour in Vietnam ensued, I and others determined his 65 percent estimate was pretty spot on.

By now, I was really stoned. And as my high increased in intensity, so did a heightened awareness of things going on around me. Like the music. The Rolling Stone's album *Let It Bleed* was playing on one of the guy's tape decks, and the cut "You Can't Always Get What You Want"—"But if you try sometime, you just might find, you get what you need"—was providing the background music for my initiation. How appropriate, I thought, as I drifted off for a moment looking for some deeper meaning to this whole experience. It wouldn't take long for me to learn what that deeper meaning was. At any rate, I was quickly learning the three Rs of the Nam—rapping, reefer, and rock & roll.

Alex, who by now was now wearing a silly grin on his face, asked me if I was sufficiently stoned. I nodded and said, "Oh yea," and suddenly realized I was wearing the silly grin as well. He struck me as the leader or "alpha dog" of the group, for as he nodded his approval to me, the rest of the group followed suit. With the formalities out of the way, the remainder of the evening turned into a heavy rap session, which consisted mostly of the guys giving me advice and recommendations for getting by in the Nam. I was told that this advice was not only based on their experiences, but was also handed down from previous "generations" of Vietnam vets. They also told some war stories about life in the field as combat engineers. These guys did everything from building bridges and working with explosives to sweeping for and detonating land mines and other devices. They had lost one of their buddies to a mine and had had their share of close calls. But they said their combat experiences paled in comparison to the stories they heard from guys who had served in the early years. The worst of it was the 1965–1966 time period, as well as the years leading up to and following the Tet Offensive. These stories were told by guys returning for a second and even third tour of duty. Yes, whether it was the adrenaline rush, the drugs, a love of war, or the military lifestyle that had developed in the Nam, more troops than you would imagine came back for more.

    I learned a little more that night about the two main divisions of troops in the Nam—the lifers and everyone else. Within the "everyone else" category, there were a number of subdivisions. There were, for example, the heads and the juicers; and the brothers, turtles and short-timers; grunts, who fought the war in the field; and REMFs (rear echelon motherfuckers, as we were affectionately known), who supported the grunts from the rear. There definitely was a subculture or military counterculture among the troops who served in Vietnam, especially among the heads and the brothers. I would continue to learn about and become an integral part of this subculture as my months in the Nam progressed.

    The enemy also fell into two categories, the NVA and the Viet Cong, with (the worst of) the lifers being the third. There were a lot of guys who thought the lifers were the only enemy, especially among the REMFs. But to be fair, as I pointed out previously, many of the career military types, like SFC Martinez, were really nice guys who were just doing their jobs and making a living in their career of choice, and they really didn't bother us.

    With the exception of the top military brass and some of the hard-core lifers, whose primary goal was winning the war and furthering their careers, there was only one goal for those of us serving in Vietnam. And that was staying alive and protecting our buddies so that we all made it back to the world after serving our 365. Forget the bullshit about winning the war or stopping communism. By 1970, that notion only existed in the minds of unenlightened politicians and career military types who still believed in the cause. But regardless of one's position on the war, dramatic changes in the mission and esprit de corps were taking place all around us.

By the time I got to Vietnam in May of 1970, it was readily evident that the military was extremely frustrated at having its hands tied by the politicians in terms of how they wanted to fight the war. And this frustration was growing with each passing month. With winning the war becoming increasingly unlikely, the military was stepping up its gamesmanship to justify its existence. Its press briefings, known as "the Five O'clock Follies," became more circus-like, with new and more creative ways to inflate body counts and combat milestones being presented (the military was known to inflate body counts throughout the war's history to justify increased funding and troop allocations). Congress, in the meantime, was divided between increased support and cutting funding and troop strength. And the cry to turn the war over to the South Vietnamese was growing louder. Unfortunately, it was the troops in the bush who were paying the real price for this vacillation. For while the bureaucrats and those who supported them watched the war on the *Nightly News* from the comfort of their living rooms, the troops in the field were still dying. And those of us in the rear paid a price as well, although for most of us, it wasn't with life or limb. Whether or not we had an active role in the war, we still had to deal with the psychological impact of what was going on around us, and with the anger and heartbreak of losing our buddies to this senseless war.

The evening turned out to be a memorable continuation of my unofficial orientation to survival, getting by, and having a good time in the Nam. But by now it was getting late, close to 0200 hours. Tom was complaining to Doc that he had an early call in the morning and wanted to get going, which made me realize just how tired I was. It had been a very long day. I thanked everyone for the refreshments and the advice, and we exchanged the handshake of our brotherhood as we made our way out the door. As we walked back to the S-2 hootch, I realized just how stoned I was. It felt good and gave me the premonition that my year in the Nam was going to be an interesting one.

The next morning, reveille sounded over the battalion PA system at 0630 hours. At 0700, we had a company formation outside the HQ building. They had these most mornings for the purpose of head count, dispensing the company duty roster for the day and to deliver any special messages or orders. It was almost like stateside, and even though we didn't have a uniform inspection per se, they still required us to be in full uniform with boots polished and the rest of the drill. After a little more than five minutes of this ritual, we were dismissed to take care of our personal needs and go to breakfast before beginning our duty.

I made my way to the latrine, a wooden building with a large step-up platform on one side with eight wooden seats lined up all in a row. The company area was also dotted with a number of strategically placed urinals. They were a crude rendition of the kind of public urinals you used to see on the streets of some European cities—little one-man kiosks that were open on the top and the bottom. They drained into a large hole in the ground that was covered with a screen to keep out debris. In the heat of the day, they provided the surrounding area with an aroma that you didn't want to be near. These facilities were a switch from the luxury of Long Binh, which had indoor plumbing in most locations. Another small building that actually had a concrete floor housed the showers. It featured a large open area with about ten showerheads protruding from the surrounding walls. We even had hot water some of the time, which was a real luxury in the Nam. After dressing and eating breakfast (Mackie was right, the food wasn't bad), I made my way to battalion headquarters to find SFC Martinez. It was time to learn my fate.

I entered the building and made my way to Sergeant Martinez's office. He was sitting at this desk and looked up as I approached the open door. "Good morning, Private Stoup, and welcome to the S-2 team," he said with a smile. My heart skipped a beat. He proceeded to tell me that the S-2 commanding officer, Captain Becker, had approved his request for assistance and that the battalion commander, Lieutenant Colonel Forrest Gaynor, had signed off on the notion as well. But what really enabled him to approve my position, he told me, was the fact that I had a secret security clearance (that I obtained when I was accepted into OCS). I never thought I'd be grateful for anything about the OCS experience—but all of a sudden, I was.

It seems that LTC Gaynor was the one who was pushing for a battalion newsletter. It wasn't that he cared that much about keeping the troops informed, mind you. But rather, he wanted one because his counterparts in other division battalions had newsletters and he apparently wanted to keep up with them. Actually, there was quite a bit of competition in the senior officer ranks in Vietnam, with everyone vying for medals and battle ribbons and promotions—and getting the division commander's attention. In those circles, if you didn't come back from Vietnam with a chest full of stuff on your uniform, it didn't bode well for your career. The same was true, but to a somewhat lesser extent, within the senior NCO ranks.

Sergeant Martinez took me next door and showed me my desk. It was right next to Mackie's in a room that housed the battalion files and its communications equipment. On top of it sat an old Remington manual typewriter that looked like it hadn't been used in, well, a long time. It seems I got the job because they had an unfilled slot for a radio operator, a combat-designated position. Mackie was apparently out running errands for the CO. Clerks ran a lot of errands for the lifers—like picking up their laundry, stopping at the PX for personal supplies, snacks, or whatever. But as soon as he returned, he welcomed me with open arms. I could tell he was happy to have someone share his office and the bullshit. And then, as if getting a desk job, which kept me out of the field, wasn't enough, Sergeant Martinez informed me that I was also getting a promotion—to private first class. I had forgotten that every private arriving in Vietnam got an automatic promotion to PFC. The ceremony for me and others getting promotions or battle ribbons would be held this coming Saturday night, at the company's biweekly cookout.

CHAPTER 4

Drugs, Sex, Rock & Roll...and Fraggings

My second night in Cu Chi turned out to be even more eventful than the first. After spending the day getting settled into my new office and getting an initial briefing on the daily routine from Sergeant Martinez and Mackie, I headed back to the hootch to meet up with Doc and the guys for dinner. Sergeant Martinez let me go at 1600 hours so I could continue to settle in (we usually worked until 1730), so I was the first one back to the hootch. The medics had gone to Cu Chi village for the day to conduct their weekly MEDCAP (Medical Civic Action Program), which was essentially a free clinic for the locals where they offered treatment for minor illnesses and injuries. The program was part of an increasing emphasis on "Vietnamization," winning the hearts and minds of the Vietnamese people. Going out on the next MEDCAP would be one of the first stories that I'd write for the newsletter.

While I waited for them to return, I wrote two quick letters, one to my girlfriend, Paula, and one to my parents. It was my first real opportunity to send them my address and tell them what unit I had been assigned to. And also to share the good news on how I had lucked out getting a writing assignment, which hopefully meant I would be spared any combat duty. So hopefully, within a week or two, I'd start receiving mail from home, which was usually the highlight of the day for most of us.

Just as I was sealing the last letter, Doc and the guys walked through the door. And just like yesterday, when I first met them, they were arguing—this time about who was the female backup singer on the "Gimme Shelter" song on the Rolling Stones *Let It Bleed* album. Tom said it was Grace Slick, and Doc claimed it wasn't but he didn't know who it was (it turned out to be a relatively unknown at the time, Merry Clayton). After exchanging greetings and brief recaps of our day, we headed out to dinner. Even though it was after-duty hours, we still had to wear our uniforms to the mess hall. We dined on mystery meat, mashed potatoes, and mixed vegetables, with applesauce and spice cake for dessert. After dinner, we returned to the hootch and changed into what I had observed to be the typical uniform of the night—fatigue pants, a T-shirt, and flip-flops (Tom let me borrow a pair until I could get to the PX and purchase my own). It was one of those items you didn't anticipate needing when packing for Vietnam. Doc added a headband to his outfit, and I noticed he was wearing two strands of beads around his neck. Many of the guys wore elements of "hippie attire," including a lot of beads and peace signs. I'd eventually get a peace sign in 18k gold on a chain (very popular in the Nam), but lost it before returning to the world. I think these necklaces were worn to express an opinion of the war—and to piss off the lifers—as opposed to being fashion accessories. Very 1960s.

We sat around listening to music on Tom's monster system while one by one, my hootch mates continued to fill me in on what a trip it was being in the Nam. I learned that two of the medics in the hootch, including Doc, were conscientious objectors. I was told that if they couldn't get out of the draft but had their CO status approved, they were assigned to the medical corps. The cut "With a Little Help from My Friends," from the classic *Joe Cocker* album, was playing in the background. That song and its line "I get by with a little help from my friends...I get high with a little help from my friends" became one of the anthems of the Nam. I met the CO's driver that night, Eric Cannon. He'd been with Captain Becker in Saigon the night before, so we were meeting for the first time. He told us about the bars he went to with the captain and what a trip it was going to Saigon—"definitely a fringe benefit of his job," he remarked. He said that while the captain was engaged in company business, he was free to do just about anything he wanted. I'd get to spend time in Saigon a few times before leaving Cu Chi and a number of times during my future assignments.

Shortly after it got dark, Doc suggested that we pay a visit to another group of combat engineers. He said it would give me an opportunity to meet more guys in the battalion. I assumed that meant it was party time again. We walked the short distance to their hootch, which was the closest to the base perimeter. Most of the base camps and outlying fire support bases in Vietnam were circular in design in order to provide a 360-degree vantage point to the surrounding area. Bunkers and guard towers were strategically placed around the perimeter. Row after row of concertina and barbed wire were placed outside the berm that the engineers built up around each base. Many types of mines were placed within the rows of wire, including the Nam-famous claymores. But even with all this protection, Viet Cong sappers routinely made their way through the wire and onto bases, using their uncanny skill and cunning to do so. These incursions by the VC often spelled disaster for the troops and their equipment, as they carried satchel charges to blow up their targets. It was not unheard of for sappers to sacrifice themselves in the process. But since airstrips, aircraft, supply and ammunition depots, and command centers were their favorite targets, I was told we didn't have to worry too much about getting hit.

Doc called out his buddy's name and announced himself as we entered the hootch and exchanged the customary greeting. He introduced me to the inhabitants, and right off the bat, I said to myself that this was the moteliest-looking bunch of guys that I'd yet to set eyes on in my short time in the Nam. They were all heavy-equipment operators, the guys who built roads and bases, did heavy construction work and the like. These combat engineers were definitely hard core—the kind of guys you definitely didn't want to fuck with. And as I was to learn, the lifers didn't want to fuck with them either. They represented a cross section of the kind of troops that were (generally) drafted and sent off to war. They were white and black and Hispanic and came from all walks of life. But regardless of their backgrounds, or where they came from, they were bound together tightly as a unit. They looked out for each other and knew they needed to protect each other, whether it was from the enemy within or outside the wire. And the enemy on the inside, for many of the troops, was the lifers. But potential self-destruction from depression, drugs, and other forces were also enemies from within, which was another reason why we all had to look out for each other.

This sense of unity and brotherhood was the most powerful force that I experienced in my year in the Nam. I had never before felt such a sense of camaraderie and shared purpose like the one shared among the troops in Vietnam—and I haven't since. The traditional barriers of race, religion, education, and social status broke down when you stepped onto Vietnamese soil. We all shared a common purpose, the most important goal in life—survival. It didn't matter if we arrived here rich or poor, black or white, PhD or high school dropout, or if we came from a city, a suburb, a farm or an inner-city ghetto. We were all in this together. Of course, it goes without saying that this kind of bond was also true in all wars where men (and women) depended on each other for mutual survival.

This sense of brotherhood and fierce independence was both good news and bad news for the army. For better or worse, the draft had assembled quite a cast of characters in Vietnam. For instance, one of the guys I met that night, who was from St. Louis, said he got there because a judge had told him it was either prison or the army (I never did ask him what his crime was because it really didn't matter). Another guy, who was from Harlem and just barely eighteen, said that he had never stepped foot out of New York City before coming to the Nam. And yet another guy, sitting in a corner of the hootch by himself, reading the *Tao*, was from Boston and had a PhD in philosophy. But we all had something in common. We were all some place we didn't want to be—fighting a war that we didn't believe in. This prevailing attitude presented an interesting predicament for the military, as it created an environment that would get increasingly hostile and bizarre as time went on in Vietnam.

As we began to rap, one of the guys pulled out the now-familiar paper bag of pot and stuffed a handful into a large ivory pipe. I was noticing that the pipes I'd seen here thus far were very ornate, with some of them looking quite old, seasoned, and pretty valuable.

Collecting ornate pipes was the thing to do in the Nam, I would learn. He brushed the overflow of pot that had fallen onto his lap to the floor, at which point I turned to Doc and commented on all the grass he was wasting. Doc laughed and said, "I thought the same thing when I first got here, but the stuff's so cheap that it really doesn't matter." He told me that the price had escalated recently to $25 a kilo (2.2 pounds), while back in the early days it went for $5 to $15 a key. My mouth dropped. He said it was still pretty easy to get. Guys brought it back from the field all the time, as you could get it from almost any villager. Vietnamese kids were often the runners, getting soda and candy bars as their reward. Or you could have your hootch maid bring it to you, although that was getting riskier, as they were searching them more thoroughly at the gate as they entered these days. There had been reports recently of VC posing as hootch maids, getting onto some of the bases with explosives, and blowing up some valuable military assets. So inspections were becoming more rigorous.

Andre, the guy from Harlem, handed his pipe and a handkerchief to Doc. I watched as he placed the cloth over the bowel of the pipe, turned the mouthpiece toward my face, and told me to open my mouth and breathe in. He proceeded to blow a blast of smoke from the bowl down my throat. I was being "shotgunned" for the first time. The sensation of inhaling this blast of smoke almost knocked me off my seat and sent an instant rush to my head. Shotgunning, I learned, was a common and popular practice among the heads, as was the use of water bowls, which cooled and soothed the harshness of the weed.

I couldn't believe what I was hearing, seeing, and experiencing. The drug culture that I had heard so much about in training was real after all, and I wanted to know more. Feeling comfortable now, I asked the group what other drugs the troops used. They told me that pot, by far, was the drug of choice and that it was used either occasionally, or constantly, by a majority of the troops. Speed was also popular, especially with the grunts in the field. While it doesn't get you high like pot, it does give you a rush, they pointed out. "It keeps you awake for long periods of time, which is why the guys in the field use it," Andre told me. "But it also gets you sketchy, which can be a bad thing," he pointed out. It usually came in liquid form, in glass vials that had numbers on them to indicate potency. All you had to do was snap the vial in half and pour the contents into a soda can and you were set. Speed was manufactured in labs in Vietnam and the surrounding Golden Triangle countries. Pills of any type were rare, as pharmaceuticals were not readily available in that part of the world. Unfortunately, they continued, speed was addictive, and someone hooked on it was not someone you wanted at your side in the bush. The number of speed freaks in the Nam was growing, and it was creating some real problems—like paranoid and sleep-deprived grunts, for example, who occasionally freaked out and started shooting at animals, civilians, or even their own men (mostly lifers).

Opium was another drug that made an occasional appearance. It came in a gummy, almost caramel-like form, and was either smoked in a small pipe or painted onto joints to create "OJs." It smelled like caramel too when it was burning and created a high that made one feel like they were almost floating off the ground. Even though many papa sans smoked opium—it was part of their culture—for some reason, it was hard to get. So it was a rare treat for the heads when they could get their hands on some. Even though acid was still popular back in the world, it was seldom seen in Vietnam, unless someone mailed some to their buddies, which did happen on occasion.

Finally, there was heroin. In my early days in the Nam, I only saw it used on rare occasions and never by my group of friends. But by the time my tour of duty was winding down, its use had grown dramatically, and it had become a real problem for the military, not to mention for the guys who were hooked on it. The troops who used it in those early days had often carried the habit with them from the States, and they had to go to great lengths to get their hands on it. But like anything else in Vietnam, or elsewhere in the world for that matter, if you had the money and a contact, you could find a way to get it. But by May of 1971, it was readily available, easy to score—and cheap.

The NVA and Viet Cong had become aware of the GI's predilection for drugs and began supporting the supply chain as a military tactic. They were aware of how drugs distracted, and in some cases, incapacitated the troops, so they became big-time suppliers. The use of heroin was ruining the lives of many of our soldiers. And if it didn't kill them in Vietnam, many GIs returned home with a nasty habit that was extremely difficult to kick. Unlike the other drugs that usually brought you up, heroin was a reclusive drug that brought you down—way down. Scenes of guys nodding off as we sat around rapping and listening to music were to become all-too commonplace in Vietnam in the 1970s.

And then there was alcohol and tobacco, the acceptable drugs that have been fixtures in the military since men started fighting wars. As it is with society in general, I witnessed more serious problems stemming from alcohol abuse in the Nam than I did by guys smoking pot. Which led me to one last question: "What about enforcement? Weren't you guys afraid of getting busted, or losing your rank, or whatever?" The question only brought smiles to their faces. Doc reiterated the unofficial rules of the game here in the 65th. They didn't come into our area at night, and we didn't come into theirs. You were careful during the day, especially when on duty. You were careful about what you used and where you got it. "If you abided by those rules," he said, "there wouldn't be any trouble." The others nodded in agreement. I guess I'd have to take them at their word although I always proceeded with caution when using drugs in the Nam. Well, at least most of the time.

Sufficiently stoned again, we bade our hosts farewell and started walking back to the hootch. On the way, Tom suggested that we stop by the EM club to get a soda. We agreed and turned down the walkway toward the club. Before I realized that anything was happening, Doc grabbed my fatigue shirt and pulled me to the ground. He and Tom hit the deck simultaneously. At that very instant, we heard a tremendous explosion and were immediately engulfed in a cloud of dust. The explosion came from the CSM's hootch to our right rear. Dirt flew everywhere, and the concussion from the blast sent a shot of pain through my ears. The three of us just lay there, frozen in place, clinging to the earth.

When the dust had settled, Doc raised his head and looked over his right shoulder. "Damn," he shrieked, "someone just fragged top's hootch" (top was the army's nickname for a command sergeant major, the top NCO in a battalion). We got up and brushed ourselves off as Doc asked if anyone was hurt. Fortunately, the only thing that hit us was dirt, and I only ended up with a brush burn on my elbow. We walked a little closer to the hootch, which still had smoke coming out of the windows. It was dark inside, and it appeared that no one was home. Before I could even open my mouth to ask what had just happened, Doc said, "That fucker must've been thrown the instant we turned the corner. Let's get the hell out of here before someone shows up." So we hightailed it out of there just as a couple of NCOs were running toward the hootch to see what had happened.

We dashed into the EM club, purchased three sodas, and grabbed a table toward the back of the room. My ears were still ringing, and I must have had a bewildered look on my face as Doc kept staring at me as if in a trance. After what seemed like an eternity of silence, he started telling me about the stories he'd been hearing about the rash of fraggings that were taking place all over Vietnam, in the bush as well as in the rear. He related that many of the troops were tired of the war, and even more tired of the bullshit and harassment they felt they were being subjected to by the lifters. And this was one way they were striking back. Of course, it took someone who was really over the edge to play this kind of game. And sadly, to many of the troops, it was a game. And apparently, more and more troops, especially grunts, were falling over that edge. Doc said he had even heard a story about an SFC in the Americal Division who had been sent to a mental ward after some of his troops surrounded his hootch with claymores and then threw a CS grenade into the hootch in an attempt to gas him out. His gas mask saved him, but he went crazy after the event and they had to take him away.

He and Tom said that this was the first fragging that they had witnessed, but it wasn't the first one to take place in the division. Doc surmised that what happened tonight was more of a warning to the lifers to cut the bullshit than an attempt on the CSM's life.

He was sure they timed the fragging for when they knew he was out, probably at the NCO club. The battalion "top," whose name was Cornelius Jeffers, was a real bastard, I was told, and had many enemies in the enlisted ranks. Even a lot of the NCOs, like Sergeant Martinez, didn't like him.

My trance and fascination with this information was broken when two MPs stormed into the club. "Did anyone witness what happened out there?" one of them asked the few inhabitants remaining in the club. No one responded. With that, they left in a huff, and I looked around and noticed that the place was almost empty. Some of the guys must have gone out to see what had happened while others just went back to their hootches to avoid the drama. I hadn't noticed. But I did suddenly realize how stoned I was and how close I had come to being injured—or killed. It was a strange sensation. Not one of fear per se, but more like a numbness—or even an obliviousness—to what was going on around me.

We got up and made our way back to the hootch. On the way back, Tom said he was going to suggest that we go see a movie at the base camp's outdoor theater that night. "It probably would have been safer," he said, "although the last time I went, the airstrip nearby was hit with two rockets, which kind of added to the show." He laughed. As I opened the door to the hootch and stepped in, I noticed that Eric had his TV on. Johnny Carson was doing his monologue. I looked at my watch; it was 2335 hours, right on schedule for *The Tonight Show*—just like home.

The next morning, I was awakened by the sound of a radio playing in the background. I looked at my watch; it was exactly 0600 hours, and at that precise moment, a disc jockey broke into the strain: "Good morning, Vietnam." I was being greeted for the first time by the now-famous AFVN wake-up call created by the former army disc jockey Adrian Cronauer (who was played by Robin Williams in the movie *Good Morning, Vietnam*). By the mid-1960s, the military had a full-blown media operation, AFVN (the Armed Forces Vietnam Broadcasting Network), established in Vietnam. Television programming was available from 0700 hours to 0100 hours. Radio operated around the clock.

There was a full slate of programming on TV, from dramas and sitcoms to soap operas and movies. We had the news at eleven o'clock and Johnny Carson at eleven thirty—just like at home. Radio programming was virtually indistinguishable from stateside stations. And almost every hootch had a television. But as you might imagine, there was also programming related to the military and its mission in Vietnam. And of course, what we saw and what we heard, in terms of news and views, was censored. Occasionally, a disc jockey or newscaster would let the truth slip out or make a comment about the war that was counter to the script or prescribed policy. It was amusing to watch the men making the "blunder" disappear from the program the next day. "What's the count on news anchors now, Doc?" Tom would remark every time it happened.

It was Friday, and this was the day that Eric was to drive me to division headquarters to get my press pass. Anyone involved in media or communications in Vietnam had to have press credentials. Little did I realize at the time, but this little card with my picture on it would be my "ticket to ride," both literally and figuratively, during my tour in Vietnam. I made my way to the office and spent the morning going through battalion files to familiarize myself with the unit. After lunch, Captain Becker and Sergeant Martinez spent an hour or so briefing me on subjects and possible stories that they wanted me to prepare for the first edition of the *65th Recorder*, the name we came up with for the battalion newsletter. As soon as we were finished, I grabbed Eric, and we headed out for the short jeep ride to make my 1500 hours appointment at division headquarters.

We pulled up in front of division HQ and parked in an open space alongside five other jeeps. As we entered the somewhat impressive building, Eric told me he'd wait for me in the visitor's lounge. A spec 4 at the reception desk pointed me in the right direction, and I proceeded to the PIO's (public information officer) office. Once inside, I handed a clerk the letter of authorization, signed by the battalion commander, that Sergeant Martinez had prepared for me. It informed the division that I would be the correspondent for the 65th

Engineers to the division newspaper and would also be writing and issuing a weekly newsletter for the battalion. He told me to follow him and led me into the PIO's office. He introduced me to Captain John Tierney and handed him my letter. I saluted, and he said, "At ease, soldier, take a seat." Captain Tierney quizzed me briefly on my background then handed me a regulation directive that stated what I could and couldn't do as an army reporter. He said I should take it back and study it carefully, but told me that it essentially said that everything I write had to be in line with army policy and had to be approved by the battalion commander and the division PIO office. He said stories of interest to the division would be picked up and used in their weekly publication, the *Tropic Lightning News*. "And if you're real lucky, your stories might even be picked up by the *Pacific Start and Stripes*," he continued. The *Stars and Stripes* was the "authorized" civilian newspaper for the military that was distributed to the troops on a weekly basis. By "authorized" they meant censored, so the only way we could find out what was really happening in the world—and with the war—was from newspapers and magazines mailed to us from back home. But at any rate, there it was in my hands—a little card that made me an official U.S. Army war correspondent.

As we headed back to the 65th Engineers' compound, Eric looked at his watch. "It's 1600 hours and I'm done for the day," he exclaimed. "Would you like to stop at the sauna before going back?" Not expecting this option, I hesitated and then asked him if he thought Sergeant Martinez would miss us. He informed me that no one would be at HQ at this hour. "We're having our biweekly cookout tomorrow night," he said, "and Martinez and the boys are out scrounging grub for the event. And it's Friday Happy Hour at both the NCO and officers clubs, so there's no need to worry."

As I had noticed at my initial arrival, the sauna was located in a sizeable building just outside the 65th Engineers' compound gate. There was a large palm tree at the entrance, next to a big sign that read, sauna bath. A number of jeeps and small trucks were parked in front and around the side of the building. As he was parking the jeep, Eric said, "Let me tell you how this place works. For three dollars, you get a towel, a locker, use of the sauna, and a massage. A girl will be assigned to you after you pay.

"If you slip your girl another two dollars, she'll give you a hand job. And if there aren't any division health and welfare inspectors around and you slip her another couple of bucks, you can get even more…if you know what I mean." I asked Eric how they got away with this kind of activity, especially considering the sauna was located on a major army base. "In this man's army, we all need a little release," he retorted. "Apparently the brass turns their heads the other way, and with inspectors making spot appearances, things generally don't get out of hand."

"What about disease?" I then asked him. He didn't answer me. And thus I made my first trip to the "Sauna Bath" and learned how it got its nickname—"the steam and cream."

On Saturday night, I attended my first headquarters company cookout. It was the company's way of promoting esprit de corps—a means for officers, NCOs, and EMs to legally fraternize…and the company's way of rewarding us for a job well done. Everyone seemed to genuinely enjoy themselves, as there wasn't the disharmony in HQ company that was often found in the engineer units. Sergeant Martinez was the real force behind the cookouts and served as its main procurer of goods—and its head chef. He somehow managed to come up with food that we didn't know existed on base. We usually had steak and all the fixings. They were cooked on makeshift charcoal grills that were fabricated out of fifty-gallon oil drums that were cut in half on the horizontal. The Sarge also managed to procure a variety of beer and sodas for the event. We usually drank whatever the weekly supply truck brought in, and often that was Fresca for soda (the first "diet" soda on the market at the time, which we hated). As for beer, it was usually either Schlitz or PBR, Pabst Blue Ribbon. To get top-grade or nonallocated food or drink in the Nam required a certain amount of skill and knowledge. Procurement games, special favors, payoffs, paybacks, and the like were often the name of the game, so getting the likes of Budweiser, Coke, and Pepsi was a real treat. And somehow, Sergeant Martinez always managed to get these items for our cookouts.

The evening also presented me with the opportunity to meet the rest of the guys in the company. And I was introduced to the company translator, Tran Pham, by Captain Becker. He said Tran would accompany me to the field whenever I was covering a story that involved the Vietnamese. He was a likeable fellow whom I guessed to be in his late twenties. He told me that he had been a schoolteacher before the war, but was now fulfilling his military obligation as a translator since he could speak English. Tran and I would become good friends, and I can thank him for getting me hooked on Vietnamese food. On days when we'd have time, I'd bring him eggs, rice, vegetables, and chicken (if I could get it) from the mess hall, and he'd cook for us at the hootch. It was incredible what he could do with those basic ingredients. But as those of us who love Vietnamese food know, it's all about the seasonings and the sauces.

At sundown, Sergeant Martinez called us all together. It was time for the monthly awards ceremony. He and Captain Becker used the occasion of the cookouts to present service medals, awards of merit, and promotions. I got my PFC stripes that night while Tom was promoted to spec 4. Two guys in the company got Bronze Stars for valor—a special event that brought the battalion commander to our little gathering. Now there was a strange man, as I was to find out later. Fortunately, he only stayed for the awards ceremony. The candidates for awards formed a straight line and waited for the CO to make the presentations. As he got to me, I stood up straight, brought my heels together, and gave him a snappy salute. God, I must have looked silly, I thought to myself. Sergeant Martinez, who followed closely behind the captain carrying all the awards and citations, just gave me a big smile.

As the cookout broke up, Doc grabbed me and asked if I wanted to join him and a bunch of guys at the EM club. The USO had booked a Philippine rock band for an evening performance. I said sure, like I had something better to do, and it would be my first taste of live entertainment in Vietnam. But first we went back to the hootch to change out of our uniforms and into our civvies—and of course, to get our heads right.

I couldn't believe how crowded the club was and how rowdy the troops were. But then again, it was Saturday night. The band was real mediocre, but a real trip to watch as they mimicked and played American and British rock from the '50s and '60s. But they had three female singers who were pretty nice looking, and that's all the crowd needed. The hoots and whistles often drowned out the lyrics, but who cared. A good time was had by all. After about an hour and a half, I had had enough, so I said good night to the guys and headed back to the hootch. I had just completed my second week in the Nam and my first with the 65th Engineers. Next week, I would begin my career as an army journalist.

As I drifted off to sleep, an empty feeling came over me. I hadn't heard from home yet, and I missed my girlfriend. And now that I knew I'd be leaving the security of the base camp for parts unknown to cover stories for the battalion, a sense of anxiety came over me that I hadn't felt since touching down in Vietnam.

CHAPTER 5

MEDCAP, Mass, and Madness at CU CHI

On Monday, I began what was to become my daily routine while in Cu Chi with the 65th Engineers—wake up to reveille, then morning formation, followed by cleaning up, breakfast, and in the office by 0730.

My office responsibilities included typing and paperwork in support of S-2 activities and putting together stories for the *65th Recorder*. But today, another task was added to my writing and reporting assignments—battalion photographer. Captain Becker asked me if I knew how to handle a camera, and I said, "Sure." After all, I had taken a lot of pictures over the years with my Instamatic and had even handled a 35mm camera once or twice. "What about developing and printing film?" he continued. He had me there, and I couldn't lie. "No, sir," I responded.

"Well, don't worry about it. They'll teach you up at the division photo lab." He handed me the battalion's 35mm camera and a box full of black-and-white film. In the coming days, I would take a lot of practice pictures in the battalion area and then Eric would drive me up to division headquarters where the photo lab was located. I was instructed by pros in the methods of processing and printing photographs, which came in handy on more than one occasion during my tour. And a side benefit was that the lab was air-conditioned!

After lunch that day, I was given another assignment by Sergeant Martinez. He said he wanted me to get a military driver's license, as it would come in handy in the future (for him and Captain Becker, as it turned out). He wanted me to qualify for both jeeps and light trucks.

"No problem," I assured him, as I tried to imagine myself driving a truck around the base and countryside.

Today, however, we were doing something different at 1600 hours. We were having drill practice (yes, marching practice) because the battalion was participating in a division parade on Saturday. It seems that the commanding general in Vietnam, General Creighton W. Abrams, was going to be paying the division a visit. So the division commander decided to have a parade so General Abrams could review the troops as they marched around the "electric strawberry" in the division headquarters circle. It seems that Major General Bautz liked parades, and I was to participate in at least three of them during my time at Cu Chi. It was indicative of the stateside mentality that he and the division suffered from, which didn't sit well with the troops.

To witness a battalion of seasoned combat engineers (not to mention the grunts)—who had either been brought in from the field for an early rotation or just for the day put into formation, by company, to practice their marching technique—had to be seen to be believed. Needless to say, getting these guys to take the whole thing seriously was a frustrating if not impossible exercise for the lifers. And it wasn't just getting them to practice marching. Cleaning these guys up with haircuts, clean fatigues, polished boots, etc., was the lifer's mission of the week. Getting them to march in a straight line was a pipe dream.

After drill practice, we had our company mail call, the most anticipated event of the day in Vietnam. In addition to letters, which were the mainstay of mail call, many of the guys, including Tom that day, got "care packages" from home. This, as I was learning, was another of the rituals of the Nam that helped the troops "make it through the night." In addition to newspapers, magazines, and books and little luxury items that were difficult if not impossible to come by in the Nam, it was all about the food items that were included in these packages. Food items like cheeses, salami and other exotic meats, cakes and cookies, canned fish and dried fruit, candies, and the like. Food that tempted the palate and satisfied those late-night munchies that most of us suffered from. Of course, these packages were shared among buddies and hootch mates, and the ritual of opening them and slowly unveiling the contents was not unlike kids gathering around the tree on Christmas morning with great anticipation. The bounty was often so plentiful that dinner at the mess hall was skipped and replaced with gorging ourselves in the hootch.

It turned out to be bonanza night for me as well, as I received two letters from home, one from my girlfriend and another from my parents. Finally, some communication from the world. I ripped open Paula's letter first and savored each of her beautiful words. Then I read the letter from my parents. It contained a piece of information that sent a chill down my spine. My mom, who did most of the letter writing in my family, informed me that I had been assigned to the same division that my dad had served in during World War II.

My father was a medic (coincidence that I was assigned to live with medics?) with the 25th Infantry Division in the Pacific Theater during the worst part of the war in that region. While treating the wounded during a raging battle with the Japanese on the island of Luzon, he was severely wounded. The battle was so fierce that they could barely retrieve the wounded and had to go back for those who didn't make it when the fighting had subsided. Presumed dead, my father lay there for almost two days. When he regained consciousness, he was able to give himself a shot that prevented the gangrene that was spreading through his body from killing him. But by the time they got him to a field hospital, they had to amputate his right arm below the elbow, as well as remove as much shrapnel as possible from his body. He also lost the sight of one eye and partial sight in the other. But he made it. I couldn't help but wonder if being assigned to the same army division as my dad was just coincidence, fate, or a sign from above. And I'll have to admit—the thought of history repeating itself did cross my mind more than once during my tour of duty in Vietnam.

The next day, I began my career as an army journalist. I was given the opportunity to accompany the medics on their weekly MEDCAP to Cu Chi village. Doc had suggested to Captain Becker that I do a feature story on their weekly clinics, and he jumped at the idea. Doc was such a bullshit artist that I think he concocted the whole thing just to get permission for me to spend the day in the village with them. But the captain loved the idea and even called the division PIO to suggest that the story be featured in the next edition of the *Tropic Lightning News*. He thought it would also be a great way to get the battalion some publicity for its pacification efforts. "Pacification" was one of two programs that the military/U.S. government tried (and failed) to implement while I was over there. Its goal was to neutralize the Viet Cong's influence with the people in the South by taking a proactive approach with humanitarian programs like MEDCAP, building schools and hospitals, and the like. The other program was "Vietnamization," which was the concept of turning the war over to the South Vietnamese. As the United States began its gradual withdrawal from Vietnam in 1970, someone had to pick up the slack against the North. Presumably it was the South, and Vietnamization was the process conceived by our government for turning the war over to the ARVNS (Army of the Republic of Vietnam). And we all know how well that went.

Before I could take the short trip outside the gates to Cu Chi village, there was one more piece of in-country processing that I had yet to complete—and that was being issued my weapon. I hadn't done it up until this point because I had yet to leave the base and didn't really need it—an oversight I was later told, for what if the base had been attacked and I needed to defend myself and others? So off I went to supply to pick up my constant companion—an M-16 semi-automatic rifle. I had learned how to use this weapon during basic training. In fact, I earned a sharpshooter medal for my prowess. It is an impressive piece of hardware that was the mainstay of our arsenal during the Vietnam War.

It felt weird carrying the rifle and a dozen clips of ammunition back to the hootch. Guys like me, who had no real combat function, still had to protect themselves and their fellow soldiers in the event it was necessary—especially outside the security of the base camp. While on base, the extent of our combat responsibility was occasional guard duty, which I was lucky enough to only pull twice while at Cu Chi. To keep our skill levels at the ready, there was required target practice at the base firing range every six weeks. There were also frequent weapons inspections to assure that our rifles were clean and in good operating condition. I never did feel comfortable carrying a weapon because the notion of doing so implied that one would have to use it. And I still hadn't rationalized in my mind whether or not I could or would be able to kill someone. But the thought of being out there without a weapon felt even more uncomfortable. So I learned to live with my jet-black buddy.

With M-16 and backpack in hand, I headed to the infirmary where my medic buddies worked. I'd spend a lot of time hanging out at this place while at Cu Chi because most of my friends were medics, and it was one of the few buildings in the area that had a concrete floor and was waterproof. As I got there, George, another one of the medics I shared a hootch with, pulled up in a ton-and-a half truck that he had just signed out from the motor pool. Now that we were all assembled, the guys began loading the truck with their gear, medical supplies, and the goodies they'd be handing out to the villagers treated at the clinic. My gear consisted of a rifle, some ammunition, and a backpack containing a notebook and pen.

As the last box was being put on the truck, Doc turned to me and asked, "Where's Tran?" I shrugged my shoulders and was about to reply that I didn't know when I turned and saw him walking down the path toward the infirmary. "Here he comes," I replied. Tran always accompanied HQ personnel on off-base missions that involved the Vietnamese. Even though some of the villagers spoke broken English or Nam slang—a combination of English, French, and Viet "Nam" jargon—you couldn't rely on them for vital communications. And treating the sick and injured falls into the vital communications category. All loaded up, we hopped into the truck and made our way to the main gate. Doc presented our travel papers to the MPs, and we were on our way to Cu Chi village, a short ten-minute drive down the road.

This was the first time I'd left the base camp since arriving. And I have to admit, being out in the countryside without a full military escort felt exhilarating.

After leaving the barren area surrounding the periphery of the base, the terrain returned to lush farmland and rice paddies. It was a beautiful day, with a big blue sky patched with fluffy white clouds. The sight of water buffalo pulling plows manned by Vietnamese farmers in traditional garb was pastoral, masking somewhat the reality that there was a war going on here. As we approached the village, the road became crowded with activity. People were walking on both sides of the main street, carrying everything from produce, water, and firewood to building materials and all kinds of personal items.

As we entered the village itself, the road became clogged with bicycles, motor scooters, Lambrettas, and other vehicles. Having only seen the village from a distance on my way to the Cu Chi base camp, I didn't realize how big it was. There were many streets with busy intersections that were lined with houses that ran the gamut from huts to small villas. And like all Vietnamese cities, villages, and hamlets, the streets were lined with vendors selling everything from food and housewares to clothing and live animals. Concessions that sold American cigarettes, soda, beer and military attire—presumably stolen or acquired on the black market—were intermixed among them. There was even a village square that was surrounded by public and commercial buildings. Picket fences outlined many of the properties, creating quite a picturesque setting. The whole scene was fascinating to me, and I couldn't wait to start exploring and absorbing the local culture.

We pulled up alongside one of the public buildings in the village square. It was the village medical clinic, which was staffed by one (what we would call) nurse practitioner. Just about every doctor and nurse in the country had been pulled into military duty, so medical care for the villagers was almost nonexistent. People who were seriously ill or injured had to travel to Saigon, as doctors only made periodic trips to village clinics. That's one of the reasons the U.S. military instituted the MEDCAP program. For even though our medics couldn't deal with serious problems, they could take care of basic medical needs.

As we started to unload the truck, I noticed that there were already people waiting in line. Others started arriving in droves, mostly mama sans with babies in arms, old papa sans, and a lot of children. They gave us big smiles as we walked by them on our way into the clinic, exposing their red, black, and gold teeth. The red was from betel nut, an herb they chewed for the same reasons I guess that people in other parts of the world chewed tobacco. But betel nut also numbed their gums, which helped relieve the pain that I'm sure many of them suffered due to poor or nonexistent dental hygiene. Black teeth were the end result of no dental hygiene. And those lucky or rich enough had an occasional gold cap on one or more of their teeth. Every now and then during my travels in the Nam, I'd see a full mouth of gold, which was almost blinding if the sun hit them the right way.

The kids seemed to love the GIs, mostly because of the handouts they usually received. Some of them were also runners for Vietnamese selling drugs or black market items to the troops. They often got a small reward for their efforts at both ends of these transactions. But Doc warned me that on MEDCAPs, we only handed out goodies to the kids who came in for treatment or to get their shots. Otherwise, most of them would never get treated.

As the medics went about their business, I pulled out my pen and notepad and began writing about what I was observing. I positioned myself next to Tran and asked him a million questions about the people and their culture, what they thought about what was going on here, how they felt about the Americans and the war, and so on. I even interviewed a couple of the mama sans and one old papa san who was more than happy to philosophize about life and all of its mysteries. Then out of the blue, a woman carrying a baby ran up to me with a look on angst on her face. She handed me her baby and began weeping. I looked down at the baby in my arms then back at her. Not knowing what she wanted or what to do, I walked over to the clinic with the woman following closely behind. I handed the baby to Tom and explained what had just happened. Tran, who was standing next to him, said he would take over from here. The woman bowed as I left, wiping tears from her eyes. I guess she didn't realize that all she had to do was get in line and that the medics would take care of her baby.

At noon we broke for lunch, and Doc, Tran, and I made our way across the street to sample some of the local cuisine from two vendors who were working side by side. It was my first real opportunity to partake of Vietnamese food, other than what Tran would cook for us at the hootch. The smells made my mouth water, but I was glad that Tran was with us to help make our selections. The Vietnamese were notorious for using all kinds of animals and herbs in their cooking, including dogs, cats, rats, and snakes; and I wasn't quite ready to go there—yet. Tom, George, and Tony stayed back at the clinic and ate food that they had brought along with them. There was no way those guys would even taste the local food, much less eat it.

Tran ordered me Vietnamese noodles, spring rolls, and some kind of fried dough that looked like corn fritters. We had warm Coke in '50s style bottles to drink (ice was almost unheard of in Vietnam, so warm drinks were the norm, except on the base camps). After he and Doc got their food, we walked to a grassy patch in the village square and sat down to eat. A common sight, which I observed around us that day and throughout my travels in Vietnam, were locals squatting rather than sitting to eat. They mostly ate their meals in bowls, which they held close to their faces, not only picking up but scooping the food into their mouths with their chopsticks. Being somewhat of a rookie with chopsticks, I followed suit, seeing that it was much easier to scoop it into one's mouth than mastering the art of picking up each item, especially rice. The food was incredibly delicious, closer to Japanese than Chinese in taste. I got hooked on Vietnamese food right from the start and would partake of local cuisine as often as possible during my travels in the Nam. For the most part, I never asked what was in the food—and I never got sick, I might add.

After lunch, I walked around the village taking in all the activity. It was extremely hot, so I unbuttoned my fatigue shirt, which must have been somewhat of a taboo as I got a lot of stares from the locals. I also had dirty blond hair. Or maybe it was just that I was a soldier walking around by himself with no weapon in hand. I had left my M-16 back at the clinic, rather foolishly I suddenly realized (this kind of stupid luck seemed to follow me throughout my year in the Nam). The sun had a mesmerizing effect on me and would often put me into an almost trancelike state when I was overexposed to it—especially if I was high—but it didn't seem to affect the locals the same way (I guess they were used to it...duh).

After looking around for a while, I made my way back to the square. I found a shady spot to sit under a tree outside the clinic and began writing my MEDCAP story. A couple of kids came over and sat next to me, observing my every move. This went on for quite some time without any of them moving.

At around 1600 hours, the medics closed the clinic and we started packing up. As we were loading the truck, I noticed that a small group of middle-aged men had gathered on the other side of the square and were staring at us. Throughout the day, we had attracted mostly women, old men, and children. But suddenly, this group of men appeared, seemingly from nowhere. I didn't say anything to the guys at the time, but I had this uncomfortable feeling about them—the kind of gut feeling that came in handy when operating in the field in Vietnam. As we pulled out, the men began pointing and talking to each other, watching our every move. The kids ran after the truck, stretching out their hands for any last handouts they might get from us. We just flashed them the peace sign as we drove off, leaving the village behind us. Doc noticed the look on my face as I continued to watch the men on the square. He didn't say anything, but put up both of his hands and made a V sign with one and a C sign with the other.

Unbeknownst to the 25th Infantry Division at the time, the village of Cu Chi was the headquarters for the Viet Cong in that region of South Vietnam. Over the years, they had constructed a massive tunnel complex right under the village—and right under our feet at the base camp, and we never knew it. The tunnel complex was so large that it housed an entire division of troops, a military hospital, as well as a command and control center. Apparently, the men we saw in the village that day had just emerged from one of the tunnel exits to observe our activity. I guessed that because we were engaged in a humanitarian activity that helped their people, they left us alone. But more likely, they didn't want to tip their hand and potentially expose their enterprise. As we learned over and over in Vietnam, passive

South Vietnamese villagers by day, even some of our colleagues and suppliers, were Viet Cong by night. Hit and run, booby traps, guerrilla warfare were all the name of the game, and it was a game that they played very well—and a lot better than us.

On the ride back to the base camp, I told the guys how fascinating I found the day and how I couldn't wait to put together the story. "Out of all the bullshit these people have to go through because of this fucking war," I remarked, "at least the army is doing some good with programs like MEDCAP." They all nodded in agreement. I also commented that I heard a number of villagers speaking French, or at least what sounded like French. Of course, I knew the history of the French occupation of Vietnam and would witness the influence of French culture throughout the country—from the architecture in Saigon and elsewhere, to the French bread that was an integral part of Vietnamese cuisine. And then there were the incredibly beautiful women that resulted from French and Vietnamese liaisons. Doc said he had been captivated by the French influence since arriving and that he wanted to learn the language. Since I had taken two semesters of French in high school, I told him that I would join him. He said they offered foreign language classes at night on base and that we should sign up. I said we should. We never did.

I spent the rest of the week putting together stories for the first edition of the *65th Recorder* and doing administrative work for Sergeant Martinez. Every time he went flying to rack up time toward his air medal—the only reason he went flying—he passed his work on to me. Evenings were spent the usual way—listening to music, writing letters, rapping, going to the EM club, and getting stoned. For the REMFs, when you left work for the hootch, it was like leaving the office and going home to your family—literally and figuratively. Doc would often stroll in the door and shout out: "Lucy…I'm home." We'd ask each other how our days went, relay war stories, and bitch about the latest directive or Mickey Mouse bullshit the army was putting us through.

We'd also talk about the war and what we'd heard through the grapevine was going on "out there." Information about combat activity was limited since we had no real source of news and were only told what we needed to know. We'd hear about casualties up north and gains the NVA and Viet Cong were making in our region. We also heard that some units were about to be withdrawn and sent home. Civilian newspapers from the world that arrived by mail were featuring stories about the pressure Congress was putting on Nixon and the military to reduce the number of troops in Vietnam. There appeared to be a growing outcry against the war from all segments of the population and an increasing frustration in Congress about the lives and the money being wasted on a war that looked increasingly like we weren't going to win.

Of course, rumors about a possible troop reduction were big news. The thought of going home early was quite appealing, especially for the grunts who'd been there for six months or longer. Since I had a job in "the media" and could snoop around and ask questions as part of my job—and because I worked in the HQ intelligence section—a lot of guys relied on me for information. I would occasionally hear or learn of things before word filtered down to the troops, but usually not much before.

Weekends were much the same as weekdays in the Nam. You worked on Saturdays, but usually had every other Sunday off. As for extracurricular activities, we had our biweekly cookouts, and there was usually a couple of movies to choose from—played at a makeshift outdoor theater. One Saturday night, they showed the movie *The Boys in the Band*, which I found to be a strange choice to play to an all-male audience in a war zone, especially in 1970. You could also take advantage of the sauna, swimming pool, snack bars (no Long Binh–style restaurants, though), dayrooms, and other base activities sponsored by the division special services group. And there was often weekend entertainment at the EM, NCO, and officers clubs as well. Occasionally, you could get a ride to Long Binh or Bien Hoa to sample what those bases and surrounding areas had to offer. And on rare occasion, you could make a day trip or even get an overnight pass to Saigon (I'd get an opportunity to sample Saigon in a couple of weeks). So considering we were in a war zone, there was actually quite a bit to choose from. And if none of these options appealed to you, one could always find a hootch or bunker party to occupy your time.

One Sunday morning, I woke up with a jolt to the sound of Tom screaming, "Gas!" As I sat up in bed, the odor hit me like a ton of bricks and my eyes began to water. Doc yelled over to me to put on my gas mask, which was part of the initial issue of gear we were given. Of course, mine was at the bottom of my duffel bag, which was under my bunk. As I struggled to find it, my eyes started to burn. And by the time I pulled it out and got it over my head, my eyes were almost swollen shut. After a minute or so, my vision started to clear, and I looked around the hootch at six guys who looked like "creatures from the Black Lagoon." The sound of each of us breathing through the face masks was eerie. I asked what was going on, and Doc told me that someone must have popped a CS grenade. It was tear gas, the same substance the National Guard threw at the protestors at the University of Maryland the week before I left for the Nam. He said this wasn't unusual, and like some of the fraggings, it was probably thrown by some irate soldier getting back at the lifers. "That's why we sleep with these things next to our beds," he continued. "You'd better get with the program, Stouper" (a pet name that Doc often called me). And believe me, from that day forward, I slept with my gas mask strapped to the bed next to my head.

It didn't take long for the gas to clear. And now that I was up, and since it was Sunday, I decided to go to Mass at the division chapel. I hadn't been to Mass in quite some time and thought it might be a good idea to do a little communing with the Creator. Besides, I was curious about how the priest would talk about the church's role in the war. I personally felt the church should have been at the forefront of the antiwar movement. After all, "thou shalt not kill" is a commandment. But then there were the Crusades, holy wars, and so on. So I guess killing was open to interpretation. I took a shower, got dressed, and made my way to the chapel.

There were two services each Sunday morning—a Catholic Mass at 1000 hours, and an inter-denominational service for Protestants and others at 1100. I took a seat in the relatively small chapel and looked around. There were about two dozen GIs present—a mix of officers, NCOs, and EMs. The priest, a chaplain with the rank of captain, and two EM servers approached the altar promptly at 1000. As the Mass progressed in its familiar pattern, my mind drifted to questioning not only the war, but also my presence in it—a feeling of "guilt by association" that came over me on occasion since the day I stepped foot on Vietnamese soil. With all the activity of the past few weeks, this thought had been shoved to the back of my consciousness. But in this setting, it began to reemerge. The guilt now turned to anger. I was angry about the war, angry with my country, and angry at myself for being a part of it. And I was angry at the church for not being an outspoken critic. While I also realized that the church had an obligation to minister to its faithful in the war zone, it still pissed me off. This chaplain was going to have to prove himself to me, and thus I eagerly awaited his sermon.

As he approached the pulpit, I sat up straight in anticipation of his words. He began with the expected discussion of the meaning of today's gospel and then turned quickly to a dialogue about our responsibility as Christians to lead by example. "We are guests in this country," he began, "and as such, we must show the Vietnamese people, through our example, what it means to lead a Christian life.

"Many of these people don't yet know Christ," he continued, "and through our mission to rid the country of communism, each of us plays a part in helping them achieve the freedom they need to be able to bring Christ into their lives." I was incensed. This guy was not only politically off the wall, but he was actually trying to convince us that one of our missions in Vietnam was to convert the heathens.

At the end of Mass, he greeted the troops as they filed out of the chapel. I wanted to tell him what I thought about the church's position on the war, not to mention his sermon, but rightfully decided against it. As I moved toward the exit, what I observed was a rather sad character, not the leader of his flock who would (or could) speak out against any perceived immorality or injustice surrounding the war. But rather, he was a sheep—an officer in this man's army, who had the misfortune of having to follow not only orders from the church, but from the military as well. He shook my hand and asked, "Where are you from, soldier?" "Pennsylvania," I replied. It was the last time I attended Mass while in Vietnam.

Later that week, I was back in the chapel, but this time it was a sad occasion. The chapel was filled to capacity, with every available member of the 65th Engineer Battalion, to attend a memorial service for one of our buddies. On Tuesday, one of the guys I had met on my second night with the 65th Engineers (in the heavy equipment operators hootch), Ken Allen, was killed when his bulldozer hit a land mine. He was clearing jungle where the engineers were building a fire support base, near the Cambodian border in Tay Ninh Province, when the tragedy occurred. He was the first person I knew who had been killed in Vietnam, and it hit me real hard. I suddenly realized that it could actually happen to me, like it has happened to countless others, causing an adrenaline rush of fear and anger to sweep over me.

The memorial service was conducted by the battalion's other chaplain, a Methodist minister. Like his Catholic counterpart, he also spouted epithets about our mission in Vietnam and about why this young soldier didn't die in vain. As if the situation wasn't tense enough, the sound of this guy's scripted dialogue brought my emotions to a fever pitch. I didn't know whether to laugh, cry, or scream. As I looked around the chapel, I could see the same tortured emotions on the faces of my brothers. I could see their tears and sense their grief and anger. Except for the few career types in attendance, we all knew that this war was bullshit, and this tragedy should never have happened.

Sensing our mind-set, Sergeant Martinez got Captain Becker to give us the afternoon off. Upon learning this, I decided to spend the afternoon catching up on letter writing and reading and catching some rays. So with the sun shining brightly, I made my way back to the hootch, stripped down to my boxer shorts, assembled my stuff, and grabbed my trusty poncho liner. A little side note here on poncho liners. They were designed, I suppose, to line the inside of the rubber ponchos that we were issued to protect us from the monsoon rains. They were made of a high-tech (at the time) nylon-like fiber on the outside with a thin fiber insulation on the inside, that kept you cool in the summer and warm in the winter. The green-camouflage-colored poncho liners were primarily used as blankets on our bunks, but could also be used as overhead shelters in the field to protect from sun and rain, or as ground covers for lying out in the sun. In fact, I learned to like them so much that I sent three of them home. And to this day, when I go to the beach, I conduct a ritualistic "unfurling" of the poncho liner, which I use as a beach blanket.

The sun in Vietnam was mesmerizing. It was incredibly hot and dry most of the time—except during the five-month monsoon season, when it was hot and humid, and you were usually drenched with sweat most of the time. So when we could get away with it, the rule was the fewer clothes the better. Guys went without wearing their shirts when they were off duty, and as I previously mentioned, almost no one wore underwear, except boxers to sleep in. With the heat and humidity, jungle rot was all too prevalent, so we wore as little as possible (which is why, I suppose, Tarzan only wore a loincloth when he was in the jungle).

I put a tape on Tom's sound system and turned it up so I could hear it outside the hootch. Then I got stoned, gathered my stuff, and made my way to a grassy patch next to the hootch. As I settled onto my poncho liner, I noticed that my tan was coming along nicely and that I was beginning to lose that new-guy look. My hair was getting longer, my fatigues were starting to fade, and I was safe—what more could a boy in the Nam ask for? The music playing was *Spooky Tooth*, a group Tom turned me on to shortly after I arrived. Between the pot, the music, and the sun, I was in a virtual trance. It was a great feeling, and one that many of us experienced quite often during our tours in Vietnam—a feeling that helped us escape from the reality of our surroundings.

As I lay there with my senses heightened, I began to notice the sounds of the war in the background. Even though they were always present, being stoned and lying there in the mesmerizing sun with my emotions still elevated from Ken's memorial service, I became aware of them like never before. Generators churning, trucks and jeeps rolling by in incessant cadence, the sound of helicopters cutting through the air, occasional gunfire and explosions—these, along with the ever-present strains of rock & roll, were the soundtrack of my year in the Nam.

A jet fighter roaring overhead broke my trance, and thoughts of the morning and the futility of Ken Allen's death once again rose to the surface. I couldn't get it out of my mind, and the more I thought about it, the angrier I got. The more I observed and experienced the insanity surrounding the Vietnam War, the politics back home, and the actions of the career military calling the shots, the more I could understand, and even condone, the actions of many of the troops. You could see why so many guys got stoned as often as they did. You could understand their refusal of duty and intolerance for authority figures. You could see why some were driven over the edge, especially those who faced the horrors of combat. And you could see, whether intentional or not, how the military played a major role in perpetuating this situation with the troops.

The career military by the end of the Vietnam era had become increasingly frustrated and demoralized. Not everything that was going on over there was their fault, of course, yet they still suffered a great sense of frustration over how the war was going. But they also, in many instances, took advantage of this situation and capitalized on the "spoils of war." In their defense, they were fighting a war that was created by politicians and was executed with faulty policy and design. In many ways, their hands were tied, and they were frustrated at not being able to fight an all-out go-for-the-win war. But as we all know, even if the policy had been different, and the military had been able to fight the war the way they wanted to, we still would have lost in the end. And there were two main reasons for this. First, we didn't have "just cause" on our side and thus we ultimately lost the support of not only of the American people, but of the troops as well. And second, we underestimated the spirit and fight of the Vietnamese people, of their ability to hold on seemingly endlessly and take everything we threw at them, and even their sense of independence and right, not to mention their cunning and skill at conducting a guerilla-style war that we had never experienced before and just didn't know how to fight or win.

As the war entered the era of the 1970s, a lot of things changed—for the country, and for the military in Vietnam. Not only did we begin losing the war, but we also began losing the spirit of the military and its troops. As I mentioned before, drugs became increasingly prevalent, and more and more soldiers were getting high. Esprit de corps was rapidly declining, especially in the rear. There were increasing refusals of duty, and even mutinies—especially in the ranks of the infantry. You could see that the lifers were beginning to sense the reality that the war was a lost cause and recognized how the situation at hand was impacting the troops. And as a result, in their frustration, some began letting up on military game playing. They started focusing on their careers and their futures instead, knowing that the end was near.

The career military in the Vietnam era had become a very fat and entrenched organization. And it was self-perpetuating, as it had been a while since career types had had the opportunity to get combat duty under their belts, not to mention combat pay. Acquiring battle ribbons, Air Medals, Bronze Stars, Commendation Medals, etc., became almost a competition among them (it was always a game). Two, three, and even four tours of duty in Vietnam were not uncommon for a lot of them. For others, who were less career oriented, whether by design or ability and mostly in the NCO ranks, two or more tours of duty in Vietnam often provided a *Life of Riley* scenario. Many career NCOs and officers lived "the high life." Some had or shared villas in Saigon while others lived in palatial quarters surrounding MACV headquarters. Even those living on base camps had plush hootches, with Vietnamese "servants" (we're talking houseboys, in addition to hootch maids). And with six out of ten troops having jobs in the rear by that time, many of these lifers had very cushy jobs with very little stress.

Of course, not all of the career military in Vietnam abused their power or situations. There were quite a few good ones, like Sergeant Martinez (lucky me to have landed with him), who treated his position more like a job than a career. Most of these guys weren't real achievers, at least from a career military standpoint. They were more concerned with the well-being of their men than scratching and playing the games necessary to get ahead. They tended to be regular guys who were grateful for their positions and for the half-decent pay, benefits, and housing that the military provided to them and their families. But understandably, they also took advantage of all that a tour in Vietnam had to offer, from the cushy jobs in an often exotic environment, to the combat pay and other incentives. Unlike the lifers who were continually in your face if you didn't toe the military line, however, these guys generally didn't get on your case if you did your job and played the game well enough to keep them out of trouble.

There was one more scenario surrounding the military in Vietnam that was the worst of all—those who profited from the war. I had been hearing some pretty incredible stories about the money that was being made by military and civilian personnel on the black market in Vietnam. And it wasn't just the lifers and civilian contractors. Enlisted men occasionally got in on the dangerous yet profitable action as well. The fact that military personnel were getting rich by shipping drugs back to the States was mind boggling. There were stories, and some firsthand, I might add, of GIs and lifers buying large stereo speakers, removing the woofers and tweeters, and then packing them with pot and/or heroin. They would then reseal the speakers (or other such item, such as porcelain pots) and ship them home, or to a designated location, and often via military transport. There was very little scrutiny of shipments for drugs, weapons, or other contraband in the early years of the war—until the military got wind of what was going on, that is. Speakers were very large in those days, and almost every guy I know sent home a large sound system from either the PX or the PACEX catalog. A two-speaker shipment of pot would be worth thousands; a shipment of heroin, hundreds of thousands. Some of those who got away with it returned for a second or third tour to do it again—and many of them retired rich on the proceeds.

But even worse and more incredible than that, if you can imagine anything worse or more incredible, was the large black market trade in weapons coming from U.S. and South Vietnamese military sources—weapons that eventually ended up in the hands of the North

Vietnamese and Viet Cong. In one (probably exaggerated) story, I heard that up to half of the weapons in the Viet Cong's arsenal came from the black market. To me, this just reinforced the notion that a country fighting a war that is not righteous—without the support of many if not most of its troops and with moral decay eating at its very core—cannot win a war. And we didn't.

The next morning, we were awakened by the sounds of explosions. They didn't appear to be real close by, yet they still shook the hootch. Doc raised his head, looked over at me, and shouted, "Incoming!" We all jumped out of bed and ran for the bunker. We waited in the confines of our refuge for a few minutes, but heard no further explosions. Even though it wasn't close, it was the first time I had actually experienced incoming—and it was a strange sensation. A little bit of fear and a lot of adrenaline-pumping excitement. As we were leaving the bunker, Sergeant Martinez was walking briskly down the path toward our hootch. He reported that the base airstrip had just been hit in a rocket attack. By this time, choppers were in the air searching for the source of the attack, and we heard outgoing artillery firing in the distance. The war I knew was out there but had never seen or heard was finally making itself known.

Now that we were up, I began preparing for the day. It was Friday, and we were having a big inspection at 1100 hours. I was complaining about the condition of my fatigues and having to polish my boots, when Doc asked me when I was going to get myself a hootch maid. "Why are you putting up with all this when you can have it done for $5 a week?" he asked. His hootch maid, a young Vietnamese woman named, oddly, Kelly, was coming this morning, and he offered to introduce her to me. "I'm sure she'll take you on," he said. "She works for three other guys in our company too, so she's always here."

The whole concept of hootch maids was fascinating to me. Here we were, in a war zone, with maid service. Most of the guys in base camps in the Nam had hootch maids, or at least shared them. Even some of the remote outposts and fire support bases used the services of the locals as well. These women, generally ranging in age from sixteen to sixty, would come to your hootch at least three times a week and provide a variety of services. They'd clean the hootch, wash and iron your clothes, make your bed, and polish your brass and boots. And depending on their age and appearance—and the disposition of the guys they were working for—they would perform other services as well (for an additional fee, of course). Some actually became "girlfriends," with a few even making it back to the States as war brides. There were other benefits to having a hootch maid as well. If you were so disposed, as I was, you could get them to bring you home-cooked Vietnamese delicacies. And depending on the time and place, they would even score pot and speed for their employers—when they could get it through the gate, that is. This was usually done in exchange for goodies they desired that we could get our hands on, like cigarettes, soap, chocolates, and other personal and food commodities that they wanted from the PX. It didn't matter whether you were an officer, NCO, or a lowly enlisted man (I must note here my continual reference to "enlisted men" when actually many EMs were actually drafted into service), these women took care of you and were a truly unique and integral part of the Vietnam experience.

Kelly arrived shortly after breakfast, and Doc introduced me to her as the new guy who was interested in her services. She was wearing a traditional yet informal white rayon top, black rayon pants, and sandals. The traditional *non la* hat that was tied around her neck was resting on her back, exposing her straight jet-black hair. I guessed that she was about thirty years old. She bowed to me upon our introduction, and I awkwardly bowed back. She then said, tongue in cheek, "that she would be happy to work for Jim-san…for beaucoup money." She had a sense of humor and a real outgoing personality as I was to learn.

There was a certain slang that existed as a means of communication between the Vietnamese and the GIs—a concocted language that evolved over time in the Nam. It was partially a combination of English, French, and Vietnamese and partially made up nonsense, probably by the GIs. I was to learn most of this language from Kelly, and it came in handy during my travels in the Nam. For example, "beaucoup" meant "very much" or "big" (obviously from the French) while "ti ti" was "very small" or "little." Those two expressions were used a lot. "Di di mau" meant "hurry up" or "go away," and "La dei" meant "come here." "Con sa" was "marijuana." The universality of numbers was also used as verbal communication. "Number one" meant that something or someone was very good while "number ten" was very bad. Everything from the taste and quality of food to the personality and disposition of people were measured and communicated by this numerical system.

Kelly and I were to get along famously during my stay in Cu Chi, and I really appreciated the human quality that she provided, not to mention what I learned from her and Tran about the Vietnamese people and their culture. They became real friends.

CHAPTER 6

Cu Chi and Saigon and Cambodia, Oh My!

Time was now passing me by in months rather than weeks. Days seemed meaningless. No one knew what day it was or what the date might be, and no one cared. The days were getting hotter, and my tan deeper. My fatigues were now faded to the point that I could be considered a seasoned REMF. The monsoon season was also in full swing, which caused a rather dramatic change in the daily weather. The humidity during the heat of the day was almost unbearable, and at around 1600 hours each day, the sky would blacken and tremendous rains would fall. Quite often, the clouds would just open up without wind, and the rain would come straight down in torrents. One day, on my way to the mess hall, a bolt of lightning hit the ground literally five feet in front of me. It freaked me out so much that I leapt into the air and fell face-first into a massive mud puddle. It wasn't unusual for the water in low-lying areas to be knee deep after only two hours of downpour. But then, a couple of hours later, the sun would be shining again, often accompanied by spectacular rainbows. This meteorological condition also produced some pretty incredible sunsets.

The *65th Recorder* was now a regular, if not anticipated, part of battalion life and was affording me an increased opportunity to travel off base to cover stories, not only for the battalion newsletter, but for the division's weekly newspaper, the *Tropic Lightning News*, as well. I typed our biweekly newsletter on a Remington typewriter at the S-2 office, cut and pasted the copy and hand-drawn graphics into a rough layout, then mimeographed the number of copies needed for distribution. The division newspaper, on the other hand, was put together professionally at a printer in Saigon. Having developed a relationship by this time with Captain John Tierney, the division PIO, I was occasionally invited along on trips to Saigon to observe and learn the mechanics of that process, which would come in very handy when I landed at my next assignment.

My first trip to Saigon was the most memorable. I got a call late in the day toward the end of July from Spec 5 Michael Bailey, the editor of the division newspaper. He said that Captain Tierney had invited me to accompany them to Saigon the next morning if I was able to go (I immediately checked with Sergeant Martinez, and he gave the okay). He said they'd pick me up in the captain's jeep at 0900 in front of the 65th Engineers battalion headquarters. Bailey said that Captain Tierney was going to an all-day briefing session and then dinner for all army PIOs in Vietnam at a villa in the Cholon district of Saigon, a very popular and trendy section of Saigon inhabited mostly by Chinese.

At promptly 0900 the next morning, we were on the road for the relatively short trip down Highway 1 from Cu Chi to Saigon. I'd been on this road before—at least as far as Bien Hoa. But heading into Saigon was a completely different experience. The road became clogged with activity as we made our way into the heart of the city. Captain Tierney dropped us off at the printer's at around 1000 and said he'd meet up with us at around 2000 hours in front of the Continental Hotel. "And don't be late," he emphasized. "I want to get back to Cu Chi before dark." As he pulled away, Bailey turned to me and said, "Something is up with the war, which is why they're having this briefing today. I don't know what it is, but I'm certainly going to do what I can to get at least a clue from the captain on the ride back tonight."

As we entered the printers, which was located on a charming side street off one of Saigon's main boulevards, Bailey informed me that it would only take us three or four hours to put the paper together. And since it was only a little after 1000, we'd have plenty of time to tour around the city. After observing for a while, Bailey gave me some hands-on experience, and it didn't take long before I got the hang of laying out the paper. It was interesting working at a Vietnamese business as well. It was a small and confined print shop, and everything looked and felt very much like the 1940s—very foreign, like we were in a black-and-white movie of that era.

We took a break around 1230 and had lunch at a little cafe across the street from the printers. The atmosphere was authentic side street Saigon, with white plastic tables and chairs both outside and inside the small establishment. The narrow street was overgrown with lush vegetation, which added to the charm of the setting. The cafe specialized in *pho*—noodle dishes of various types with locally grown vegetables and either beef, chicken, or pork served in large bowls, which is just what I was hoping for, having only had Vietnamese noodles once before. And what a treat! The dish reinforced my love of Vietnamese food and increased my desire to sample a multicourse dinner later in the day if we had the time.

By 1400 hours, we were finished with our work, just as Bailey had predicted, and were told as we were leaving that the papers would be delivered to the base early the next morning. Bailey suggested we take a rickshaw into the heart of the city and do a little shopping. I was always up for some shopping, especially in a strange and exotic locale. So we flagged down a bicycle-driven rickshaw and made our way toward the center of the city. The streets were crowded with all kinds of vehicular traffic, not to mention people and vendors pulling carts of varying kinds. The noise and pollution from the Lambrettas and motor bikes was stifling. People approached us at every stop, trying to sell us either some kind of food, product, or service. It was fascinating.

The day was hot and sunny, but we were shaded by our boonie hats and the top of the rickshaw. As we rode along at a slow but pleasant pace, taking in the colorful scenery along the way, I asked Bailey where he was from and what he did before joining the army. He told me that he was from New York City but had been living and working in Washington, D.C., for the *Washington Post*. Like many of us, he had been drafted. I was going to meet and learn a lot from guys like Bailey during my tour in Vietnam—a side benefit of serving during the period of the draft—as opposed to serving with the much-younger and less-educated all-volunteer force that followed when the draft ended. As time and history would tell, the contrast between the two couldn't have been greater. An "all-volunteer" force joining to fight for love of country or a cause they believed in (or were duped into, like Iraq) or to start a career versus drafting men out of high school and college, or off the street, or on their way to prison against their will to fight a war they either hated, didn't believe in, or knew nothing about. The contrast couldn't have been more different.

We rode through city streets and boulevards crowded with shops, cinemas, bars, and restaurants. Street vendors clogged the roadways, with many locals preparing food right on the sidewalks outside their homes or shops. We also rode through lush residential neighborhoods lined with palm trees and villas. The influence of French architecture and style was very evident in many parts of the city. It was classic and beautiful, but sixteen years of war and neglect had taken its toll. Many buildings and public areas were in a state of deterioration while others were surrounded by barbed wire—some taking on an almost fortress-like appearance.

We made it to the city's central plaza area in about twenty-five minutes. Bailey paid the driver in piasters, the Vietnamese currency, although the driver asked him for MPC. I suddenly realized that all I had with me was MPC, not thinking to change some military money into piasters before making the trip. Bailey told me not to worry, as MPC was worth its weight in dollars on the black market. Besides, he said, he could spot me some Ps if necessary.

We began browsing our way through the vendor stands and shops along the main street leading away from the plaza. The place was teeming with activity, a virtual bazaar like the kind you'd see in movies of places like Istanbul or Tangier. It was hard to fathom that this was a country besieged in war. Anything and everything was for sale from the street vendors, and you could often get items for half the asking price—or less. There was everything from fans, radios, housewares, and food of great variety, to exotic caged birds, fowl, and even live animals. There were a lot of American-made products, like cigarettes, liquor, and cases of soda and beer, as well as military clothing and accessories. The vendors had acquired a lot of the stuff on the black market or directly from U.S. or ARVN supply sources by whatever means. The shops were interesting as well, and the atmosphere in most of them was very friendly. As you entered, you would be greeted by one or more of the proprietors, who would bow and give you a big smile. They'd often offer you something to drink, like hot tea, warm beer, or soda, and then they would go to great lengths to convince you to buy something.

One particular shop caught my eye. It contained Vietnamese art and artifacts. Oriental art had always appealed to me, and with opportunities like being in Saigon quite often, in Bangkok on R & R (which was ahead of me), and the PACEX Catalog, I had made the decision to acquire as much as I could during my year in Southeast Asia. We entered the shop and were greeted by a stylish older gentleman wearing a long white silk robe, with a white goatee to match. I caught myself staring at him for a moment, as he reminded me of photos that I had seen of Ho Chi Minh. Unlike many of the shopkeepers, he wasn't pushy, but rather stood silently by waiting to serve us. The shop was lined with glass cases holding a variety of art and objects crafted from materials that ranged from jade and ivory on the high end to soapstone, bronze, and cast iron. There were many sculptures, mostly of Buddha figures, in various sizes, forms, and positions. After great consideration, I selected a verdigris bronze Buddha head with eyes closed that was about eight inches tall and was mounted on an ebony pedestal. I was thrilled! I had my first piece of Oriental art and a beautiful memento of Vietnam.

After spending a couple of hours wandering around the streets and shops, and being hustled for just about anything one might desire, from sex to drugs to rock & roll (cassette tapes of all kinds of music), we decided to find a restaurant and indulge in some more Vietnamese culinary delights. Bailey had been coming to Saigon on a regular basis for about eight months, so he had a couple of favorites to recommend. I told him that I was just along for the ride and let him make the decision. We proceeded down Tu Do Street toward one of the more fashionable parts of the city. Tu Do Street, of course, was infamous for its bars, clubs, and girls that attracted GIs like a magnet. They hung in clusters in the doorways of the bars, calling out at us as we passed and trying to tempt us with their wares. At this point, we really didn't have the time for both girls and dinner—or the money in my case—so we hurried on by before our appetites shifted from our stomachs further south. And there would be other days in Saigon.

The restaurant Bailey selected was located in a villa, just a couple of blocks off Tu Do Street. When we arrived, he asked for a table on the outdoor terrace, which was surrounded by palm trees and a beautiful tropical garden. Two peacocks and other exotic birds wandered on the grounds of the villa. We ordered drinks and sat there, mesmerized by a brilliant stream of setting sunlight filtering through the palm trees, illuminating birds-of-paradise and other exotic flora. It was warm, but overhead fans created a gentle, cooling breeze. For a few moments, neither of us spoke. I don't know what was going through Bailey's head, but I was in a state of twisted nirvana, finding the surrounding environment more than a little hard to believe. It's not like I was an officer assigned to the press corps in Saigon who might be used to this kind of scene. Or a grunt who might freak out at this kind of rear echelon opulence in contrast to the horrors of the field. No, I was actually somewhere in the middle of those two extremes. And even though I was enjoying the experience of dining among Saigon's elite, I still felt a little uneasy—and very much like I didn't belong here. But I wasn't going to let that spoil the moment.

After a two-hour dinner that was one of the best of my life, it was time to head to the Continental Hotel to meet up with the captain. We grabbed a rickshaw and headed for the city's central square where the hotel was located. As we rode up Tu Do Street, we again passed by the club district, with the girls whistling and waving to us as we passed by. Maybe on my next trip to Saigon I'd get a chance to see a little more of that side of the city.

When we arrived at the hotel, the captain was waiting for us in his jeep. I looked at my watch—it was 2001 hours. Fortunately, we were on time (I didn't want the captain to be pissed off by our being late and possibly blow future opportunities to get into the city). "So what did you think of Saigon," he asked me.

"Pretty incredible," I replied. I told him how we had spent our day once we were finished putting together the paper and how much I had enjoyed the experience—and what a good tour guide Bailey was. When we hit the city's outskirts, Bailey spoke up and asked the captain how his meeting went and if there was any news that he could share with us. "Pretty damn interesting," he responded. "There's a lot of shit coming down, but unfortunately, I can't share it with you right now. But rest assured…we'll all be involved covering what's about to happen." We made it back to Cu Chi just as the sun was dropping below the horizon.

Even though my press credentials indicated that I was a "combat correspondent," I was fortunate in that I really didn't have to cover combat. That doesn't mean I was never "in harm's way" (an expression we never used, to my recollection, during the Vietnam War period; I think it started in the post-9-11 era), for I did experience a few tense situations during my year as a correspondent. I probably could have covered the limited amount of combat that our battalion witnessed during the latter part of 1970, but I didn't have to—didn't want to, and therefore didn't. Rather, I was a feature writer and columnist who wrote stories about the guys in the battalion, the battalion itself and its history, and the army and Vietnam in general. Let me cite an example of the type of cover stories that I wrote for the *65th Recorder*, this from the first issue dated June 7, 1970:

65TH ENGINEERS AID IN RECOVERY OF DOWNED AIR FORCE OV-10

Engineers from Bravo Company, 65th Engineer Battalion, were called into action recently to aid in the recovery of an Air Force OV-10 that crashed in the 25th Infantry Division AO near Cu Chi. The crash occurred on April 29, 1970, and the Engineers were called in the next day to begin the recovery operation. The cause of the crash still remains a mystery. CPT Lawrence Oliver, Company Commander

> of Bravo Company, explained that his company's mission was to recover the aircraft, and although the mission was accomplished, it was not accomplished without some difficulty.
>
> The Air Force, which usually handles its own recovery operations, called on the Engineers because of the swampy terrain and readily available equipment. And what a job it was. Captain Oliver related that the plane was doing 240 knots at the time of impact, and entered the ground at an 85 degree angle with such force that only the tail section of the plane remained above ground.
>
> Because of the conditions under which the men had to work, the mission took a good two weeks to complete. The men of Bravo Company could only work in six-hour shifts because of the danger of immersion foot, and because the JP4, a fuel that contains a mixture of kerosene and alcohol, burns the skin.... and so on.

Other early headlines (and accompanying stories) included the following: "A Peaceful Mission for the 65th Engineers," "'Bridge over Troubled Water' Becomes New Swimming Pool at Waikiki East" (the base camp's name for its new swimming pool), "River Boats Turned Over to ARVN's in 65th Engineer Vietnamization Move," and "Engineer Officer 'Soft Soaps' His Way into the Hearts of the Vietnamese." The latter story was the first of mine that was picked up by the Pacific Stars and Stripes, the "Authorized Unofficial Publication for the U.S. Armed Forces of the Pacific Command." In volume 26, number 236, dated Tuesday, August 25, 1970, the article read as follows:

VIET OFFICER "CLEANING UP"

> *CU CHI, Vietnam (Special)*—The 25th Inf. Div.'s APO is considering setting up a special mail room for a lieutenant from the 65th Eng. Bn. In little

> *more than a week, 1st Lt. Stephen K. Rhyne has received more than 10,000 bars of soap, hundreds of toothbrushes, and hundreds of tubes of toothpaste. Rhyne, a native of Stanley, N.C., serves as the assistant Civic Affairs officer for the 65th Engineers. He heads the battalion's MEDCAP (Medical Civic Action Program) team which has recently been handicapped by a lack of soap and dental supplies. Rhyne wrote to his parents asking them to stir up public interest in the MEDCAP program in his hometown. A few weeks later, the contributions started pouring in from churches, church-sponsored groups, and even his mother's bridge club.*

The above article was condensed by the *Stars and Stripes* from a longer article that I wrote for *the 65th Recorder*. In addition to writing and publishing the newsletter, I also disseminated military bullshit and propaganda as I was directed (or ordered) to do so. So that was my job during my days, weeks, and months with the 65th Engineers in Cu Chi.

Life on the Cu Chi base camp was almost second nature to me now, and the rigid military "drill" had slackened quite a bit from when I first arrived. With exceptions to be described as my story continues, the days had become pretty much routine. When reveille sounded, we dragged ourselves out of bed and threw on almost anything for the daily formation, which was more for head-count purposes than anything else—except for the once-weekly uniform inspection (which we actually had to dress up for). Then off to the latrine and bathroom for whatever kind of cleanup we felt necessary (we didn't shower every day). Then breakfast at the mess hall. And finally, off to the office by 0730, which usually was more like 0800. There was almost no fear of danger, and there were enough creature comforts to make life at Cu Chi almost enjoyable. Mail call was still the anticipated event of the day; I was getting letters from my girlfriend, family, and friends almost daily at this point. And per our requests home for gourmet items and other goodies, care packages were now getting almost ridiculous in their frequency and extravagant contents.

Of course, there was still the occasional army bullshit to put up with, like formations, police calls, inspections, starched fatigues, and polished boots. But those of us who escaped the stress and dangers of combat figured we were lucky to be where we were, so we just put up with the lifers and the bullshit. And after the recent series of fraggings and tear gas incidents, the "off-the-record" protocol that had been observed between the lifers and the EMs had now become more like a truce. After hours, they didn't bother us and we didn't bother them. They didn't come into our living areas, unless necessary, and we stayed out of theirs. In other words, the troops could drink their beer, smoke their pot, and do their drugs in their haunts without fear of harassment or being busted. And the lifers could get falling-down drunk in their clubs without our snickering at them as they tripped and fell on their way back to their quarters.

As my time in Cu Chi progressed, I became aware of, and eventually participated in, another interesting Vietnam phenomenon—pets. Believe it or not, some of the guys had pets—mostly dogs. But there were also a handful of monkeys and parrots, and even some more exotic species like snakes and lizards—and even a lynx. One evening, as I lay in bed reading, I had an interesting experience. The door to the hootch opened, and a monkey walked in and jumped up onto my bed. As he walked toward me, he looked me straight in the eye, as if sensing what kind of person I was. Apparently satisfied, he curled up alongside of me (he obviously had done this before) and spent the night. I assumed it was someone's pet, as this monkey's behavior was way too domesticated for it to be wild. And sure enough, the next morning, its owner walked by the hootch calling its name. With a bolt, he jumped out of bed, opened the door, and took off. Strange indeed, but one learned to expect and accept the unusual in Vietnam.

On another day, on my way back to the hootch from work, one of the engineers who had just returned from the field called me over to show me what he had brought back with him. It was a box full of puppies—cute-as-can-be mutts that looked like they came from a real mix of backgrounds. He asked me if I wanted one, and after a moment's hesitation, thinking the hootch could really use a dog, I responded, "Sure!" I gravitated to the smallest of the litter, a fluffy black guy with white markings on his forehead and chest. Using a piece of rope for a leash, I took him to the hootch to meet the guys, wondering to myself if what I had just done was such a good idea. For the most part, they welcomed him warmly. Even Doc, whose initial reaction was "Stoup, you've got to be out of your fucking mind," warmed up to him rather quickly. We put our heads together and came up with a name for him: Sergeant Pepper. From that moment forward, Sergeant Pepper was our constant companion—at least until the final days of Cu Chi.

As the weeks went by, I got into yet another unique aspect of Nam culture—shopping via the PACEX (Pacific Exchange) Catalog. Actually, I was introduced to this feature of Nam culture shortly after arriving, but didn't realize the full extent of its offerings until I was settled at Cu Chi. Unlike other wars, where the PX was the primary or sole source of necessity items—like toiletries, snack food, cigarettes, books and magazines—the larger PXs at Vietnam base camps and headquarters locations were a shopper's paradise. In addition to a wide variety of food and necessity items, one could purchase cameras, stereo equipment, music, liquor, jewelry, and a variety of Vietnamese and Asian souvenirs. Yet this was nothing compared to what was available through the PACEX Catalog.

The PACEX Catalog, which was updated a couple of times a year, was available to all military personnel, government and civilian contractors serving in the Asia-Pacific theater. It was almost as thick as the Sears mail order catalog and was amazingly diverse in its offerings. You could get anything from televisions, cameras, and stereo equipment of a great variety, to an incredible selection of jewelry, silks, artworks, and native crafts from all over Asia. Even automobiles, as I recall. And the prices were incredible. Just about every guy I met over there brought back a full component stereo system. It was the beginning of the Japanese era of dominance in electronics, and we were introduced to names like Pioneer, TEAC, Sony, and Kenwood. Between the PX, the PACEX Catalog, Saigon, and R & R in Bangkok, I sent so much stuff back that when I returned home from my tour, my parents said they were tempted to erect a banner that would have read, "Welcome Back from Your Shopping Trip to Vietnam."

Another regular part of social life in the Nam was "hail and farewell" parties. Most often, when someone new arrived, and almost always when someone was leaving, a hail and farewell party was thrown to mark the occasion. These events were especially popular with officers and NCOs, although most units invited their EMs as well, and often coincided with the weekly or biweekly cookouts. If you're beginning to get the impression that there was a lot of partying going on in the Nam, well, you'd be right—there was. At the event on this particular Saturday night, I was surprised to learn that three guys from my OCS class had just arrived at Cu Chi, and one of them was assigned to the 65th Engineers. As we were catching up, he informed me that only seventy out of the two hundred that started the program made it through to commission. And those poor suckers were now being assigned to infantry units throughout the Nam—except for the lucky few that got assigned to either Germany or Korea.

Other than trips to Saigon and the base camps and villages in and around Cu Chi, Long Binh and Bien Hoa, I didn't make many trips into the field, or the bush as some called it. Those that I did make were exciting, though, with my first trip being especially memorable. Rumors had been floating around, especially in intelligence circles like the S-2 section where I worked, that certain American units (I should note here that our allies from other countries also had units in Vietnam, like Great Britain and Australia) were conducting "hit and run" missions into Cambodia. The 1st Infantry Division (Big Red One) was one of them, and who knows if others were involved as well. Officially, these units were only operating at or near the border. But in reality, they were going into Cambodia, and without legal authorization I might add. At this point in the war, Congress had turned down the military's request to enter Cambodia to cut off supply routes to the South that North Vietnam and the Viet Cong were using to fortify their troops. Congress feared that an expansion of the war into Cambodia would be disastrous, not only for the allies, but for the Cambodians as well. At least that's what they claimed. But with antiwar sentiment exploding in the United States and elsewhere in the world, and the subsequent outcry coming from the electorate, fear of losing their jobs in the next election was an even greater concern to Congress.

As if gearing up to participate in the anticipated push into Cambodia, the 25th Infantry Division was putting the finishing touches on a new fire support base near the border in Tay Ninh Province. On a Monday morning late in June, Captain Becker called me into his office. Without indicating that he fully knew what was going on, he told me that the battalion commander wanted me to travel to Fire Support Base (FSB) Dorn and write a story about the battalion's involvement for the division newspaper. Of course, the 65th Engineers had built this pivotal "springboard" base, and apparently it was important to the CO to get coverage of this fact. Something was about to happen there—and they knew it. Not getting many opportunities like this, I jumped at the chance to get my first big feature in the *Tropic Lightning News*. And besides, I was up for a little excitement and a chance to get a real taste of the field. He proceeded to inform me that a convoy was leaving first thing in the morning and that I should plan to be on it. He said Sergeant Martinez would fill me in on the details.

That night, I packed my gear for the trip. I was hoping to get up and back in a day—if I could hitch a ride back on Lieutenant Colonel Gaynor's chopper. He was planning to tour the FSB late tomorrow afternoon, but just in case I had to spend the night and wait for the next convoy back, I packed my shaving kit, along with my camera, film, and some C rations...just in case. Needless to say, my M-16 would accompany me on this trip, so I cleaned it and packed a couple of clips of ammunition. Doc and the guys ridiculed me the entire time I was packing, singing songs about the Viet Cong that we learned in training. Actually, I think they were a little concerned for my safety, knowing that I wasn't exactly "combat ready."

But they continued the ribbing anyway. "Hey, Stouper," Doc yelled out, "I want dibs on the AK-47 from the first Cong you get…It'll probably be my only chance to get a souvenir of the war."

The convoy pulled out of Cu Chi at 0600 hours sharp the next morning. I rode in a deuce-and-a-half truck with a couple of engineers who were being sent up as replacements for the guys who'd been there since ground breaking two weeks ago. The truck was also loaded with ammunition, which made me a little more than nervous (as one guys in the truck pointed out, if we hit a land mine, we'd all be blown to kingdom come—which is one surefire way of getting out of this place). From what they told me, FSB Dorn was now almost fully operational. The infantry had moved in three days ago, and artillery units were put into place yesterday. By 0800, the sun was already blazing. We were now well into the countryside, which was dotted with small dwellings and an occasional church, temple, and graveyards. Rice paddies and farm fields being worked by papa sans and their water buffalo were now a common yet still-beautiful sight. Back in the world, it would have been a three-hour drive to the base. But on these roads, it would take us six hours or more. In addition to having to share the narrow roads with all the local traffic, there were often massive potholes to navigate, many of which looked like small lakes due to the monsoon rains.

About midway through the trip, we stopped for a piss break. The convoy pulled off to the side of the road in an area that was pretty much deserted. Most of the guys just hung around the trucks smoking cigarettes or walked along the roadway stretching their legs. I was told the sector we were travelling in, between Cu Chi and Tay Ninh, was relatively secure, but that there was always the potential for danger. The infantry unit we were travelling with was our safety net, and these guys took their role pretty seriously. They were never without rifles in hand, especially when we stopped along the road.

After relieving myself, I began walking up the road to stretch my legs. By now, the heat of the day was stifling. After walking a short distance, I paused in the middle of the road, closed my eyes, and tilted my head up toward the sun. It was mesmerizing. And then, all of a sudden, I was struck with a powerful sense of déjà vu. I swore that I had been in this exact spot before…everything was incredibly familiar. This was the first time I had experienced this sensation in Vietnam, but it wouldn't be the last. The sensation was overwhelming, and remarkable in its intensity. Being in a strange and exotic land…with senses heightened due to the ever-present possibility of danger…coupled with the intensity of the sun (and sometimes the buzz that many of us often had on)…it was no wonder that many of us experienced this mind-racing phenomena.

After passing through Tay Ninh City, a fairly large and picturesque town, the terrain began to change. The foothills of small mountains began rising in the distance, and the trees and foliage became thicker and more jungle-like. We arrived at FSB Dorn without incident around 1300 hours. The base was nothing more than a large, barren piece of land that had been carved out of the surrounding landscape. On it was erected a tent city with a few wooden structures surrounded with sandbags, a command bunker, latrines, a few sheds, bunkers, and storage areas for fuel, ammunition and supplies. There was also a small landing pad for helicopters. As with all bases in the Nam, FSB Dorn was circular and was surrounded with layers of barbed wire. As we drove through the gate, I observed combat engineers carefully placing claymore mines within the wire. After we pulled to a stop, I hopped out of the truck and headed for the command bunker to find Major Tom McKendrick, the head honcho at Dorn. Captain Becker said he had notified McKendrick that I was coming and that I should check in with him as soon as I arrived. He also advised me to clear my plans with him and to get his ideas for the story as well. I had no problem with that.

I entered the bunker and was greeted by a first lieutenant. I rolled off a quick salute, which I think caught him by surprise. As he responded in kind, I introduced myself as a correspondent for the division newspaper and asked where I could find Major McKendrick. He pointed to a man standing in the corner of the bunker screaming at someone on a field telephone. McKendrick looked my way, but didn't miss a beat in his conversation. "He'll be with you in a minute...I'm Lieutenant Smith," he said, extending his hand in a friendly gesture that caught me by surprise. "What brings you to FSB Dorn?" I told him why I was here and was about to describe my mission when Major McKendrick finished his call and barreled our way. "Here's the guy the 65th Engineers sent up to do a story for the division newspaper," Lieutenant Smith informed him. I started to salute the major, but was quickly cut off. "We don't bother with those formalities out here," he said, extending his hand instead. Again, I was taken aback by this unfamiliar informality, but quickly recovered to give the impression that I was used to this kind of treatment. Yea right!

I told the major that I was sent to cover a story on the 65th Engineers' role in constructing the base by LTC Gaynor and that I would like to interview him and anyone else he might suggest. He grumbled something about not thinking publicity of any kind was a good idea at this time, even if it was for an internal publication, but then added, "I suppose we both have to follow orders." I sensed by his comment that there was more to the mission at FSB Dorn than just supporting combat operations for the 25th in IV Corps.

As I got out my pad and pen, he and the lieutenant rattled off information and statistics about the fire support base, as if reading from a prepared text. I learned about its size and construction, how long it took to build, what units were supporting it, but otherwise, nothing of great interest. And of course, there was no mention of the fact that the base was practically sitting on the Cambodian border. When they were finished briefing me, Major McKendrick suggested that I walk around to take some pictures. "And feel free to talk to the men," he offered enthusiastically, leading me to believe that the average soldier residing here knew nothing about the real mission of the base.

I left the bunker to see what I could learn from the "average" soldier. It was now almost 1400 hours, and I had missed lunch. Fortunately, I had packed some C rations in case of an emergency, not that this qualified as an emergency. I made my way to an area of tents, figuring I'd catch someone at home. The barren ground of the base was mostly mud, often ankle deep, because of the daily monsoon rains. Boards and scrap lumber were used as walkways in areas where it was particularly bad. I was told on the ride up that if we got a lot of rain today, the convoy might be stuck here, perhaps for a day or more, and that I might have to spend a night or two before getting back. But that didn't concern me too much, as I was planning to hitch a ride back on the CO's chopper.

As I maneuvered the planks walking toward the center of the base, I noticed an artillery unit with a couple of big guns just on the other side of what I guessed to be the residential tent area. There was a virtual frenzy of activity as the guys from 2nd Battalion, 77th Field Artillery, prepared the guns for action. The size of these guns for such a relatively small FSB seemed a little strange to me. But then again, what did I know. So I decided to do a little "digging" and headed past the tents for the artillery battery. On the way, I dug into my backpack and pulled out my compass. I held it in my hand and pointed it in the direction the guns were pointing. And sure enough, they were pointing west…into Cambodia. I put the compass away and approached two shirtless guys stacking shells near one of the guns.

I introduced myself as a division reporter doing a story on FSB Dorn. They seemed eager to talk to me and immediately extended their hands in the Nam brotherhood handshake. Even though I was wearing jungle fatigues with a U.S. Army patch, PFC stripes, and the division insignia, they asked me if I was a civilian. I replied, "Unfortunately, no. I'm with the 25th. I'm attached to the 65th Engineers and am here to do a story on the base for the division newspaper."

"Bummer," one of them blurted out.

Although this was the first time that I was asked this question, it wouldn't be the last. For as my time progressed in the Nam, and as I wrote more stories and interviewed more guys, more often than not they would ask me if I was with the civilian press. The confusion usually occurred because the civilian press often wore nonissue military jungle fatigues that were either given to them by someone in the military or were acquired on the street in Saigon via the black market. And introducing myself as a reporter often got their hopes up. It seems a lot of GIs were more than willing to spill their guts about "what was really going on" to the press, which is why the media was monitored and guarded so closely when traveling in the field and among the troops in Vietnam.

"Looks like you guys are preparing for a little action," I remarked.

"More than a little," one of them responded. "We're going to be firing out all night." Since I sensed we were operating on the same wavelength, I commented that the guns appeared to be pointed west. "Do you know how close we are to the Cambodian border?" I asked. One of them, a corporal named Anderson, looked me right in the eye and said, "We're practically inside Cambodia, man!" I was taken aback by his comment.

"They think we're stupid," he continued, "but we're not. We know exactly what's going on here, and a lot of guys are really upset about it." He and his buddies proceeded to tell me about the hit-and-run missions that had been going on for weeks. He said units assigned to this base had been participating in the missions and that some of the grunts had refused to go out, knowing we had illegally crossed the border. "In fact, some of them are here now," he said, pointing to the tents I had just passed.

"You should go talk to those guys," Anderson suggested. "They'll give you a real story. And if you're planning to spend the night," he continued, "be prepared for some real noise." I thanked them for the information, wished them luck, and headed back toward the tents.

The first tent I came to was set back a bit from the others, which were lined up in two rows. And interestingly, a gasoline-operated generator was cranking away alongside of it. The tent flaps were closed, but with the generator running and music coming from inside, I figured someone must be in there. I approached the entrance and yelled, "Hello, anybody home?" "Come on in," someone yelled back. I pulled back the left flap of the tent, bent my head down, and went inside. As the flap fell shut behind me, I couldn't believe what I was seeing. First, I was amazed to find the tent illuminated by a black light, highlighting Day-Glo posters of Jimi Hendrix and Janis Joplin hanging on the tent walls. Then there was the full component stereo system stacked on ammunition boxes that was cranking out Hendrix's version of "The Star Spangled Banner" (thus the reason for the generator). And finally, there was what I presumed to be a soldier wearing an unbuttoned fatigue shirt with all the right army, division, and unit badges, including his spec 5 rank, but without a name badge. He was sitting in a lounge chair—the kind you take to the beach—and, other than his fatigue shirt, was wearing only boxer shorts.

He had wire-rimmed sunglasses on his face, and a colorful headband adorned his temple. A large silver peace sign was hanging around his neck, and the inside of the tent reeked of pot and incense. "Welcome to Haight-Ashbury East," he greeted me.

It appears I had walked in on a soldier who was living in his own world and apparently somewhat outside the realm of military control—at least while at FSB Dorn. I was dumbstruck…and fascinated. After introducing myself, he proceeded to tell me he was a code specialist working for division intelligence. He didn't tell me much more and just smiled every time I asked him a question about what was going on here. "This is a far-out place," he responded, "far away from the bullshit of the rear." This was the first time I had witnessed such a blatant aberration of military discipline, but it wouldn't be the last. Something indeed was going on at Dorn, and I was going to find out what it was (although I think I already knew). The guy asked me if I wanted to smoke a joint, and although tempted, I wisely declined, knowing I had to keep my head straight if I was going to survive this increasingly bizarre experience. I thanked him for the offer, wished him luck, and left shaking my head, still trying to absorb what I had just witnessed.

As I made my way to the first row of tents, I noticed a bunch of grunts sitting outside of the one on the end, huddled together in conversation. But as I approached, they stopped talking and turned around to look at me. Again, I couldn't believe what I was seeing. This was the most seasoned-looking bunch of men that I had seen since arriving in the Nam—even more seasoned than the combat engineers in my unit when they returned from an extended stay in the field. One guy's hair was long enough to be pulled into a ponytail, and most had at least two weeks' growth of beard on their faces. They were all wearing copper bracelets on their wrists, and either had peace signs, crosses, or other emblems hanging around their necks. Some wore headbands to keep the sweat from running into their eyes while others wore them as fashion, or more likely protest statements as in "I dare you to tell me to take this headband off my fucking head."

I introduced myself as a reporter for the division newspaper, which immediately broke the ice. "I don't know what kind of story you're writing," one of them commented, "but if you'd like to cover a real story, then step into the circle." They invited me into their group, and we exchanged names and handshakes. They then proceeded to tell me horror stories about what's been going on in the area.

They were foot soldiers, grunts, from the 1st Brigade (Lancers) and had been involved in hit-and-run missions into Cambodia for the last three weeks. They had been operating out of the Tay Ninh base camp or living in the bush until Dorn was built and were now waiting for replacements so they could be rotated back to Cu Chi before being sent farther north to even more rugged quarters in Dau Tieng. "We're not going anywhere until that happens," one of them piped in. The most talkative of the group, a corporal named Scudder, told me that they had refused to go into the bush that day and were waiting to see what was going to happen to them. As he spoke, another guy started passing around a joint, and I took a hit as it came around to me as a gesture to gain their confidence. "I don't think they're going to do anything to us," he continued, "'cause the lieutenant's sick of this shit too. He's lost five men since this bullshit's started, and he doesn't want to lose any more. I think he's covering for us. We're all sick of it."

The pieces of the puzzle that I had been gathering (and observing) at Dorn were beginning to fit together. It appeared that the mission at FSB Dorn, and elsewhere in the region, was falling apart—or at least wasn't going well. Major McKendrick's attitude and posture were now beginning to make sense. But I still couldn't quite figure out why he seemingly gave me carte blanche to walk around so openly, unaccompanied, with such free access to, well, anyone. You would have thought the opposite would have been true, especially considering the circumstances, and what I was hearing and seeing.

Apparently, he had a problem with the "mission" as well. And besides, I wasn't a civilian reporter, so he probably figured I wouldn't be able to do anything with what I was learning anyway. And if I tried, either no one would believe me or I'd be stopped dead in my tracks as my copy went up the chain of command for approval. Like any of this had a remote possibility of making it into the press, military or otherwise. But later in my tour, a lot of this kind of stuff did make it into the civilian press, as I and others like me did what we could to inform the media of what was going on in the field and behind the scenes in Vietnam.

I hung around with the grunts for about two hours, getting high and listening to their harrowing stories about life in the bush. Listening to them made me feel real guilty about my cushy life in the rear, but they didn't resent me. That was one of the curious things about the Nam. The unity among the troops in resisting the common enemy, the military (or at least the asshole lifers), was strong because we supported each other. The guys in the rear, especially in admin, did what they could, when they could, to get guys out of the field. And the guys in the field did what they could to get themselves back to the rear, sometimes taking rather risky and drastic measures to do so. The way everyone figured it, we were all in this together, and we needed each other to survive. Many of us didn't choose to be here, and many of those who did regretted their decision to enlist once they learned the reality and the ways of the Nam. And speaking of the ways of the Nam, I asked Scudder what was up with the guy in the tent with the generator. "Oh, you mean Smylie," he replied, pointing to the tent. "The guy's an intelligence specialist they brought in from MACV headquarters to try to break the enemy's code. He's so specialized that they can't touch him…and he knows it. The dude lives in his own little kingdom," Scudder added, somewhat bitterly.

It was almost time for dinner, served around 1600 hours in the field, and the grunts asked me if I wanted to join them. It was also starting to rain hard. I pulled out my poncho and tucked my camera into my backpack. Just as we were starting to make our way to the mess tent, I noticed Lieutenant Smith running toward me—carrying an umbrella. As I walked in his direction, he yelled out to me, "We just got a call from LTC Gaynor. The weather's gotten bad and he won't be able to make it in today. Said he might try again tomorrow. If it's not too muddy, the convoy will be leaving early tomorrow morning, but I'm afraid you'll have to spend the night here, Private Stoup." Great, I thought to myself.

After dinner, which actually wasn't bad, I did a little more walking around, taking in the sights and smells. But the rain was falling even harder now, making walking increasingly difficult, so I decided it was time to find a place to bunk for the night. I wandered over to the command bunker and walked in. Lieutenant Smith was by himself. "Any suggestions on where to bunk?" I asked him.

"I'm afraid the place is full," he responded, "so I guess you'll have to fend for yourself." Great, I thought to myself again.

Being in a strange place on the edge of who knows where, with danger a strong possibility, not knowing anyone or where to go, gave me an empty feeling. My stomach was suddenly in knots. But I wanted this assignment, right? And I wanted to know what it was like being in the field, right? Darkness was falling, and from what I had been told, the Nam became a different place at night—especially in the field. I trudged around, looking for a place to bed down. Being a REMF, I didn't want to intrude on anyone's space or appear as though I couldn't make it on my own. So I avoided the tent area. I wandered over toward the artillery battery, where a dump truck was parked. Its driver was settling down in the cab, and his buddy was fastening a hammock under the truck's body. I tapped on the window and asked the guy if he knew of a spot where I could park for the night. "You can sleep in the truck's bed," he responded. "I have a tarp you can try tying from the back of the cab to the rear dump door. That should help keep out some of the rain." His buddy then chimed in, "Since I'm using my hammock tonight, you can use my air mattress to sleep on." I thanked them both profusely and began the task of preparing my sleep area for the night—in the back of a dump truck. Fortunately, the rain had let up, at least long enough to let me try to pull things together.

As I was preparing my bed, I noticed a flurry of activity around me. A couple of platoons of grunts were preparing to head out on a night mission (in the rain and mud, to face certain danger if not death—how miserable it must have been for them), and the artillery battery next to me was gearing up for action as well. Then I remembered what someone had told me as I was preparing for my first trip to Cu Chi village: "Villagers by day, Viet Cong by night." I was beginning to get a little nervous.

It started to rain again as I attempted to settle down for the night. I was a little depressed, a little scared, and very much alone. You might say that I was down in the dumps. The tarp over my head covered about three-quarters of the top of the truck and was thus far keeping out most of the rain. The last thing I had to do was blow up the air mattress, and I was now wishing I had brought along my poncho liner, as I was getting wet and it was a bit chilly. My M-16 was close by my side.

It was now around 2300 hours and I was finally beginning to drift off to sleep, when an explosion jolted me back to reality. I peered out from the bottom of the tarp to see what was going on and was immediately thrown back by another strong concussion. It was the big guns of the artillery unit next to me firing out. Was this going to go on all night, I wondered, congratulating myself for my selection of sleeping quarters. Then I had a horrifying thought. What if the enemy was able to pinpoint the position of these guns and started firing back in an attempt to take them out? If that was to happen and they were successful, I was a goner. I considered trying to move to another part of the base, but really didn't know where to go. And besides, it was dark and raining, so I decided to stay put.

It started raining hard again, and water was now pouring in from the rear portion of the truck that the tarp didn't cover. I crawled to the back and tried to adjust the tarp toward the rear, but without much success. While attempting this adjustment, I looked out the back of the truck. I hadn't noticed when I climbed in, but the rear of the truck was actually extended out over the first row of barbed wire on the base perimeter. I suddenly got very paranoid and started imagining a Viet Cong sapper crawling through the wire and into the back of the truck to slit my throat. With that thought in mind, I crept slowly back toward the front of the truck, knowing I probably wouldn't be getting much sleep that night.

The truck was now slowly filling up with water—about two inches deep at this point. I tried to settle back down on the air mattress, which had been keeping me afloat and semidry. But as I did this, I noticed that it had sprung a leak. Before long, I started sinking into the water and getting wetter as a result. And the tarp above me was starting to sag from the weight of the water that was accumulating on it. It wouldn't be long before the whole thing came down on me. Knowing there was nothing I could do about my situation, I just lay there, frozen in place, hoping and praying that I would make it through the night. After a while, I must have fallen asleep. I know this because I was jolted out of my reverie by the sound of the big guns firing out once again.

Finally, at around 0600 hours, the sun started to rise, and FSB Dorn slowly came to life. But unlike the frenzy of activity that occurs in the rear at that hour, there was little noticeable activity. I was soaked, cold, and numb, but didn't move from my position. When the sun got brighter, I finally jumped out of the truck. I looked at my watch; it was now 0715. I took off my shirt, wrung it out, and put it back on. A few guys were walking around, but the two in the truck continued to saw wood. I made my way to the mess tent in the hope of getting something hot to eat and drink. And as good fortune had it, both were available. Lieutenant Smith was in line for coffee when I got there. He turned and looked at me as I approached and asked, with a smile on this face, "How'd you sleep?"

"How does it look?" I responded. "No one told me to expect this kind of hospitality," I continued. "You guys even got me a water bed."

Smith proceeded to tell me that he had just received a call from Cu Chi and that LTC Gaynor would be here by 1000 hours. "He's just making a quick in-and-out stop, so you'd better be here and ready to go by that time." Now this was good news. The lieutenant then invited me to join him for breakfast in the command bunker, which I gladly took him up on. After breakfast, I decided to try to hook back up with the grunts, as I wanted to hear more stories about their experiences in the Nam. The sun was shining brightly now as I walked toward their tent area, and my clothes were beginning to dry out.

The grunts I met at Dorn were a diverse bunch of genuinely nice guys, from college graduates to high school dropouts, who made me feel like I was one of them. The stories they told were both disturbing and fascinating and made me realize how lucky I was to be hearing about them rather than experiencing them firsthand. These guys made me feel comfortable and less guilty about my cushy life in the rear than I probably should have. "More power to ya," one of them said. "You got over, and that's good. More of us should get over…We all should get over." As the rest of the guys nodded in agreement, Scudder lit a joint and started passing it around. *Oh well,* I thought. *Why not be stoned for the ride back to Cu Chi.*

When LTC Gaynor arrived, I followed him around on his brief inspection tour of the base. He asked me if I had gotten all the information I needed for my story, and I responded, "Yes, sir." But in reality, I had no idea what I was going to write about other than the obvious—we came, we cleared jungle, and we built a base. The real story of FSB Dorn couldn't be told, at least not in an army publication. As we headed for the chopper pad to depart, we passed the group of grunts who were still hanging around outside their tents. In silence, they watched as we passed by. I turned and looked their way and caught Scudder's eye. He smiled and flipped me the peace sign. Out of the corner of my eye, I noticed that LTC Gaynor had observed the exchange. So I gave the guys a "thumbs-up" and kept walking. "Good bunch of men," I remarked. He turned away without commenting and continued walking toward the chopper.

I climbed into the back of the UH-1 (Huey), rifle and backpack in hand. There were already five men aboard, so the only place for me to sit was next to the door gunner. He had an extra belt and put it around my waist and pulled it tight. "Hang on," he said. "It's going to be quite a ride before we get to Cu Chi." It was my first ride in a helicopter (although in the latter part of my tour I'd become a real frequent flyer), and I couldn't wait for the experience…not to mention being happy to get the hell out of Dorn. Before I could even lay down my gear, the chopper lifted off the ground, dipped its nose slightly toward the ground, and then took off in a straight line shot. LTC Gaynor was copiloting the craft. Door gunners on each side of the rear compartment were manning M-60 machine guns. More and more choppers had been shot down by snipers in recent weeks, so door gunners were now mandatory on all flights.

Within moments, we were far above the treetops and gaining altitude. The sight of the countryside from this elevation was breathtaking, especially looking west into Cambodia. As I sat back to enjoy the ride, LTC Gaynor's aide, Second Lieutenant Levy, leaned over to inform me that we were going to make another stop before returning to Cu Chi. He had to yell to be heard above the noise of the rotor. "We're going to make a quick inspection tour of a communications outpost," he said. "It's about forty clicks due east, on the III Corps border." I just nodded, suddenly realizing I was still stoned from my farewell conversation with the grunts. "No problem," I yelled back. Besides, from this vantage point, I'd be up for some new scenery. And I was up…and smiling!

As we flew east, the land became less wooded. A lot of defoliation had obviously taken place in the area, with large sections of land practically barren. We were good at stripping the land of vegetation, thanks to an effective arsenal of chemical agents like Agent Orange. Occasionally, the terrain was pockmarked with craters from B-52 bombing raids. But by and large, it was rice paddies, small farms, and villages that dominated the landscape in this part of the country. After about thirty-five minutes of flying, the land became noticeably flatter. And then all of a sudden, I saw it in the distance. At first, it looked like a large mound of dirt on the horizon. But the closer we got, the larger and more ominous it became.

"What's that!" I yelled to Lieutenant Levy, pointing to the landmark we were approaching.

"Nui Ba Den!" he yelled back.

Nui Ba Den was the tallest mountain in the southern half of South Vietnam, rising 3,268 feet above sea level. It was unusual, not so much because of its size, but because it stood alone on the landscape. It wasn't part of a range, but rather was a haunting and dominating feature on the face of an otherwise totally flat terrain. Its presence on the landscape and its natural beauty was impressive, and approaching it by air made it even more spectacular.

Levy leaned over and yelled the lowdown on Nui Ba Den into my ear. It seems the mountain was considered sacred by many Vietnamese. But it was also considered strategically important by both sides of the war. As unbelievable as it sounds, Levy told me that we controlled the top and bottom of the mountain while the Viet Cong controlled the middle. We had a fire support base near the bottom of the mountain and a communications outpost on the top while the Viet Cong had a tunnel system in the middle leading down the side opposite of our FSB. The two sides were constantly engaging each other in bloody skirmishes over the real estate, he went on to say, and many troops on both sides had lost their lives as a result. "It's nothing like Hamburger Hill…mostly hit-and-run activity," he explained.

"You mean we're going to land on top of that mountain?" I exclaimed, looking at him with what felt like bug eyes.

"You're damn right we are!" he yelled back at me. I picked my M-16 up from the floor and put my finger on the trigger.

We continued to gain altitude and in another couple of minutes were parallel to the top of the mountain. As we approached, we penetrated a cloud that engulfed the top of the mountain in a shroud of fog. We landed on an extremely small flat surface near the pinnacle. Communication platforms and radar towers were everywhere. A small building was tucked next to a wall of rock. "We'll be back in a few minutes," Lieutenant Levy yelled, as he and LTC Gaynor made their way to the communications center. The pilot cut off the engine, and it suddenly became silent…very silent. The only thing you could hear was the wind, and there was a biting cold to the air that penetrated my still-damp fatigues. I rolled down the sleeves of my fatigue shirt as the pilot stepped away from the chopper to have a cigarette.

The silence, and the very unusual environment, put me into a very pensive and almost dreamlike state. Here I was, on top of a mountain, towering over the war, wondering what it was all about—and wondering what the rest of my tour had in store for me. It was a very strange way to be ending my first big adventure in the Nam—on top of this world, on top of Nui Ba Den.

CHAPTER 7

The MARS Call, Scrapbooks, a Buddhist Wedding, and a Two-by-Four

We were now well into summer, and the monsoon season in the south was nearing its end. It was almost three weeks since my big adventure at FSB Dorn, and nothing real exciting was happening in and around Cu Chi. The base had been hit twice with rocket and mortar attacks, but neither near the 65th Engineer's compound. I had my second experience smoking an "OJ." And oh yes, what we had known for some time finally became official—the United States was conducting operations in Cambodia.

After information was leaked to Congress, and subsequently to the media, about our hit-and-run incursions, a great furor arose over this "illegal" (not sanctioned by Congress) activity. In the debate that ensued, the military apparently convinced Nixon and Congress that operations in Cambodia were essential if the United States was to meet its withdrawal objectives. The military insisted that cutting North Vietnamese supply routes to the South that were running through Cambodia (and Laos) was vital to the success of the "Vietnamization" of the war. Otherwise, they were told, Vietnamization would fail, and it would be more difficult for the United States to make a graceful exit from the scene. Their rationale was begrudgingly accepted, and the incursion into Cambodia was officially sanctioned. It did, however, have a time limit attached to it.

The 65th Engineers were supporting Cambodian operations in the usual way—by clearing jungle, sweeping for mines, building bridges, and the like. But for me, it was life in the rear as had become usual. I went to work in the morning, came home at night, read the paper, played with the dog, and rapped with the guys. And all, of course, while listening to music and getting stoned. But every now and then, there was a little diversion. For instance, one morning, shortly after arriving at work, Sergeant Martinez asked me if I wanted to call home. "What do you mean?" I asked.

It seems there was a ham-radio-operated phone network called MARS, the Military Auxiliary Radio System. Some guy in Hawaii was spearheading the operation, picking up calls on radio frequencies from the Nam and transmitting them to the phone company in California. From there, it was a standard toll call to the final destination. I said, "Sure, I'll give it a shot," and decided to try to reach my girlfriend.

The weird thing about the process was that the radio operator in Hawaii had to monitor the calls and manually switch back and forth between the two parties. So when you were finished with a sentence, you had to say "over." Having someone listening in on your conversation and having to say "over" all the time made intimacy a little difficult—but it was worth it. It was still live communications and an opportunity to hear the voice of someone you dearly missed.

Considering the time difference and the lack of advance notice that the call was coming, I had no idea if I would reach her. But in a stroke of luck, the call succeeded, and we had a brief five minutes to fill each other in on our lives. After completing the call, a wave of depression came over me, as it made me realize how much I missed her and home. It was a strange feeling, having the Nam life that I had become accustomed to, broken by a taste, or tease, of the world that I had left behind. But it was an interesting experience nonetheless. After the call, Captain Becker called me into his office and gave me a command information project to write, which amounted to writing an update of battalion regulations that had just been handed down from division HQ. The project would take up all my spare time for a couple of weeks, so it was back to the reality of army life just that fast.

There were a few other happenings and occurrences that broke the monotony during this time period as well. For one, there had just been a big drug bust in the battalion area. It seems one of the lifers had uncovered a hidden stash of about ten keys of pot in an equipment storage area. It was apparently hidden by one of the engineers, but no one got nailed as they couldn't find the "owner." The incident did, however, create a mad scramble as each of us sought to find a safer place to hide our personal stashes before the inevitable battalion-wide search of each hootch began. Although infrequent, these types of drug searches of our personal belongings were increasing as more and more pressure was placed on the lifers to conduct them due to increased drug use among the troops and all the publicity it was generating back in the world.

Another strange incident occurred when an engineer who had just returned from the field stumbled into our hootch one night. He was acting strange and said he was feeling funny and admitted to Doc that he had dropped a hit of acid that morning. At that point, he collapsed into my arms. The medics put him to bed and watched him closely throughout the night, but didn't report the incident to the authorities. Doc said he had dealt with this before. He was seemingly recovered and back to normal the next day. In another incident, a heavy drug user in the battalion "burned out," and they had to take him to the psych ward at Long Binh. The guy was a "speed freak," addicted to an amphetamine that came in liquid form in glass vials that some guys (especially those who had to spend extended periods of time in the bush) would mix with Coke to keep them awake—for long periods of time. Speed, like heroin, was taking casualties at an increasingly alarming rate as time went on in the Nam. And in another speed-related incident, a guy on the drug in one of the infantry units tried to shoot his company commander. Fortunately he missed and was taken away to LBJ (the Long Binh Jail).

Toward the end of summer, I also got a temporary job working as a bartender at the officers club while the regular guy went home on emergency leave. The job kept me off KP and guard duty, and I was able to drink for free (and grab a couple of 5ths to bring back to the hootch). This took about two evenings a week of my time until it ended when the regular bartender returned from his leave. Nice duty, huh.

And during that same month, I got to spend two days in Bien Hoa researching a story on Vietnamization. I took an interpreter with me, as the story revolved around teaching ARVNs how to operate river boats. So in addition to writing the story, I got to take a scenic boat ride on the Saigon River. And to add to the excitement, while we were on the river, a couple of fighter jets and B-52s flew by, dropping their payload in an area not far to our south. We could actually feel the earth quake, and the water in the river rippled with waves from the concussion. And finally, I got to make two trips to Dau Tieng (a former 1st Division, Big Red One, base camp) to take photographs and write a story for the division yearbook (yes, every division published a full-color yearbook each and every year they were in the Nam). On one of the trips, I flew in a Huey with a stunt pilot (or so he claimed). To show me his "stuff," we flew for ten miles at ninety mph, only ten feet off the ground. Then we did loops and spins. I was fully strapped in, of course, and loved every minute of it—which made me begin to wonder about my sanity.

I couldn't wait for work to end one Friday in mid-September, as there were big doings going on that weekend. Tom was about to leave us, and it wasn't just DEROS (duty ended return from overseas service), but ETS as well (estimated termination of service). Two big acronyms in the Nam. Yes, Tom was going home, and we were having a big party to send him off. Of course, the company was having its usual "hail and farewell" for all the guys who were on their way home. But our party was going to be a lot more interesting, at least in terms of refreshments.

When I got back to the hootch, Tom was packing, with direction being provided, of course, by Doc. Even though we were all going to miss him, it was Doc who was feeling it the most. The two of them had been inseparable since I arrived, sort of like Mutt and Jeff. The one thing I wasn't going to miss, however, was all the short-time jokes. Tom, with his usual deadpan sense of humor, had played his "shortness" to the hilt. For the past couple of weeks, every night when we got home from our respective jobs, he would hit us with another one. As I walked over to observe his packing ritual, Tom looked at me and said, "I'm so short that I couldn't go anywhere today. I had to spend the entire day hiding under a small rock so no one would step on me."

Tom had his stuff spread out all over the place and had Doc assisting him with what looked like a craft project. I asked them what they were doing, not knowing that I was about to learn yet another of the customs and rituals of the Nam—preparing a scrapbook for the return trip home. *(I should point out here that not every returning soldier participated in this custom…but a hell of a lot of them did, especially the die-hard heads).* Just about every guy I knew in the Nam kept a scrapbook, which was actually a photo album that one filled with not only photographs, but also newspaper clippings, MPC and piaster samples, short-time calendars, unit insignia patches and other miscellaneous items that ranged from empty Cambodian cigarette packs that had contained prerolled joints (that you could buy on the street in Saigon), to peace signs, "Mr. Zig-Zag" paraphernalia, and the like. Any interesting tidbit or souvenir that would fit under the clear plastic sheets that covered each sticky album page was included. These spiral-bound photo albums, with padded fabric covers, were sold in the PX and on the street in most large cities in the Nam, and often had maps of Vietnam on the cover and titles like "Souvenir of Vietnam." But the key to sending the albums home, at least for the heads, was the padded front and back covers of the albums.

I don't know how or when the custom began, or whose bright and inventive idea it was, but for the guys who wanted to bring back a sampling of Nam pot and who hadn't shipped any back by other means, the Vietnam scrapbook was the chosen vehicle. Using a razor blade, one carefully opened the glued inside seams of the fabric covering the scrapbook. Next, you removed the paper padding and the cardboard that supported the front and back covers. Then you glued prerolled joints to the cardboard in rows of two or three (you could get up to sixty joints on each cardboard insert if they were small enough). Finally, you covered the joints with a thin piece of padding that had been presoaked in cologne to cover the odor of the pot and placed the cardboard back inside the fabric outer covers. And finally, you reglued the seams, and your padded souvenir scrapbook of Vietnam was ready for the trip back home. Most guys shipped their scrapbooks home, but some (like me) carried them in their duffel bags for the trip back to the world. Risky business for sure. But then again, that's what the Nam was all about.

On Monday morning, I was a little hung over and spaced out after a weekend of seeing Tom off in true Vietnam style. I was also a little sad as I realized that my friends, the first guys I really got to know since arriving in the Nam, were starting to make their way back home. After dragging myself out of bed and going through the morning rituals, I made my way to my office at battalion HQ, where I was greeted by a cheery Sergeant Martinez. He slapped me on the back and said, "I have some good news for you, Stoup." I asked him to speak a little softer as he proceeded to tell me that my promotion had gone through and that I would be getting my specialist fourth class stripes this Saturday night at the company cookout. Finally, I was moving out of the private ranks and into the specialist category. The only bad news was that I couldn't get my MOS changed to information specialist with this promotion. I was getting promoted in the slot I was filling at Battalion S-2, which was combat radio operator. I found it interesting, but not unusual for the army, that I was now a combat radio operator by military occupational specialty, even though I had never trained for or even held a combat radio. But at least I was no longer a combat engineer.

After a week of writing mostly command information bullshit, the weekend arrived, and it was going to be an interesting one for a change. For starters, I was getting promoted at the company's biweekly cookout on Saturday evening. But the event I was really looking forward to was happening on Sunday. Sergeant Martinez and I had been invited by Tran to attend his brother's wedding in a little hamlet not far down the road from Cu Chi village. It would be a real Vietnamese experience, including a Buddhist ceremony and a reception at the home of Tran's parents.

I spent most of Saturday just hanging around the hootch—cleaning, writing letters, and organizing my laundry. I mowed the lawn around the hootch (which had been neglected for weeks), then set up a cot and lay in the sun. Today's music selection was the Guess Who's "American Woman." It was so hot that afternoon that I swear I must have lost a gallon of sweat. Getting a tan and having the right look was essential in the Nam. To that end, I laid out two pair of my baggy fatigue pants so Kelly could take them to a tailor in the village to have them tapered and form-fitted. A lot of guys did this—really.

That night, LTC Gaynor pinned the Spec 4 insignia on my collar, and we ate steak and baked potatoes. It was a typical Saturday night as I had come to know it at Cu Chi. A little bit of army ceremony, a cookout, and a show at the EM club that featured yet another Filipino group with three female singers mimicking the Supremes. And finally, we ended the evening with our usual "nightcap" of getting stoned in someone's hootch while listening to some incredible music of the era (I referred to the music of the late '60s and early '70s as the Renaissance period of rock & roll) on a mind-blowing sound system. And one more important note: Doc was leaving in the morning for his long-planned and anticipated R & R to Bangkok.

R & R was a real big deal in the Nam. A week away from it all, especially for those in combat, was second only to going home in anticipation. And the options provided by the military for that one-week all-expenses-paid (transportation) vacation were, admittedly, spectacular. If you were married, you could meet your wife (or family) in Hawaii. But if you were single (or married and wanted a no-holes-barred getaway) the options were amazing. And making the choice was extremely difficult, with opinions and recommendations coming from all directions, especially from those who had already been to one or more of the locations. The options included Sydney, Australia; Hong Kong; Seoul, Korea; Tokyo, Japan; Manila, the Philippines; or Bangkok, Thailand. Other than Hawaii, the two most popular destinations were Sydney (for guys who craved "round-eyed" women for a change) and Bangkok for its exotic location, women, and "anything goes" reputation. Guys who were on their second (or third) tour would either try someplace new or go back to a favorite location. And a few lucky guys, most of whom worked in admin where they cut the travel orders, actually finagled the system and got two R & Rs in one year.

BEHIND THE WIRE

On Sunday morning at 1100 hours, I went to meet Sergeant Martinez at his hootch. He wasn't there when I arrived, but pulled up a few minutes later in Captain Becker's jeep. "The captain's letting us use his jeep for the day," he informed me with a sense of pride in his voice (I guess it was a big deal for an officer to give an NCO his jeep on the weekend). We loaded the jeep with the gift he purchased at the PX (a set of dishes) and our M-16s and headed out the main gate toward Cu Chi village.

Tran had given Sarge directions from Cu Chi village to his hamlet, so hopefully we wouldn't get lost. We obviously didn't have our translator with us, so if we lost our way, it might have been difficult to communicate our dilemma with the locals. Although surprisingly, quite a few Vietnamese could handle enough of the English language to get by, as opposed to the 99.9 percent of Americans who spoke no Vietnamese (other than the slang we adopted from their language). I rode shotgun for once, literally, with loaded M-16 in hand. Even though I had never had to use it, there was always the possibility of a first time. In fact, that week, we were graphically made aware of how close the enemy was to us. It seems the local ARVN militia got lucky and ambushed seven Viet Cong as they emerged from one of the Cu Chi tunnels. To make a point to the local villagers (some of whom were Viet Cong "by night"), they beheaded all seven and placed their heads on fence posts in the village square. The ARVN kept the heads on display for forty-eight hours, and many of the guys from the base camp went to the village to witness and photograph this bizarre scene. I passed on the opportunity.

Driving through the Cu Chi village square caused me to imagine what the faces on those heads might have looked like. The thought caused a chill to run down my spine, and I quickly shifted my focus to the surrounding environment. It wasn't often that us REMFs actually thought about the clear and present danger that lurked just about everywhere. Unlike our brothers in the field, we were usually in well-fortified areas, with hundreds if not thousands of troops and unlimited firepower around us. But once outside the security of a base camp, there was a mind-set that one had to quickly adopt. The only thing I can imagine comparing it to is the mind-set (or instincts) of a deer in the wild. You had to be alert, with all your "antennas" tuned to the surrounding environment at all times—always knowing that a hunter or natural enemy could be lying in wait, watching your every move. Yet you also had to realize that this was the day-to-day environment in which you lived and operated and that life, the search for food and companionship and all that nature provided, had to go on. So you learned to live with that potential danger. Those who managed to stay mentally healthy didn't think about it, or at least didn't dwell on it. They just prepared themselves as best as they could, mentally adjusted to the situation, and went on with their business.

We arrived at the small hamlet, which was located in a wooded area about five miles to the west of Cu Chi village, just before noon. As we pulled up, Tran came running out of one of the buildings, waving his hands. The hamlet consisted of about fifteen buildings, all of which I believe were houses. Even though they weren't "grass huts," they were very modest in terms of their construction. Tran greeted us warmly and led us into his parents' home where the ceremony was going to take place. In the corner of the main living area was a Buddhist shrine, surrounded with flowers and candles. The smell of burning incense permeated the air. A white cloth was on the floor in front of the shrine, presumably where the bride and groom would be standing for the service. As often happened to me in Vietnam during unfamiliar or strange occurrences, I momentarily lapsed into a state of unreality. My senses were overwhelmed by the sight, smells, and sounds of what was going on around me. It's as if I was watching a documentary about a Buddhist wedding ceremony rather than actually being there to observe one.

I snapped back to reality as Tran touched my shoulder, asking me if I wanted something to drink. I said, "No, but thanks, Tran," and walked to the other side of the room to where Sergeant Martinez stood, talking with one of Tran's relatives. Before long, the room began to fill with friends and relatives of the family, most of them from the hamlet. After the ceremony, we moved to Tran's house for the wedding reception. Everyone in the hamlet had prepared something for the occasion, and when the aroma of the food reached my nose, I knew we were in for a treat. As soon as all the guests had assembled, Tran handed out small shot-type glasses. He then poured a clear liquid from a large bottle into everyone's glass. When this task was completed, he raised his glass into the air and delivered what I presumed was a toast to the newlyweds. When he was finished, everyone clicked glasses, bowed, and downed the contents. I didn't know what I was drinking, but it burned all the way down. I later asked Tran what it was, and he said rice wine (of course, and homemade to boot).

Tran's grandfather, who looked like Ho Chi Minh, came over to where we were standing and had Tran fill both of our glasses. He then clicked my glass, muttered something in Vietnamese, and downed his drink. I just nodded and, so as not to insult him, did the same. He motioned for Tran to fill the glasses again and began talking to me in Vietnamese. I nodded again, as if I understood what he was saying. Tran intervened at this point and said, "My grandfather wants you to match him drink for drink." I gave Tran a look as if to say, "This could be trouble, please help me." This old guy wanted to outmacho me. We downed another shot as I looked around the room for some reason to escape. It was customary in Vietnam (as in many cultures) to match drink for drink in a situation like this. And I knew that if I didn't get out of there soon, I was going to pay a big price a little later. Tran picked up on my unease and led me away toward a table filled with food.

Sergeant Martinez was standing at the table, stuffing himself with all kinds of local delicacies. As I was feeling the effects of the rice wine, I decided to do the same. Everything looked and smelled delicious, although there were a couple of items that looked a little "risky." The tastes of the now-familiar seasonings were wonderful as I moved from item to item. Sergeant Martinez looked at me and said, "You better not ask what you're eating. These locals cook with just about anything that runs or crawls."

I thanked him for his words of wisdom and continued feasting. He then looked at his watch and said we had better start heading back to base. "I promised Captain Becker I'd have the jeep back by 1700 hours," he remarked.

We found Tran and had him take us around to say our goodbyes. When we got to the wedding couple, I handed the groom a hand-painted Vietnamese card that I purchased at the PX. In it was $25 in greenbacks that I had borrowed from the Sarge (Sergeant Martinez always seemed to have a few greenbacks in reserve to dip into). He opened it and bowed in grateful appreciation. I bowed back, and we continued bowing to each other until Sergeant Martinez and I made our way out the door. Tran followed and walked us to the jeep, which was being "guarded" by some of the youngsters from the hamlet. I looked at Sergeant Martinez, as I could tell that they wanted us to take them for a ride. He picked up on this and said, "We gotta get going, Stoup," as he shooed the kids out of the jeep.

On the relatively short ride back to the base, Sergeant Martinez and I didn't say much to each other. I don't know what he was thinking, but I couldn't help but reflect on the experience we had just been through and on the vast differences between our two societies and cultures. These people were so materially poor, yet so spiritually rich. As human beings, I know that we shared many of the same life goals, values, and desires. But culturally and intellectually, we were worlds apart. To me, it was a cultural experience that I found fascinating. But Sergeant Martinez, being Hispanic, was a lot more accustomed to cultural differences than I was. And this was his second tour of duty in the Nam, so I'm sure events like this were no big deal to him. Rather than reflecting on the event we just attended, he was probably thinking about being short. He only had two weeks left on his rotation, and I could tell he was mentally gearing up for the trip back home and what his next assignment might be. I was really going to miss him, and that's something I never thought I would say about a lifer.

On Tuesday, Sergeant Martinez's replacement arrived to be oriented to his new job. At first meeting, I knew this guy was going to be trouble. Sergeant First Class Ralph Brady, a real lifer, was definitely not the caliber of his predecessor. It was readily apparent that he was a mean son of a bitch who was carrying some kind of chip on his shoulder. But in reality, he merely represented the lifer mentality that had taken hold in Vietnam during this particular point in the war's history.

The war in the south had come to a virtual lull, and there were a lot of career soldiers, especially the asshole lifers, who were looking for ways to vent their frustration at not being able to fight the war and garner more ribbons, citations, and promotions. Unfortunately, the REMFs often bore the brunt of this frustration in the form of harassment and military gamesmanship. But by this stage of the war, the troops were just as frustrated, and they had a way of getting their revenge if things got out of hand (as many of the lifers would soon learn if they hadn't already). Rumors were also circulating again that the division was about to be withdrawn, but nothing that could be confirmed. So it appeared that we were going to have to live with SFC Brady for a while, and we weren't looking forward to it.

As it turned out, Sergeant Brady would become my nemesis during my final weeks in Cu Chi. For some reason, he was always on my back, as if he had some kind of personal vendetta against me. I think it was because, in his mind, I represented the soldier who "got over" rather than the soldier that put his life on the line almost every day. He often referred to me as a pothead because I lived and hung around with the medics, who were notorious drug users. One day, his fantasy of busting me was almost fulfilled. I was processing film and printing photos from a recent shoot in the makeshift lab I had put together in a small shed just behind the battalion HQ building. I had just finished smoking a joint (to make the task of dealing with the processing chemicals a little more pleasant—my excuse du jour) when he busted through the door of the shed. He screamed at me that he smelled pot to which I responded, "Someone must have been smoking outside the shed, Sarge, because all I can smell in here are these stinking processing chemicals," which fortunately did permeate the air. Since he didn't catch me in the act and since I had nothing on me, there was nothing he could do but grumble. "I'll catch your sorry ass one of these days, Stoup, and when I do, you'll know what trouble is." With that, he stormed out the door. Now that was a close call, and I cautioned myself to be a little more careful, as the times they were a-changing in Cu Chi. Sergeant Brady continued to hound and try to pursue me as the weeks went on, but he never succeeded in catching me, or anyone else for that matter, with anything.

Doc returned from R & R the following Sunday. He loved it so much that he said it had "balanced out" his time in the Nam, and that's saying something, especially coming from him. We spent the night on top of the bunker, getting high and listening to story after story about his adventures and dalliances. The ARVN compound outside our base camp was hit with mortar and rocket fire that night, so we had a light show to watch while we listened. By the time he was finished with his stories, I was convinced that Bangkok was the place I wanted to go (with Sydney coming in a close second). And besides, I was fascinated with Asian art, culture, and food and had already been leaning toward Bangkok. I'd have to wait until late February, though, before making the trip.

239 days. Racial tensions between black and white troops were also building to a dangerous level during this time period. There had been a lot of publicity back in the world recently about "race wars" breaking out among the troops in Vietnam. I personally hadn't witnessed any problems and had only heard about isolated instances of racial tension. Even though, to a certain extent, the brothers did tend to hang with each other, as did the Hispanics for that matter, there was still an overriding social harmony that existed among all the troops. Regardless of race, we all pulled for each other, especially when dealing with the enemy on both sides of the wire. But lately, with the lifers increasingly taking their frustrations out on the growing troop population in the rear, tensions were high and level heads often didn't prevail.

On my way back to the hootch one afternoon later that week, I witnessed an altercation among a small group of enlisted men. They were divided by race, black on one side and white on the other, and they were yelling taunts at each other. Two of them appeared to have been fighting, and just as I was passing through the crowd, the black guy who apparently had been fighting picked up a two-by-four that was lying on the ground and slammed it onto the head of his white antagonist. As he was hit, the guy's knees buckled and he fell to the ground, bleeding from the head. Before anyone could react to what had just happened, a jeep full of MPs came speeding down the company street toward us. Someone must have called them when the fight broke out.

Four burly MPs jumped out of the jeep and into the center of the fracas and immediately grabbed and handcuffed the guy holding the two-by-four. They told everyone in the area to freeze and began taking names and questioning the participants. As I was the only witness outside of the group involved in the confrontation, I was questioned as well. After I told them what I saw, I was told that I'd have to testify at a court-martial against the guy who was arrested for assault.

Two weeks later, the court-martial was held in a small air conditioned prefabricated metal building near division headquarters. I sat in the back of the room as the proceedings began, waiting to be called to testify. The room was freezing (it was rare to be in a totally air-conditioned building). As I sat there, I periodically noticed the accused glaring at me. He was a big guy and looked real unhappy. I began to shake. I don't know if it was the freezing temperature in the room or the fear of retribution, but I was shaking. But I did what I had to do, stuttering and shaking occasionally, and told the court what I had witnessed. The trial ended with the judicial panel finding the defendant guilty. He was sentenced to two years of hard labor and given a dishonorable discharge. The whole experience added yet another facet to the gem of my life in the rear in Vietnam.

CHAPTER 8

The Bridge at Memot, Cambodia, a Desperate Attempt for an Early Out, and the Final Days of Cu Chi

October arrived in a blaze of sunshine, and with it came a rash of activity. For starters, Sergeant Martinez was leaving later in the week, and we had his "hail and farewell" to prepare. The guys in the company wanted to send him off in style since he was one of the good guys. So we decided to have a big blowout in his honor—one last megaparty before Sergeant Brady took over and ruined our social life. No one could predict what life would be like under this bastard, but it was pretty obvious to all of us that he was just chomping at the bit to get control of the company and make our lives miserable. Anticipating this, I had made a point of late to get chummier with Captain Becker, hoping that I could go to him to counter any problems that I might have with Sergeant Brady.

New division regulations came down that week saying that all dogs had to be tagged and tied, and only ten dogs were allowed per company. SGT Pepper made the cut, but he hated being tied up. He was constantly trying to get loose and actually did so one day. Today he is hiding under my bed and won't come out. I let him run free at night, but have to keep him tied up during the day. And then one day, a "last gasp" monsoon storm moved in, dumping almost twelve inches of rain in a three-hour period of time. When I got back to the hootch from work that afternoon, wading through knee-deep water in some places to get there, I heard a whimpering coming from under the hootch. It seems that SGT Pepper had gone under the hootch, probably freaked out by the thunderstorm, and his rope got caught on one of the beams and he couldn't free himself. The water was up to his nose and he almost drowned. Needless to say, I kept him in the hootch from that point on, tied to my bed for protection. Besides, my office was close enough to the hootch to be able to let him out to pee at lunchtime.

At mail call that day, I got a letter from my college roommate John Stahura who had also been drafted after completing his master's degree at Indiana University. It seems that he broke both of his ankles during training at Fort Lewis, Washington, and now has a permanent medical profile, which means no combat duty for him. As he has degrees in both sociology and statistics, he'll probably get some kind of cushy job, like working as a statistician for the army. Lucky bastard, but more power to him.

On one of my visits to the captain that week to discuss party details, he hit me with a piece of news that added a twist to the weekend events. "You and I are going into Cambodia," he informed me. "We're leaving by convoy on Sunday and will spend the night at Tay Ninh. Then we'll catch a convoy into Cambodia on Monday morning and make our way to the village of Memot." He proceeded to tell me that the battalion was donating a bridge to a Cambodian hamlet. He said the division's heavy equipment going in and out of Cambodia during Operation Bold Lancer had destroyed one of their bridges, and the 65th Engineers were going to construct a new one and leave it behind as a gesture of goodwill to the Cambodian people. "And of course, they plan to milk the occasion for all the PR value they can get out of it," he continued. "LTC Gaynor wants you to write the story," he added, "and he wants me to go along because of the importance of the event. There will be an official ceremony, and Colonel Gaynor will be flying in with some division brass…So this is an important one, Specialist Stoup."

I began my preparations for the trip the next day. Since I planned to take a lot of pictures of the event, my morning began with a trip to the division PIO to score a load of film. As for conducting interviews for the story, Captain Becker said I would be provided with a Vietnamese translator that spoke both English and Cambodian. So that I'd have everything ready to go before the big party that night, I packed my knapsack, cleaned my rifle, and loaded about a dozen clips of ammunition. And this time, I packed my poncho liner. I was ready to go and was both exhilarated and apprehensive at the thought of making the trip into another foreign land—even though it was only a few hours' drive to the border.

The night of Sergeant Martinez's farewell party arrived, and we did, indeed, send him off in style. We all chipped in and bought him a new set of luggage for his trip (I could tell he was touched when he made his farewell remarks). One by one he said goodbye to his troops, and his Puerto Rican eyes were glazed over when he got to me and we shook hands for the last time. I didn't even want to think about what life in Cu Chi was going to be like without him.

The next morning, at a civilized 1100 hours (being Sunday), Sergeant Brady took us in Captain Becker's jeep to meet up with the convoy. He brownnosed the captain with his lifer bullshit jargon for the entire ride to the other side of the base, which practically made me sick. As he pulled away after dropping us off, Captain Becker turned to me and said, "I don't know if we're short enough to survive this guy, Stoup." At that point, I knew I had an ally.

When it came time to saddle up, Captain Becker was invited to ride in a jeep driven by a second lieutenant while I hopped into a deuce and a half with a bunch of grunts. I was hoping for some (more) good war stories on the four-hour ride to Tay Ninh. I wasn't disappointed. They were participating in the final phase of Operation Bold Lancer, the 25th Infantry Division's name for its Cambodian operation, which was coming to an end. The deadline imposed by Congress for the U.S. military to be totally withdrawn from Cambodia was only days away.

The grunts told me about the difficulties fighting in Cambodia and of the losses they were taking. They told me that unlike the southern sector of South Vietnam, which had been gradually defoliated over the past five years or better, the Cambodian landscape was thick and lush, which made it easy for the enemy to hide. A system of good roads was also nonexistent, so it was difficult for the United States to use APCs and tanks to a large extent. And those that did make it in were tearing up the roads and bridges they encountered (and thus our bridge replacement mission). It was definitely a hit-and-run operation, they told me. Tunnels, ambushes, mines, and booby traps were the modus operandi.

We arrived at our destination right on schedule, and I was assigned to a tent for the night that housed rotating enlisted men. The Tay Ninh base camp had quite a storied past, and I learned some interesting facts about it during my short stay. It was originally an enemy base camp that was taken over by the Americans when troops from the 196th Light Infantry Brigade arrived in Tay Ninh City on August 14, 1966. Many a decisive battle had taken place in and around this base camp.

At 0800 hours the next morning, we boarded a new convoy that was heading into Cambodia. This time, I was allowed to ride in the jeep that had been assigned to Captain Becker, which was being driven by a second lieutenant Paul Bugos. It was a two-passenger jeep, so I had to sit in the small cargo compartment in the back. I climbed in, put my gear next to me, and positioned my M-16 between my legs. I then loaded a clip of ammunition into the rifle and placed two more within easy reach. Moments later, we headed out.

After only about thirty minutes on the road, we crossed the border into Cambodia, and it wasn't long before the landscape began to change—dramatically. I had this weird feeling, like I was entering a strange and very foreign land, which, of course, I was. I guess I had grown accustomed to the relatively flat South Vietnam landscape that was dominated by wide open fields and rice paddies. But what we were now entering was a land that was a lot lusher and exotic—like parts of South Vietnam, I would imagine, before we bombed and defoliated the hell out of it.

The gravel road we were traveling on was lined with palm and banana trees and took us through bush that was so thick with foliage that you couldn't see in more than a few yards. I started thinking about what the grunts had said, about how the thick jungle growth made it ideal for enemy ambushes, which caused me to pull my M-16 closer to my body in an almost reflex action. As we made our way down the road, we came upon a group of combat engineers walking toward us with minesweepers in hand. They were being covered by a platoon of infantry, who were walking the perimeter with rifles and grenade launchers at the ready. The engineers were wearing headsets and barely looked up to acknowledge our presence.

Lieutenant Bugos, who had said very little up to this point, casually turned toward me and Captain Becker and said, "You know, the convoy we're in makes this run to the division's main base in Cambodia every day." He then continued, almost proudly. "And it's been either ambushed or hit land mines for the past five days in a row. So keep your fingers crossed," he said, smiling, before he turned his attention back to the road. Now, I thought to myself, that was a comforting piece of information. I started to tense up, but then looked out at the engineers sweeping for mines and at the grunts. I could have been out there with them; I could have been one of them, which made me feel a little better, but not much.

We passed fields of sugarcane and pineapple that were lush from the monsoon rains. Natives started appearing along the road as the terrain changed from thick jungle to fields of tropical fruit. Some were carrying large baskets on their heads while others had large sacks slung over their shoulders. Their skin was darker than that of the Vietnamese. And many of them, including the men, wore wrap-around skirts known as *sampots*, which was a carryover from the days of the Khmer dynasty. As we approached a pineapple field that was being worked by the locals, a group of them started running toward the convoy with big smiles on their faces. They had fresh pineapples in both hands and were giving them to the GIs, who reached out for them as they passed by. It looked like they were happy to see us, but then again, looks can be deceiving—for even though they had smiles on their faces, some of them also had a look of fear in their eyes. There had been a lot of massacres of villagers and locals on all sides of this war, and I'm sure these people were well aware of it. So rather than being happy to see us, I think they were more likely trying to appease us in the hope that we would pass them by without incident.

About fifteen minutes later, we came to a fork in the road. The convoy proceeded along the right fork, but our jeep suddenly broke away from the group and took the left fork in the road. When I realized that we had left the convoy, my heart skipped a beat, and there was an immediate lump in my throat that rendered me almost speechless. "What are we doing?" I asked Lieutenant Bugos in an almost hysterical tone.

"We're heading to our destination, Memot village," he replied. "The convoy's heading to the base camp, which is north of here. The village you're going to is a bit to the southwest. And you do want to make it to your destination so you can get your story, don't you, Specialist?" He gazed at me with a smug look on his face. These fucking lifers loved this stuff. Scaring the shit out of REMFs was one of their favorite pastimes. Captain Becker didn't say a word.

Actually, the thirty-minute-or-so drive from the time we left the convoy to when we reached the village was one of the most memorable experiences of my year in the Nam. I can't fully explain it, but the combination of fear and adventure, coupled with the unbelievable beauty and uniqueness of the countryside, put me into a near state of hypnosis—an almost out-of-body experience as if I was looking at everything I was seeing through someone else's eyes rather than my own.

Much of the ride took us through one of the Michelin rubber plantations. For miles, we were in a shrouded forest, with nothing but row after row of perfectly aligned rubber trees. As we drove along at a somewhat leisurely pace, I kept imagining that Viet Cong were going to jump out from behind the rows of trees and ambush us. It was actually the perfect place for an ambush to take place, and we were an easy, solitary target (even though the convoy was a bigger and better target, I thought to myself). But just in case, I took my rifle off safety and put my finger on the trigger. If ever I was going to face the enemy and have to use this thing, I thought to myself, this was it. As we continued down the dirt road toward our destination, sunlight streamed through the treetops, lighting our way through the dark forest of rubber trees. It was magical. Nothing happened.

Within minutes of leaving the thick of the plantation, the village came into sight. We crossed over a small river on the Bailey bridge that the 65th Engineers had built and entered Memot village. I couldn't believe my luck. We had made our solo journey through the plantation without incident, and Captain Becker had made radio contact with the base camp and learned that the convoy had arrived without being hit for the first time in five days. I was beginning to feel like someone was actually watching over me.

The commander of Bravo Company, 65th Engineers, First Lieutenant Lawrence Washington, was there to meet us. He was accompanied by a couple of NCOs from the company and our translator. They saluted Captain Becker as we approached, which seemed a little unnecessary, considering what I had learned about the field. Also assembled was what appeared to be every old man they could rustle up—a lot of papa sans and village elders standing in a group, with questioning looks on their faces. Lieutenant Washington informed us that LTC Gaynor and the division chief of staff, Colonel John Hughes, would be flying in at around 1300 hours. I looked at my watch. It was a little past 1100, so I had a little less than two hours to conduct my interviews and take pictures. Lieutenant Washington then introduced me to the Vietnamese translator, Nguyen Chi. "Nguyen will help you get your story," he said, as he walked off with Captain Becker to inspect the bridge.

As Nguyen and I walked toward the center of the small village, I explained to him why we were here and the nature of the story I was told to write. I gave him as much background as possible without getting too "political" and avoiding all the military details that had been drilled into me. I had a very basic set of questions in mind and knew I had to keep it simple with these people. Nguyen nodded that he understood as we made our way to where the elders were gathered.

Nguyen greeted the group with a bow and spoke to them in Cambodian. He must have introduced me, as I heard my name in English, which prompted the group to bow to me as well, which I returned. He then must have invited them to sit, as the elders sat down on chairs that had been provided for the ceremony. He then grabbed chairs for the two of us, and we sat together facing the small group of men. I asked them right off the bat if they were pleased that the Americans had replaced the bridge leading to their village. The oldest and most distinguished of the group stood up and started speaking. At first, he looked at Nguyen as he spoke, but quickly turned his head toward me and looked me in the eyes as he continued. He said, "The Americans had destroyed their ancient bridge when they came to the area, so it was the honorable thing for them to do to replace the bridge, even with one this crude." My reaction to his words was delayed as Nguyen translated his comments. I tried not to smile even though I liked what he had to say, or at least the way he said it. He continued standing after he spoke, so I assumed he was the head elder in the village and was probably going to do all the speaking for the group.

As a follow-up, I asked him if the military action that had taken place in the area had an impact on the village and its people. His face reddened as he responded, "We are a peaceful people and do not want to be involved with any people coming into our land. We did not want the soldiers from Vietnam who came and damaged our farmlands and roadways. And we did not want the Americans who came after them," he continued. "We don't support either side and wish for all foreigners to leave our land so we can live in peace, as we are accustomed."

I could see where this was going, or wasn't going, so I decided to ask one last question. "Are you at least pleased at the gesture being made by the Americans to repair the damage they caused by leaving the bridge behind as a gesture of goodwill?"

"As I said before," he commented, "all we want is peace, and for all foreigners to leave our land." And that was that. I stood up, and Nguyen followed suit. I asked Nguyen to thank them for their time and for answering my questions. The senior elder turned to his colleagues and nodded, and they all stood and bowed. The two of us returned the bow then turned and walked away. "That was interesting," I said to Nguyen as we made our way toward the river. He looked at me and smiled, but didn't say anything.

When we reached the banks of the river, Nguyen asked me if I knew anything about Buddhism. I said that I didn't know much, but that it had always interested me and that I had read some of the teachings of Buddha. I thought for a moment that he might be a missionary for Buddhism, about to try to convert me much like the Catholic missionaries that had converted great numbers of the Vietnamese people.

But rather, as I had expressed an interest, he asked me if I wanted to visit the local Buddhist temple, which was on the other side of the village. I told him that I would love to, and with that, he stood up and I followed him for the short walk to the temple. It was a small unassuming building, but very ornate, especially its pointed and tiled roof. Once inside, an aura of silence and the smell of incense greeted my senses. A beautiful golden statue of a sitting Buddha surrounded by flowers dominated the front of the small room. A few monks in saffron robes were sitting in their prayer positions in front of the shrine. I stood there in silence for a few moments as Nguyen bowed his head in reverence. He then raised his head and turned to look at me with a smile on his face. I followed him out of the temple, and we made our way back to the river's edge without speaking.

When we got there, I looked at my watch and realized that it was lunchtime. But my stomach had already told me that, as it was grumbling, and I was hungry. So I found a place to sit on a wall that ran along the river on one side of the village and opened my knapsack. Nguyen excused himself and walked over to talk to a Vietnamese friend he had traveled with. I pulled out a couple of cans of Cs, and as I was opening them, I noticed out of the corner of my eye that a small group of kids were watching my every move. They probably had never seen an American before the engineers moved in, and I could tell they were fascinated. What an odd and interesting lot we Americans must have seemed to this homogeneous race. Just in the group they were observing: I was somewhat blond and Anglo of average height; Lieutenant Washington was very black; one guy was six feet four inches tall, while another was five foot four; Captain Becker had a pudgy belly, while an engineer PFC was skinny as a rail; the lieutenant's NCO was Latino; and so on. And of course, we walked tall and carried a big stick. I decided to go over and try to talk to them, but as I moved closer to where they were standing, they backed up proportionately. So we just stayed where we were and enjoyed watching each other.

Just as I began to eat, I heard the sound of a chopper in the distance. It was a Huey, with its now recognizable sound. I wolfed down the canned ham and peaches that I had opened and repacked my bag. Then I got out my notepad and camera and walked toward a clearing that I presumed would be used as a landing area. Captain Becker and Lieutenant Washington arrived a minute later.

The Huey touched down, kicking up a dust storm that caused the kids to run off shrieking in what sounded like a mixture of terror and glee. I had to hold my boonie cap on, which I had been wearing to block out the intense sun. Before the blades came to a halt, the two colonels jumped out of the aircraft and made their way to where we were standing. Colonel Hughes's aide followed closely behind, carrying a package under his arm. Captain Becker bolted forward and greeted them both with a snappy salute.

It was the most strack I'd ever seen the captain, and I planned to tease him about it a little later.

My amused reaction to his demeanor made me realize that I was actually getting close to Captain Becker, the first "almost friend" that I had made in the officer corps, which leads me to a topic that has always interested me about the military—its class structure. It's the rule that says that officers can't fraternize with NCOs, who can't fraternize with enlisted men, and so on. I had become friends, of sorts, with Sergeant Martinez, but that was more of a friendly boss/employee kind of relationship. Just because of rank, I couldn't socialize with an officer or an NCO—at least not officially. I mean, there were a lot of officers (lieutenants and captains) in the Nam who were my age, or close to my age, many just serving their time and not career types. And for the most part, I was their intellectual and social peer (at least in civilian life). There were even a few NCOs around my age, but not nearly as many, as most of them were career types. But because of that rank distinction, it was taboo to get involved with any of them. So I constantly found myself suppressing my feelings, opinions, and even my normal reactions to things. Even though I understood why the military had established this policy, it didn't mean that I had to agree with it. And in the coming months, like everything else in the Nam, I would work around this policy and develop a number of friends in both the NCO and officer ranks.

Lieutenant Washington led us all to the central building of Memot village. The local hierarchy were assembled and waiting patiently for the American officials to arrive. As the brass made their way toward them, the Cambodians bowed in deference. LTC Gaynor and Colonel Hughes greeted them politely, but did not bow in return. As they all stood there, conducting their official "small talk" through interpreters, I snapped a few pictures. Then the colonel's aide unwrapped the package he was holding and handed it to LTC Gaynor, who began to speak. "On behalf of the 65th Engineer Battalion, 25th Infantry Division, and the government of the United States of America, I'd like to present you with the title to this Bailey bridge." He concluded his presentation by pointing to the structure that all of a sudden looked very much out of place in the exotic setting of the hamlet. Can you imagine what these people must have been thinking, being presented the "title" to a Bailey bridge in the form of a framed certificate, a piece of Western culture at its finest? I'm sure, to this day, that it's hanging on a wall of the government building in that small Cambodian village.

Acutely aware of the absurdity of the situation, the village elders responded to the presentation with forced politeness. When asked for a reaction through the interpreters, they merely thanked the colonel for his gesture of kindness—as opposed to the comments they made to me when I interviewed them. The whole event was very strained, even though I don't think the colonels realized it. They were too caught up in their magnanimous gesture of goodwill and in meaningless ceremony that was so much a part of their lives.

When the ceremony ended, a couple of village women appeared, carrying baskets of fruit, some kind of biscuits, bottled water, and warm soda. While those in attendance enjoyed the refreshments, I approached Colonel Hughes to get a few comments for my story. "Colonel Hughes, why did the division donate this bridge to Memot village?" I asked.

"It's a symbol of the spirit of cooperation between our two countries," he responded, "and another example of the successful execution of our pacification program." Nothing like a little propaganda to spice up a story, I thought to myself. It was going to be great fun writing this one, and even more fun getting it approved—if I wrote it the way I wanted to.

Just as I was about to ask him another question, his aide appeared and informed him that it was time to leave. "Sorry, Specialist, but we have to move out," he said, as they walked toward the Huey that was starting to crank up its engine. At the same moment, Captain Becker came running over and told me to grab my bag. "We're flying back to Cu Chi with the colonel," he informed me. Now that was a piece of good news. I wouldn't have to spend the night at the base camp under who knows what conditions. I wouldn't have to drive back through that rubber plantation, and I was going to get to see Cambodia from the air.

As we rushed toward the waiting chopper, I turned and looked back at the scene we had left behind. Lieutenant Washington and his NCOs were standing there, along with the group of village elders, children, and others who had gathered for the occasion. They all had puzzled looks on their faces as they watched us lift off the ground, as if they were wondering what the hell had just happened. I was wondering the same thing.

Three days later, I was sitting at my typewriter putting the finishing touches on the latest edition of the *65th Recorder*, having submitted my bridge story for approval the day before, when Sergeant Brady approached my desk with a sadistic look on his face. "Colonel Gaynor wants to see you in his office ASAP," he sneered. "And in case you're wondering what he wants, it's about that story you wrote on the bridge." Even though Sergeant Brady caught me by surprise, being called into the colonel's office didn't. I had a funny feeling this might be coming, as I took a chance and wrote the bridge story as I saw it. And I did something novel for army journalism—I told the truth.

No one else was in the office and the colonel's door was open, but I knocked anyway. He looked up and told me to come in. I walked up to his desk, stood at attention, and saluted. He returned the salute and asked me to have a seat. My article was lying on his desk. He looked me in the eye, then picked up the article and waved it in front of my face, saying, "What the hell is this, Specialist Stoup!"

"It's my story on the Bailey bridge, sir," I replied.

"I thought you were smarter than this, Specialist," he continued. "If you think I'm going to send this to division reading like this, you've got another thing coming. I want you to cut the peace shit out of this story and rewrite it the army way. And I want it on my desk by 1500 hours this afternoon. And this better be the last time this happens, or you're going to be spending a lot more time in the field," he concluded. I didn't say a word when he finished his tirade. I just stood up, saluted, turned, and walked out the door. I was angry, but not surprised. I knew I was taking a chance by telling it like it was—by quoting the village elders verbatim. And I knew I shouldn't have expected more from a lifer. But this guy was supposed to be a highly intelligent and well-rounded man—and maybe he was. But he was also a pompous asshole. He was afraid of his own shadow, or at least the shadow of the division PIO, who might have actually accused him of letting the truth slip out of the bag. But in reality, it was me who had the problem. By this time, I knew how the game was played in the military. I knew that the truth and military policy in Vietnam were at opposite ends of the spectrum. I just happened to disagree with the policy and thought maybe I could slip one by. Well, I couldn't. I rewrote the article, taking the "peace shit" out of it, and had it back on the colonel's desk by 1500 hours. This is how the final story read on the front page of the *Tropic Lightning News*, Vol 5, No. 27, 1970:

ENGINEERS BUILD CIVILIAN BRIDGE

Memot, Cambodia—One of the first casualties of operations in Cambodia was a light, French- built bridge over a stream that bisects this prosperous city. But when U.S. troops withdrew, they left the busi-

ness community a new bridge built especially for commercial use.

After the first bridge was destroyed, Alfa Company of the 65th Engineer Battalion quickly replaced the span with a tactical bridge to permit military traffic to pass. Later, as the deadline for American troop withdrawal drew near, it became apparent that the tactical bridge would have to be removed for future use. An order quickly went out stating that some provision would have to be made to bridge the stream so that normal civilian commerce could continue. The engineers answer was to replace the tactical span with a Bailey Bridge. Alfa Company removed the old span, while Bravo Company constructed the new.

The villagers took in the event with all the excitement of a national holiday. The bridge site was constantly surrounded with hundreds of onlookers, while other villagers prepared native dishes and peddled their wares as if the Engineers' presence was cause for a village-wide celebration.

Bravo Company, under the leadership of Captain Lawrence Washington, and well-organized from previous experiences, completed its mission in less than six hours. When asked their reaction to the bridge building by the engineers, a group of elders bowed vigorously and repeated, "Thank you, Thank you."

I might have lost the battle, but I wasn't ready, just yet, to give up the war. I'd have an opportunity to have my way with the military a little later in my tour. But for now, I didn't want to risk being reassigned to the field, so I acquiesced. Staying alive, at this point, meant a little more to me than writing the truth. And besides, with all the other work I was doing for the battalion, plus the articles I was getting placed in the division newspaper, my standing in the battalion was pretty good. I was even able to finally get Sergeant Brady off my back about drug use (still implied because of my association with the medics), as I had recently encouraged one of the guys in our company to turn himself in to mental health to deal with his heroin addiction. I also wrote an article on the increasing prevalence and dangers of heroin use for the division newspaper. And I really was trying to encourage guys to give up smack, especially the short-timers who were about to make their way back to the world.

Life at Cu Chi was getting progressively worse. The glory days—at least my glory days—were rapidly becoming a memory as the bullshit and game playing continued to increase in frequency and intensity. Sergeant Brady was doing his best to make everyone's life at headquarters company miserable, and he was succeeding. Starched fatigues, polished boots, and the like were once again being enforced. The troops were restless, and I was expecting another fragging incident, or worse, at any time. And about a week later, another fragging did, indeed, occur in one of the infantry units.

At mail call one day that week, I received a letter from my friend Dennis (the guy who I went to basic with who I ran into at the PX in Long Binh shortly after arriving in the Nam). He informed me that his unit was being withdrawn and that he was being transferred to the 1st Air Cavalry Division in Phuoc Vinh. I didn't think much of his news at the time. But then, one Wednesday afternoon in early November, a rumor spread around the base camp like a wildfire. The 25th Infantry Division was leaving Vietnam! It was being withdrawn from active duty and would be heading back to its home base of operations at Schofield Barracks in Hawaii. I was at division headquarters working on a story for the *Tropic Lightning News* when I heard the news. And the way everyone was talking about it, this time it appeared to be more than a rumor. As soon as I was finished with my work, I raced back to the battalion to see if Captain Becker could confirm what I had heard. He did. The division would be withdrawn within thirty days, and everyone with seven or more months of Nam duty under their belts would be going with it. My heart sank, as I only had a little more than five months under my belt. "What happens to those of us with less than seven months?" I asked, holding back tears of fear that were forming in my eyes.

"You'll be reassigned to another unit," he responded.

Within a few days, the pieces of the withdrawal puzzle started coming together. From civilian newspapers and magazines that made their way from the world into our hands, to classified pieces of information passed along by dissident members of the officer corps whom I had befriended over the months (and a couple of NCOs), I got the full story. It seems that Congress, not to mention the American people, was becoming increasingly impatient with the war. Even though the nation had committed nearly 500,000 troops and untold resources to the effort, we weren't winning, or even gaining ground. The country had apparently come to the conclusion that it was time to get out and cut our losses, which by this point were already extremely high. Legislation had just been passed requiring the military to reduce troop levels by 150,000 within ninety days, and the 25th Infantry Division would be one of the first to go. Additional cuts were to follow closely thereafter, giving me hope that maybe my days in the Nam still might be numbered. But for now, I was in limbo. I had to wait for the orders that would determine my fate and would tell me where my next great adventure would be in the Republic of Vietnam. But just as I did when I arrived at the 65th Engineers Battalion (with a little cunning and a lot of luck), I once again wasn't about to let the army determine my destiny without trying to do something about it.

Two things happened during that thirty-day period of withdrawal preparation that helped distract me from the agonizing anticipation of my fate. The first was more symbolic than essential to my fate while the second was not only essential, but also critical to the goal of getting me the hell out of Vietnam—and possibly the army. The second required a bold move on my part, not to mention a lot of hasty planning and execution. But first, let me describe the little surprise that was laid on me by one of the officers from the division PIO office—an officer that I had become close to over the course of the past two months.

First Lieutenant Jack Kraley was not only about to go home, but he was also about to ETS from the army after a four-year ROTC enlistment. Despite the taboos, he would visit our hootch on occasion to smoke a joint (which was a little more difficult in the officers' quarters), and we'd chat about our mutual dislike of the army and hatred of the war. One evening, shortly after the withdrawal announcement, he joined me and Doc for a smoke and pulled a card out of his wallet to show us. It was a membership card to the Vietnam Veterans Against the War organization. He told us how he had gotten together with friends the last time he was home on leave and that they convinced him to join. He said the organization was the brainchild of a couple of Vietnam vets from New York, who formed the group to lobby against the war. He also told us that a lot of troops serving in Vietnam were "card-carrying" members and that it was safe to do so as all the information regarding the organization and its activities (including membership cards) was sent through the mail, which was secure (believe it or not, they didn't censor our mail). He said it was a good way to get firsthand news, and the truth, about what was happening with the war rather than the limited and censored information we got from the military. He asked Doc and me if we were interested in joining. Of course, we jumped at the opportunity, so he gave us the name and address information so we could contact them and become members. So I can proudly say that I became one of the card-carrying members of Vietnam Veterans Against the War while still serving in Vietnam. *(Note: Rather than being disloyal, I found joining this organization to be patriotic. And I was in good company, as Secretary of State John Kerry, a decorated Vietnam War veteran, was also a member of VVAW back in the day.)*

As nice as it was finding an antiwar organization to join, it still wasn't helping my current situation. But Lieutenant Kraley gave me another piece of information that I found very useful. He had met a few other soldiers during his duty assignment who were also saddled with that extra year of service for having dropped out of OCS. He told me that the regulation on OCS service had changed a couple of times in recent years and that the extra year requirement for dropouts had recently been rescinded to help the army achieve its troop reduction mandates. I couldn't believe what I was hearing. He said, however, that a dropout date of this past March or later was required to have the extra year removed. So I, as he put it, was in a "catch-22" situation and didn't qualify for the drop as currently written. But he strongly recommended that I contact whoever I could—Congress, the Department of the Army, whoever—to see if the regulation could be changed or amended. "And the more the merrier," he said, encouraging me to find others in the same situation to join in the effort.

I thought about what he had to say for a long time that night and came up with a plan. There were a lot of unhappy troops in our battalion with less than seven months of service in the Nam. And as I was to learn, there were a lot more men than I realized who shared my situation—guys who had also enlisted for OCS and then dropped out and, like me, were stuck with that third year of service beyond the two years required by the draft.

The next morning, I visited a fellow soldier that I had met at a hootch party who worked in battalion admin, Spec 4 Allen Domb. I remembered having a conversation with him about my OCS experience and learning that he too was an OCS dropout. Since he worked in admin, I asked him if he could go through the battalion records and see how many other guys were in our situation. He got right on it and that evening brought me the information. I was amazed to learn that there were thirty-nine of us, and we decided to contact every one we could find that fit the profile and ask others to help us with the task of finding the rest. Allen and I then drafted a letter that we would have each of the thirty-nine sign, which we would then copy and mail using our free-mail service. We even came up with a name for the endeavor: "Project Year Drop." Here's how the letter read:

October 1970

Congress of the United States of America
Department of the Army, Department of Defense
Washington, D.C.

Dear Sir:

We, the undersigned, are writing to call your attention to a situation we believe is deserving of your serious attention. This is not a petition, but rather a letter written by a group of concerned young men who share a common plight. All of the undersigned are currently serving with the U. S. Army with the 65th Engineer Battalion, 25th Infantry Division, in the Republic of Vietnam. The circumstances leading to the drafting of this letter are related to our enlistment in the U. S. Army for the purpose of receiving a commission through the Army's OCS program.

Having enlisted for three years to obtain the OCS program, we chose not only to serve our country, but also aspired to serve as officers in the U. S. Army. We did not resist the draft or seek other evasive action to avoid the military. All of us have a college background and most of us are college graduates. Since we have been in the U. S. Army we have compiled unblemished records. We are all serving in the Republic of Vietnam despite any personal, moral, or political beliefs to the contrary. However, we believe that we are being treated unfairly, or at least have not been given due consideration. Most of us have been in the U. S. Army for over a year now, and are still at the rank of Private First Class. It appears that those with fewer qualifications are given greater opportunity for advancement than us.

A few months prior to our enlisting in the service, the Army pursued the policy that anyone enlisting for OCS, should they complete the program or not, would only have a two year commitment to complete their service. This policy was changed in March of 1969. After March of 1969, anyone enlisting for the OCS program had a three year commitment, regardless of whether they completed the program or not. Then, in July of 1970, the U.

S. Army once again changed the policy to a two year commitment in order to discourage candidates from completing the program. The reasons: to aid in the overall troop reduction; to cut back on a surplus of officers; and to aid in the Department of Defense's cost reduction program (RECON). The above is a good and logical plan; however, our question is, where does that leave us?

Soldiers in basic training and in the advanced training stages who enlisted for the three year OCS program are now given the option of dropping OCS, having a year cut from their service agreement, and in addition, they are given their choice of duty assignment anywhere in the continental United States. We were not given that option. Neither were those who enlisted for OCS prior to March of 1969. Candidates currently in the program, including those who were in our own classes and who resigned from the program after the latest change in policy, also were given the new options. We did not have this opportunity.

Our term of enlistment in the U.S. Army, as are all others, is based on a contract. However, the Department of the Army has waived that contract for those now in OCS. That was not done for us. It is also stated that our term of enlistment and duty assignment is also based on the needs of the service. If indeed the current purpose of the Department of Defense is to reduce troop strength, then why has the possibility of reducing our service commitment to two years not been acted upon? We are all volunteers, and are serving in the Republic of Vietnam, and we feel that both the needs of the U. S. Army and our request could be served by the rectification of this inequity.

Prior to entering OCS we were given a combat MOS, and consequently are now finding ourselves in a situation where our educational backgrounds are not being utilized. The only opportunity we had to change our MOS was through reenlisting in the service. Since the great majority of us plan to continue our education, this choice was found to be unacceptable. For one reason or another, the undersigned withdrew from the OCS program because we firmly believed, after having experienced the program, that we would be unable to serve to the best of our ability as officers in the U.S. Army.

A number of us have written our Congressmen and have been answered promptly and courteously. However, the letters we received did not solve our problem, nor did they shed any light onto possible future action. We now have come to the realization that if any action is to be taken, it must be initiated at the level of the Department of the Army.

We have chosen the only means we know to communicate the circumstances of our plight to those who can help us. We are certain that the government of our country, a country we chose to serve, has our best interests in mind, and will respond positively to our plea. We ask only to be given the same opportunities that those before us and those after us have been given.

We have served our country well, and like those before us and those after us, we ask that our commitment with the U.S. Army be reduced to two years so that we can begin to shape our futures as citizens of the United States of American.

Anticipating a favorable response, and with heartfelt appreciation, we remain

Very truly yours,

We actually got everyone to sign the letter—even a few nervous nellies that feared retribution from division brass if they learned of our endeavor. But I assured them that I had cleared the project with an army lawyer, which was sort of true. I did take the letter to a member of the staff judge advocate's office at division headquarters to see if it was "legal" to send. I knew that this lawyer had been drafted and that he was not a big fan of the army since they sent him to Vietnam instead of to the Pentagon, as he had been "promised." *(A note here: I knew about this lawyer thanks to a tip from Lieutenant Kraley. It's yet another example of how we took care of each other in the Nam and how the whole Vietnam brotherhood thing worked.)* After examining it, he "unofficially" told me it was legal, as long as the document was signed by everyone participating and was in the form of a letter (it was illegal to initiate or sign a "petition" in the military).

In the time frame we had, and with all the logistics involved pulling it off—finding everyone, using army equipment and materials, and all while we were working our regular day jobs—it amazes me that we were able to accomplish our objective. But we somehow managed to send out nearly eight hundred letters to 435 members of the House, 100 senators, to every agency at the departments of the army and defense, as well as to a number of publications and news agencies. And we actually got a few responses—from a number of members of the House and Senate, including Patsy Mink from Hawaii; Howard Baker from Tennessee; Margaret Chase Smith of Maine; Harrison A. Williams, Jr., of New Jersey; and a few others. Each of them acknowledged our letter and said they would send inquiries to the appropriate agencies. Some even promised responses. If nothing else, as we figured it, we had made a valiant attempt to alter our destinies. Our group of thirty-nine hoped that the Department of the Army would grant our request, based on the logical and just grounds that we presented for "Project Year Drop." And if not on those grounds, then we hoped the eight hundred letters and the swarm of red tape it would generate in required responses from Congress and others would cause the army to grant our request just to get us off their back.

The next three weeks were spent in agonizing anticipation of our fates and in misery from all the bullshit being dealt out by a frustrated military that was trying to adjust to leaving a war that it hadn't been able to win. The lifers were pissed off! To many of them, it meant no more Air Medals, Bronze Stars, service ribbons, and combat pay. The troops, on the other hand, were elated. They could have cared less about the war. All they cared about was getting the fuck out of Dodge. As a result of these opposing attitudes, the tension between the two groups was high. And speaking of high, it was getting increasingly difficult to do so. Old turf barriers were now ignored, and the lifers began searching everything and everyone that came on and went off the base. This situation just increased the tension between the two groups. And when you add to that the fact that everyone was now either short or being reassigned, you can imagine what the esprit de corps was like. Tensions were so high, in fact, that many feared incidences of fraggings or worse would increase in the final days of Cu Chi.

An interesting article appeared in some of the stateside papers during the latter period of the war. It cited examples that occurred during the time I spent in Vietnam. I can't remember who, but someone mailed it to me while I was serving as editor of the base newspaper at Fort Jackson, South Carolina, in early 1972. It eerily confirms, from a career military officer's point of view, what I witnessed and heard about during my tour in the Nam. I thought this would be a good spot to insert Colonel Heinl's message.

VIETNAM WAR HAS DESTROYED THE ARMY
by Colonel R. D. Heinl, Jr.

WASHINGTON—Anybody who thinks we still have some kind of a serviceable army left to execute national policy abroad or restore domestic tranquility at home had better read the January 8, 1972, "Saturday Review."

Under the provocative title, "Fragging and Other Withdrawal Symptoms," the Review—not ordinarily a disinterested source on military matters of the Vietnam War—presents a chillingly detailed, unquestionably authentic and quite dispassionate study on the army's newest lethal fad—the casual murder (known as "Fragging" from Fragmentation grenade) by soldiers of unpopular officers and NCO's.

Since January 1970, writes author Eugene Linden, 45 American army officers and noncommissioned officers have been murdered by their own men in Vietnam alone (the geographic area to which his lengthy article is confined). Linden does not extend his study to widely and credibly reported murders and assaults on officers and noncoms in Europe.

Besides the 45 officer homicides, he reports, the army has recorded 363 assaults (not lethal except in intent) using explosive devices, plus 118 similar cases of "possible assaults," whatever that means.

THESE DIRE statistics deal only with grenades and mines, and do not extend to murders or assaults by soldiers using rifles, pistols, or other lethal hardware, such as for example, the 1970 incident in which black soldiers gunned down their battalion's executive and operations officers for turning off an ear-splitting hi-fi in camp at Quang Tri.

Describing fragging as part of an "intra-army guerrilla warfare," the article states that "virtually all officers and NCO's have to take into account the possibility of fragging before giving an order to the men under them."

This grisly game of psychological warfare, writes Linden, results from what he characterizes as the "the procedural, disciplinary and morale breakdown of the army."

This army, he points out, is sharply different from any we have ever fielded before, manned by privates who are at best alienated and unmotivated and at worst, drug-using, race-tormented, anti-authoritarian, and in consequences often mindlessly murderous.

NO ONE SEEMS to know how common fragging's really are. The statistics given in this study are only illustrative, for it is the consensus in Vietnam, as observed by this reporter, that by no means all of such assaults end up on record, let alone before court-martials.

Linden quotes army legal sources as saying that no more than 10 per cent of all fraggings result in court-martial proceedings.

Major General James Baldwin, who commanded the ill-fated Americal Division, which in 1971 was said to be averaging one such attempted murder a week, found the practice so common even a year ago that grenades were called in from the hands of all troops outside of combat and no longer issued even to sentries on defensive posts.

One observer in Vietnam described fragging as "the troops way of controlling officers." It goes without saying, of course, that an officer who is "controlled" (i.e. rendered gutless) by deadly fear, is no longer of any use to the army because he is incapable of issuing or enforcing orders necessary to the discipline or performance of a fighting force.

BEHIND THE foregoing horrifying facts, and even behind Linden's penetrating analysis of the psychological and environmental factors that have made fragging an awful reality, stand several home truths the country should be thinking of.

Vietnam—whatever our ultimate successes in pacification and Vietnamization—has virtually destroyed the U.S. Army.

> *If only for the army's sake (and behind that, of course, the common defense) it is imperative to get the troops out as soon as possible to keep them from murdering themselves morally if not physically.*
>
> *No matter what the cost, and even if it means a half-sized army for the next generation, the draft must be gotten rid of, and our armed forces recruited exclusively from among men who want to be soldiers, sailors and airmen.*
>
> *Until the Vietnam-poisoned, draft-embittered, antimilitary junior enlisted men are, with their cancerous grievances and influence, purged in entirety from the military services, the latter cannot again be considered credible, reliable, non-political instruments fit or safe to be wielded by the United States.*

The final days at Cu Chi base camp were unsettling, but never let it be said that the troops in Vietnam didn't party until the end or let a little uncertainty dampen their spirits. There were parties almost every night somewhere on the base camp. And a flurry of movies was being shown almost every night at the base theater. I took in two—*Butch Cassidy and the Sundance Kid* and *Gailey, Gailey*. Go figure. The base camp also instituted "Friday Night Fights" in those final weeks. We now had spectator sport boxing as an added entertainment feature. And we started visiting other units, conducting our own unofficial farewells. One night, we went to an admin unit party that was a tribute to the passing of Janis Joplin and Jimi Hendrix (we had just lost those two giants of rock & roll music). On another occasion, the artillery units pulled together and threw a Halloween party unlike any I'd even attended. Where these guys came up with the "accessories" for their costumes was a mystery to me. But then again, creativity and ingenuity were the hallmarks of Nam vets. Needless to say, everyone got trashed.

191 days. In other news during this waiting period, two guys from my company were arrested in Saigon for possession of drugs. The one guy had two keys of grass on him, the other a couple of bags of heroin. They were really stupid for carrying that stuff around with them. Drug busts, both on and off base, were increasing every day, with heroin the biggest problem. I just don't get the appeal of that drug. Two of us are trying to convince one of our medic friends to get help, as he can hardly walk he's so stoned most of the time. On a lighter note, I bought an aluminum lounge chair from a guy who was leaving so I could get my short-timer's tan in greater comfort. The monsoon season is now over, and it is hot—between 95 and 100 degrees almost every day. And oh, I'm losing weight rapidly—I'm down to 135 pounds. Eating obviously isn't a priority, at least the stuff they're serving in the mess hall.

And speaking of eating, I was standing in the chow line one night for a steak when someone tapped me on the shoulder. I turned around to see who it was and almost fell over. It was Dennis, my friend from basic and AIT days. He had the day off and came to Cu Chi with some buddies who had to pick up a truck from the division motor pool. He came along to see me, he said, and as usual, he was dressed in civilian clothes. I don't know how he does it, but Dennis refuses to wear a uniform—and seems to get away with it (although I'm sure there are times when he is required to wear one). We agreed to see each other as much as possible in the coming months (depending on our fates, of course), but wouldn't arrange our R & Rs together, as he was desperate to hook up with round eyes in Sydney and I was planning on Bangkok.

I kept hearing from other basic, AIT, and OCS classmates as well. One friend, Jerry O'Malley, an OCS classmate and graduate, was assigned to an infantry unit in the 23rd (Americal) Division, Lieutenant Calley's unit. Jack Koscuiska, a fellow basic and AIT classmate from Upper Darby, Pennsylvania (we went into the army together in Philly), was with an engineering battalion in the 4th Division working as an assistant demolitions expert. And Chuck Lofty, I learned from O'Malley, made it all the way through OCS.

But the day before he was to get his commission, he told them to stick it up their ass. Not sure where he ended up.

In preparation for moving, I was sorting, packing, and shipping stuff I didn't want to carry with me. I shipped a forty-pound package home in preparation of leaving Cu Chi. It contained two poncho liners, a gas mask, various jungle fatigues and uniform accessories, a single round of M-16 ammunition, photography and press clippings, books, and a Spiro Agnew watch (a unique antiwar souvenir produced by the "Dirty Time Company" that a friend traded me for a pack of prerolled joints).

I was told I probably wouldn't be leaving Cu Chi until at least December 1 at the earliest, December 5 the latest. I sent a letter to Paula asking her to start preparing a package of civilian clothes to send to me for my R & R. I had already saved $200 of the $400 I wanted to take with me. I was also very busy with all the final writing projects and photography assignments they were giving me, both at battalion and division level. I was writing the battalion history, creating a "Memorial Edition" for the newspaper, and photographing just about every bigwig on the base camp for the division yearbook. I also learned, by taking photos of everyone in the officer corps, that my TAC officer from OCS, First Lieutenant George Hilton, was a grunt lieutenant with the 25th. Who knew! It couldn't have happened to a nicer guy.

The base camp was being dismantled piece by piece, and every day, more and more people were leaving. Since we were not permitted to take them with us, the dogs that had been our pets were now roaming the base in packs, scavenging for food. It broke my heart having to let Sergeant Pepper go to join his canine friends and fend for himself. I considered having him put down, but resisted, hoping someone might want him for a pet. It was sad, as I knew the Vietnamese generally didn't keep dogs or cats as pets and that he would probably end up in some Vietnamese family's dinner.

Observing the Vietnamese during this pullout period was also sad. They still came to the base each day to perform their duties, but in decreasing numbers as the base population dwindled. They often looked lost and seldom had smiles on their faces. On the one hand, I felt sorry for them for they were about to lose their jobs and an important source of newfound income for their families. But on the other hand, they were also being freed from the bondage of civilization rape that we had inflicted on them and would once again be able to live their lives according to their culture and traditions. But then again, there was the ever-increasing encroachment from the North. I think everyone knew it was only a matter of time before North Vietnam would prevail over the South. And I think the Vietnamese who worked for the Americans, especially in higher level positions, were more than a little concerned about their futures. Fortunately, most of them would only have to suffer through a period of "reeducation" after the nation was reunited in 1975.

My orders finally arrived on November 24. I had been assigned to the 1st Air Cavalry Division, one of the most respected divisions in the U.S. Army. They were still intact in the Nam, with their headquarters in Phuoc Vinh, which was at the foot of Vietnam's central highlands. I was to report to the 15th Replacement Detachment on December 1, 1970. Until then, I was free to move around and do pretty much anything I wanted. Captain Becker gave me a three-day pass to go either to the beach resort at Vung Tau or to Saigon. As often as I'd been to Saigon, I still hadn't reached my fill, so I decided to go to the big city one more time and enjoy the clubs, restaurants, and do a little more shopping. A couple of guys said they would come with me although most were headed to the beach at Vung Tau. I figured I'd wait for my R & R to hit the beach, as I planned to spend a couple of days at Pattaya Beach on the Gulf of Siam, which was just a few hour's drive south of Bangkok.

Saying goodbye to the guys was tough. The night I got my orders, as we were planning our farewell bash, Sergeant Brady popped into the hootch and informed us that we were going to have a little ceremony. It seems that Captain Becker was able to get each of us an Army Commendation Medal, my first real medal of the war. The idea of our getting these medals, however, really pissed Brady off. "You peace-loving sons of bitches don't deserve these medals," he told us, shortly before Captain Becker arrived. He was one unhappy lifer. The division being withdrawn had really messed up his plans in terms of combat time and his potential for medals. He had only been in the Nam for a little over two months and was hoping to get reassigned to another engineering unit. But because of his rank and in-grade position, he was forced to follow the 65th Engineers and the Tropic Lightning Division to Hawaii.

So it really got his goat to have to watch us get medals pinned to our chests. We, of course, loved every minute of it.

We decided to combine our final bash in Cu Chi with Thanksgiving dinner. We gathered all the food we could find and had an incredible meal. There was a lot of drinking going on but not much pot, as we had all gotten rid of our stashes in preparation for moving. The next day, there was nothing left to do but finish packing and lie out in the sun. By this time, my tan was deep and my hair was turning blond. It certainly was nice having sunny days most of the year. On November 28, I moved to the transient hootch to await my shipment, which was two days away. I was saddled with two large duffel bags and a fan (I had to dump the lounge chair), so I was glad that I had shipped the rest of my stuff home. It's amazing what one can accumulate in a little under six months in the rear in a war zone.

163 days. The next night, I said goodbye to my few remaining friends in Cu Chi. Captain Becker invited us to his hootch and treated us to cheese and crackers, whiskey, and beer. We had a great rap, reminiscing about all that we had been through while at Cu Chi. As I was about to leave for the transient hootch, he offered (more like insisted) to drive me to Bien Hoa in his jeep the next day to catch my plane to Phuoc Vinh. Like the rest of us, he had little left to do but pack and wait for his plane to Hawaii. He'd be one of the last ones out… remembering the battalion's motto of "First In – Last Out."

The next morning, the captain picked me up at 0800, and we made our way out of the main gate and onto Route 1 south toward Bien Hoa. It would be the last time I'd see Cu Chi (until 2007, that is, but more on that later). We barely spoke on the drive to the air base. I guess we had pretty much said all that there was to say the night before. When we reached our destination, I grabbed my bags and the fan from the back of the jeep, then threw him a snappy salute, followed by a peace sign. He just smiled. At this point, my emotions were all over the map, from fear and longing to sadness and anticipation. Cu Chi had been home for more than five months, and I had made a lot of close friends there.

He came over to me and extended his hand in the handshake of the Nam brotherhood. I could see that his eyes were filling up with tears. Noticing this, I quickly remarked that I hoped to see him back in the world, then turned, grabbed my belongings, and started walking toward the 15th Replacement Detachment building. Without turning around, I could hear the sound of gravel under the tires of his jeep as he drove off.

CHAPTER 9

Welcome to Phuoc Vinh and Merry Christmas

I had always wanted to fly in a C-130. It looked just like a combat aircraft should—rugged, with mud caked in its tires and painted in the green-and-tan camouflage pattern of jungle warfare. Its primary function was hauling equipment—in this case, a load of GIs and their gear. As we waited for the order to board, I reflected on my Cu Chi experience, but mostly on how much I was going to miss Sergeant Martinez and Captain Becker. I was going to miss a lot of the guys I met there, of course, especially Doc, but it kind of boggled my mind that the two I was going to miss the most were both lifers. Just goes to show you, never judge a book by its cover. As far as I was concerned, they had redefined the strict military class structure that prevailed in the military in their own manner. And as a result, they had gained the trust and respect of their men, which is as it should be. But then again, in the Nam, nothing was as it should be, so I guess I had lucked out. And I knew that I would be fortunate to find superiors—leaders—in Phuoc Vinh that I would like and respect as much as those two men.

When the order came, we walked in single file onto the tarmac and entered the aircraft from the rear, walking up the large ramp that had been lowered to the ground. Once inside, we were directed to bench seats that lined both sides of the aircraft. We were then instructed to secure ourselves with shoulder strap seatbelts that were fastened to the fuselage at each location. None of the guys on board said much during the ninety-minute flight north, primarily because the engine noise was so loud that we had to shout to be heard. There weren't any windows either, so we could only imagine what kind of terrain we were flying over. Everyone just kind of stared straight ahead…or slept. I'm sure most of the guys had their next assignment on their minds. I know I did. A combat radio operator—shit! I thought to myself, *There's no fucking way I'm going into combat with the 1st Air Cavalry Division.* So I began planning my strategy for getting a writing job. This time I had a portfolio (of sorts) to show, and I would go right to the division PIO office and present my credentials.

We touched down smoothly and quickly taxied to a halt. As soon as the fasten seatbelt light went off, the guys stood up and started gathering their gear. But unlike the flight to the Nam, which was deadly silent once we landed, this time there was a lot of chatter among the troops. There wasn't the look of fear or panic on most of their faces. It was more like a sense of mild impatience, as if to say, "Just get us to our next assignments and hootches as quickly as possible, please." Most of us were seasoned by this stage of the game, or at least as seasoned as one could be considering the uncertainties of the Nam.

As I stepped out of the aircraft and looked around, I knew that I wasn't in Kansas anymore. On first glance, this place was definitely different than Cu Chi. It had a distinct look and feel, and I immediately sensed that my Phuoc Vinh experience was going to be very different from that of Cu Chi. For starters, we had landed on a dirt airstrip, as opposed to a paved runway. And there weren't any large hanger or terminal buildings. Just a few mid-size structures, and a lot of helicopters emblazoned with the 1st Cav emblem.

The terrain surrounding the airfield was also very different. It was hilly and wooded, a stark contrast to the flat farm fields and rice patties that surrounded the Cu Chi base camp. But as we drove off in the buses that were waiting to take us to the replacement detachment, I noticed that many of the trees didn't have leaves. As I was to learn, the 1st Cav's base camp at Phuoc Vinh was located in the center of a defoliated rubber plantation. I was told that the defoliation took place when they were building the camp a few years back, so the thought that I might suffer from the effects of chemical poisoning never even entered my mind. (Note: It wasn't until many years after the war that the effects of Agent Orange poisoning started to appear in veterans, myself included).

As we drove toward the center of the base camp where the replacement company was located, I couldn't believe the contrast between this place and Cu Chi. For one, it was considerably smaller and had an almost "small town" feel…at least as military base camps go. The streets were lined with (mostly barren) trees, and the place was a lot less developed than massive facilities like Long Binh and Cu Chi. And the streets weren't paved, and there were no sidewalks, except in the area immediately surrounding division headquarters.

Another thing that struck me was how casual everyone looked walking around. They were strolling leisurely…more like they were on a college campus than a military installation. As officers and enlisted men passed each other, no one saluted. And people were even smiling. Yes, this place was definitely different than Cu Chi, and I had a hunch that I was going to like it here. Presuming, that is, that I would be able to stay here, as opposed to being shipped out to the field as a combat radio operator with some infantry unit.

As far as processing went, things moved a lot faster in Phuoc Vinh than they did at either Long Binh or Cu Chi. It took a little more than a day for orientation and to process my orders, which meant I only had to spend one night at the replacement company. But that also meant that I was going to have to act fast if I was to avoid being assigned to an infantry unit. As soon as I turned in my paperwork and was assigned to a hootch, I dropped off my gear and immediately inquired as to the location of the division PIO. One of the admin clerks told me that the 1st Cav referred to it as the IO (Information Office) and not the PIO as with the 25th. And as luck would have it, it was less than a three-block walk to the division IO from the replacement company. So I pulled out the envelope that contained my writing samples and press clippings and made my way down the road to my destination.

As I walked along what appeared to be the main street of the base, I continued to marvel at the sights. Guys would flip you the peace sign as you walked by, smiling like Cheshire cats. The state of most of their uniforms was also a lot more, shall we say, casual. For example, fatigue shirts were often rolled up to a very hip short-sleeve length. Boonie hats were worn in a number of individual and stylish ways, many of them sporting a variety of pins and patches. Some of the guys' fatigue pants were cut off above the ankle, and quite a few of them wore sandals rather than combat boots. I almost had to rub my eyes to make sure I wasn't imagining what I was seeing. So far, this place certainly didn't reflect the fearsome and gung-ho image that the 1st Cav's reputation called to mind. It was more like a scene from the *4077 M.A.S.H.* unit that in later years would become famous, thanks to its film and television success (even though the TV series, *M.A.S.H.*, was supposedly set during the Korean War, many think it was actually a more accurate depiction of the Vietnam era).

I was excited and could feel the adrenaline pumping through my veins as the IO came into sight. There was a big sign on top of the building that read: "First Team Press Camp." The "First Team" was the nickname of the 1st Air Cavalry Division, and its soldiers were called Skytroopers, as I was to learn. I walked up the path leading to the main entrance of the building and opened the door. Inside, there were a number of desks scattered throughout the large, open room. The entire building was open air—without windows—giving it a distinctly tropical feel. There was a large drafting table for artists at one end of the room, and a small, partitioned office at the other end. Two ceiling fans were churning away, causing a mild breeze to flow through the hot afternoon atmosphere. There were only two guys seated at desks in the otherwise empty room. Both of them were shirtless. As I approached, one of them looked up, smiled, and said, "Can I help you?"

"I'm looking for the division information officer," I responded.

"Then you want Lieutenant Garcia. He's in his office," he said, pointing to the other end of the room.

I walked up to the entrance of the partitioned office, knocked on the wall, then stuck my head around the corner. The door was open. "Lieutenant Garcia," I inquired.

"That would be me," he replied, his face lighting up in a broad smile as he gestured for me to come in. I didn't know whether or not to salute him, but before I even finished the thought, he stood up and extended his hand. He was wearing shorts and flip-flops. As I shook his hand, a warm feeling came over me, and I knew for sure that I wasn't in Kansas anymore.

"I'm Specialist James Stoup, and I've just been assigned to this division from the 25th Infantry Division in Cu Chi," I blurted out. "The 25th was withdrawn, but I wasn't short enough to go with it so they sent me up here," I continued. All of a sudden, I realized that I was rambling—and talking a mile a minute. Lieutenant Garcia sensed my nervousness and asked me to sit down. He then asked me if I was thirsty, and before I could answer, he pulled two Fresca's out of a little refrigerator next to his desk. Feeling a lot more relaxed now, I proceeded to tell him my story, about how I arrived as a combat engineer five-and-a-half months ago, and talked my way into a writing position. I showed him my "portfolio" of writing samples and press clippings, including copies of the *65th Recorder* and *Tropic Lightning News* with my bylines. And then I boldly asked him if he needed another combat correspondent. He looked at me and smiled (as I was to learn, he was always smiling) and said, "As a matter of fact, I was just about to put in for someone like you. Your timing couldn't have been better, Specialist Stoup…Let me see what I can do."

Second Lieutenant Jose (Joe) Garcia, from San Antonio, Texas, was the division command information officer. He was an exceptionally friendly Chicano who would become a good friend—and save my ass from the field. He would also teach me a great deal and help guide the rest of my army (and subsequent) career as a journalist. And as if that wasn't enough, we also shared the same opinion of the army and the war, and he could have cared less about the military class structure.

While I was sipping my Fresca, Lieutenant Garcia picked up the phone and made a call to a friend of his in admin at division headquarters. He asked his buddy if he could assign me to the division IO in an information specialist slot. He told him that I had been with the 25th and had just arrived from Cu Chi, and that my paperwork was probably still being processed at the HQ transfer company. I sat there staring at him, trying to hear the responses coming from the other end of the line. He nodded his head once or twice and said "uh-huh" a couple of times. While all this was transpiring, I felt little beads of sweat starting to form on my forehead. "His current MOS is combat radio operator," he added. And then, after a pause that seemed like an eternity, he let out a big "Yes!"

He hung up the phone and looked straight at me as another big smile came across his face. "You're in, Specialist Stoup. It'll take a couple of hours, but my buddy told me to tell you that it's as good as done. And don't worry about that 05Bravo20 MOS. If you're as good as I think you are—or will be—we'll get you promoted to Spec 5 in an Information Specialist MOS. Welcome to the First Team Press Camp."

"I can't thank you enough," I said, at least twice, as far as I can remember.

After he told me the good news, he stood up and grabbed my hand, this time in the Nam handshake of brotherhood. "Let's head over to my hootch and celebrate," he almost yelled, as he put his arm around my shoulder and led me out of his office. As I was soon to learn, Lieutenant Garcia liked to drink. He also liked to party and was real good at finding almost any excuse to do so. In essence, Lieutenant Garcia liked to have a good time, and he was one of the most relaxed and easy-going guys that I had ever met—anywhere—but certainly in the Nam.

By the time I got back to the transfer company, they had my orders ready to go. There's nothing like having connections, even if new-found. I had been assigned to Headquarters and Headquarters Company, 1st Air Cavalry Division, in an information specialist slot. I couldn't believe my luck. For the second time in a row, I had beaten the system and had once again been saved from duty in the field. The gods were definitely looking after me. And this time, if I was fortunate enough to get another promotion, it would not only guarantee me an information specialist MOS, but would also elevate me to E-5 status as a specialist, the equivalent of a sergeant, and it would give me a nice jump in pay. I was going to make sure that I lived up to expectations and made this happen and was looking to Lieutenant Garcia as the means to this end.

HQ and HQ Company was scattered throughout a roughly three-square block area and was comprised of a variety of support functions, like admin, legal, finance, and the like. As luck would have it, I was assigned to a hootch right across the company street from the First Team Press Camp, which was going to make commuting to work very convenient. Lieutenant Garcia even arranged to have a jeep pick me up at the transfer company and drop me off at the front door of my new home. It was all so unreal that I feared waking up the next morning and realizing that it was all just a dream.

The hootch I was assigned to was similar to the one I had in Cu Chi, but not as open air as those further south, as the winters got a little colder in this part of the country. The construction was a little better as well. And there were more bunkers scattered throughout the company area than there were in Cu Chi, and they were all of fortress quality. When I asked why, I was told that the base got hit regularly with mortars and rockets. Based on its locale, this didn't surprise me.

The outdoor showers and latrines were a lot more primitive than those at the much more developed Cu Chi base camp. For instance, I learned that if you wanted hot water, you waited until the end of the day to take your shower. This was because it took that long for the sun to heat the water in the fifty-gallon drums that were positioned on the roof of the wooden and metal shower structures. Water trucks filled the drums each morning, and it usually took all day for the sun to heat the water to a comfortable temperature.

After getting oriented to the immediate area, I got my bedding and started unpacking my bags and settling into my new quarters. The hootch was still empty by the time I had finished, and the whole area was very, very quiet. It was also starting to get dark, so I figured everyone was either at dinner, out partying, or at the EM Club. I don't know if it was the silence, or the change of environment, but all of a sudden a wave of depression swept over me. Without warning, I suddenly realized how lonely I was and how much I missed my girlfriend and family. It was also nearing Christmas—a particularly difficult time to be without friends and family—and I had left the only friends I had in the Nam behind when I left Cu Chi, and had yet to make new ones here. So it was probably a combination of all those factors that caused me to hit rock bottom. I guess I was also coming down from the euphoria of being spared from the field again and getting an information specialist assignment. So I decided to hit the sack and save discovering my new surroundings and finding new friends until the morning.

Life in Phuoc Vinh turned out to be amazing—almost a total contrast from my Cu Chi experience. It was casual and laidback to an extent that I didn't think possible in a war zone, and certainly not what I had envisioned by reputation for the headquarters location of the strack 1st Air Cavalry Division. But that was part of the enigma of Phuoc Vinh, because the 1st Cav had its shit together and was really an impressive outfit. They took their role as soldiers seriously, but played it out in the field, not in the rear. They were impressive and successful in combat and had an awesome arsenal of men and equipment. But they were equally impressive as party animals. When they were in the rear, they chilled out, and the command appeared to generally let its men do their own thing—as long as it didn't get out of hand. You were expected to do your job, and do it well. And if you did, you were pretty much left alone.

My first day in the office was pleasant. I arrived in full uniform (fatigue pants, shirt, and jungle boots), which is what I wore to work at Cu Chi. But I immediately felt out of place as I walked into the press room, since everyone else was dressed a lot more casually. Two guys were wearing T-shirts, fatigue pants, and sandals, which I was to learn was pretty much the uniform of choice. One guy was wearing shorts and a T-shirt; another was bare-chested with fatigue pants, and yet another was wearing what appeared to be pajamas. As in Cu Chi, no one wore underwear. I couldn't believe my eyes.

As soon as Lieutenant Garcia saw me he came running over, wearing only shorts and a T-shirt…and his big Chicano grin. He greeted me warmly, then took me around and introduced me to my new colleagues. The first guy I met was Sergeant John Seawall, the IO's head artist. Next was Spec 5 Bob McKowen, the editor of the *Cavalier*, the division's newspaper. The 1st Cav's IO put out a weekly two-color newspaper, as well as a full-color monthly magazine, and an annual yearbook. I then met PFC Pat Cassidy, one of the IO writers. A few more introductions followed until I had met everyone on the staff. After the introductions, the lieutenant led me into this office to discuss what he had in mind for me.

Lieutenant Garcia assigned me to a desk next to Spec 5 Bob McKowen. He told me to "hang close" to him, as he had his shit together and really knew what he was doing. McKowen hailed from Richmond, Virginia, and had been a reporter for *The Washington Post* before getting drafted. And Lieutenant Garcia was right. I would learn a lot from him and really develop as a journalist during my days at Phuoc Vinh, thanks in great part to his tutelage. At the desk on the other side of me was Pat Cassidy, a happy-go-lucky kind of guy from Grand Rapids, Michigan. He was short and stocky, with a distinctive port-wine mark on one side of his face. He was like a puppy dog, for as time went on, he would follow me everywhere. He would become a real good friend, and we'd often laugh about the guys jokingly accusing us of typing in two-part harmony on our slightly rusted Remington typewriters. And across the room from my desk, sitting at the big drafting table, was John Seawall, a quiet, soft-spoken guy from San Clemente, California. He was a very talented artist who would teach me a lot about print layout and design.

After spending my first night in the hootch alone (I fell asleep before the guys got back from the EM Club), my second night there was considerably more memorable. I shared the hootch (which was divided into rooms or areas with privacy dividers, like Cu Chi) with Pat and John; with Tom Greer, the HQ and HQ company driver who was a genuine southern boy from Georgia; and with Bill and Buddy, two guys from finance. Bill and Buddy had invited some guys from their office over to do "a little partying" that night and asked me if I wanted to join them. I said sure, figuring this would give me a first taste of the party scene at Phuoc Vinh. Besides, Pat and John were going to a movie that I had no interest in seeing on the other side of the base, and Tom was driving them over in his jeep (having a driver living in the hootch would come in handy on more than one occasion).

We sat on the bunks in the small room that Bill and Buddy had constructed out of plywood in the hootch. When their buddies arrived, I was introduced, and a friendly conversation ensued. They asked me where I had come from and what it was like there. While making their inquiries, one of them lit up a joint. As I proceeded to tell them about my Cu Chi days, the guy sitting to my right handed me the number that was being passed around the room. I took a hit, not realizing what I was getting myself into. Almost immediately, my head felt like it was shooting up through the roof. At that moment, I realized that what I was smoking wasn't *con sa* (the Vietnamese slang word for marijuana that I had learned in Cu Chi).

I was taken aback by both the immediate effect of whatever it was that I had inhaled and the realization that I wasn't smoking grass. I guess I was distracted by my new environment, as I hadn't even noticed the absence of the distinctive smell of burning pot that always permeates the air when smoking weed. Out of both embarrassment and stupidity, and not wanting to appear uncool to my new colleagues, I took another hit from the joint when it came around again. But this time I barely inhaled and quickly passed it on to the next guy. Being alert to the difference, this time I focused my senses on the very strange taste and smell. Whatever it was, it was mixed with tobacco in a cigarette. It made me instantly high but not a pleasant high like the one you experience from pot.

I asked Buddy what we were smoking, and he replied, "Skag." Skag, of course, is slang for heroin. My stomach turned, and a horrible feeling came over me. I couldn't believe I had smoked heroin. Almost immediately, I started feeling sick. Without hesitating, I excused myself and walked out of the room and then ran out the back door of the hootch. I leaned on the sandbag wall that stood as a barrier on the back side of the hootch and puked my guts out. My head was spinning, and I was getting increasingly sick to my stomach. And then, all of a sudden, out of nowhere, Tom appeared.

He asked me what was wrong, and I relayed to him what had just happened. He just shook his head. "That stuff's nasty," he told me. "I gave it a try when I first got here. In fact, I almost got hooked on it. But I was smart enough to give it up before it got to me too bad. And let me tell you about sick. I was so sick when I started, that..." He was interrupted by one of the guys walking out of the hootch, who wanted to know why I had left so abruptly. "What's up?" Bill asked. He appeared to be nervous and had a defensive manner about him. "Stoup here's a little sick," Tom informed him in his charming Georgia accent. "It's his first time."

Then the other guys came out and took turns describing to me how you always get sick to your stomach the first couple of times that you used, as I continued to wretch my guts out. But they assured me that it was worth it. "For once you get past the sick part and get to the high, there's nothing like it in the world," one of them told me. Well, I decided at that very moment that this was one world that I wanted no part of.

I continued to puke for what seemed like an eternity and then started dry-heaving, as there was nothing left in my stomach. Tom stayed with me and tried to make me feel better, while the other guys disappeared. We went back into the hootch and I lay down on my bunk. The room was spinning, and I felt worse than my worst hangover. "I can't imagine why anyone would use that stuff," I told Tom. He told me that it was becoming more and more prevalent in the Nam, and that most guys who used it snorted the drug. Some guys, who could get their hands on sticks (needles), would shoot it right into their veins, like my medic friend had in Cu Chi. While others, he noted, smoked it mixed with tobacco in a cigarette like we had done. I remembered the heavy equipment operator at the 65th Engineers who did the stuff, and how he nodded off into his drug reverie the night the rest of us sat around getting stoned on pot, rapping and listening to music. Right now, they seemed like the good old days. My mind was racing. I was sick, and I felt very much alone. Eventually, I fell asleep.

The next morning I practically crawled to work. My stomach was still queasy, so I skipped breakfast. Shortly after I got there and secured myself a cup of coffee, McKowen came over to discuss my assignments. He lit up a cigarette and offered me one. I had recently taken up smoking (right after the announcement that the 25th Division was leaving Cu Chi), but even the mention of a cigarette started my stomach churning. It immediately triggered a reaction to the poisoning I had experienced the night before from the skag, so I turned down his offer. In fact, I never smoked a cigarette again—at least not in the Nam.

McKowen told me that he and Lieutenant Garcia were impressed with my writing samples and that they wanted me to write a Command Information Program for the division similar to the one I wrote for the 25th. They also wanted me to be a feature writer for the *Cavalier*, as they thought I'd be a good interviewer, and there were a couple of articles they wanted me to start on right away. "The first one," he said, "with Christmas approaching, was to interview the base chaplains on their role in bringing the true meaning and spirit of Christmas to the troops." He then rolled his eyes, shrugged his shoulders, and said that request came right from the division executive officer, Major Barry Winslow. The second, believe it or not, was to write a series of articles on drug abuse. The 1st Cav, like every other unit in Vietnam, had been ordered to do something about the drug problem. But unlike the brass at Cu Chi, they planned a soft approach to the subject. Lectures and articles rather than busts and harassment were their plan, to be followed by a "no questions asked" access to counseling and even rehab. I found all this ironic, especially after my experience of the previous night, not to mention my fondness for Vietnamese pot. But, quite obviously, I was more than happy to accept the assignment.

Our conversation was halted briefly when Lieutenant Garcia, wearing nothing more than his usual T-shirt, boxer shorts, and flip-flops, came bounding through the office door. He gave everyone his big, smiling good morning, grabbed a cup of coffee, and joined McKowen and me at my desk. "Are you giving the Stoupman his assignments?" he asked McKowen. "Yes, sir," he responded. We talked for a while about the series of drug articles and kicked around other subjects that I could possibly write about. And then Lieutenant

Garcia came up with another idea. He said he had wanted for some time to add a little levity to the paper, some "light" material that would be of interest to the Skytroopers. He wanted it to be a weekly feature, almost like a silly gossip column, and that the guys in the office would help me come up with ideas until I got to know the place. We brainstormed the subject for a while, and as he got up to leave the office to go back to his hootch to "get dressed," he exclaimed, "We'll call it *Stoup's Scoop*."

Here's my first *Stoup's Scoop* column:

Newbie vs. Papa-san...No Contest

The scene, I'm sure, is familiar to most of us, for we all have gone souvenir shopping in Vietnam at one time or another. Shopping in Vietnam, as in many countries throughout the world, is governed by the three B's: bargain, bicker, and buy.

Even though the "newbie" is warned by his companions of the shrewd maneuvering of the Vietnamese merchant, it still takes some doing to "get over" on this native mastermind of merchandising.

Let's drop in on a local village scene, where Pfc. Newman is about to match wits with a local papa-san:

Pfc. Newman: Wow papa-san, you really have some groovy things here!
Papa-san: You want, you need, I show, you buy. Best pries in Vietnam. Papa-san give you good price, save you beaucoup money. You new in country GI? Fatigues look mighty green.
Newman: Me? New? I've been here for six months. Tell you what I need papa-san. What do you have in beads or necklaces?
Papa-san: Ah, I have what you want. Love beads, hate beads, peace symbol, war symbol,

black-power symbol, Irish-power symbol, Polish-power symbol…papa-san even have yellow-power symbol for ARVN. Me sell cheap for you—4,000 P!

Newman: 4,000P! What do you take me for, anyway?

Papa-san: Me take you for about 3,500 P, hee hee…Tell you what GI. I sell you peace symbol for 100 P and watch you wear.

Newman: No deal, papa-san. How much do you want for the love beads?

Papa-san: Love beads very special. Come from ancient temples in Vietnam highlands. Monks spend many years finding precious gems to string into beads. This only place in Asia where you find these beads…

Newman: How much…?

Papa-san: Papa-san sell you for 500 P.

Newman: 500 P, that's great papa-san. Give me two pairs.

(Back at the base camp)

Newman: Hey Sarge, dig the groovy beads I picked up in the village…they're made out of precious gems from the Vietnamese highlands!

Sgt. Short: Precious gems from the Vietnamese highlands! You didn't fall for that line did you? That's Vietnamese plastic coated with enamel…What'd you pay for them anyway?

Newman: Gee Sarge, I gave the papa-san 1,000 P for two pairs…

Short: I thought the guys warned you about shopping in the village…Joe picked up the same beads yesterday for 100 P and a can of C's!

Another feature of the paper that existed before I arrived was a questions and answer column entitled: *From the Horse's Mouth* (a horse head is prominently featured on the 1st Cav emblem, as the 1st Air Cavalry Division traces its roots back to the days of the U. S. Cavalry...horses then, helicopters now). I took over that column as well...here's a sample:

FROM THE HORSE'S MOUTH

Dear FTHM:

A few months ago I purchased a complete stereo set-up from PACEX. The system is with me in Vietnam, and since I will be DEROSing in a little over a month, I was wondering what would be the best way to send this equipment home? Any suggestions would be appreciated.

B.M.J.

Dear B.M.J.,

Unless you are independently wealthy, forget mailing your system first class. If you have a year to wait for your equipment to make it half way around the world by ship, then send it fourth class. There is, however, a way that you can get your equipment home free; and it will arrive approximately the same time you do. I'm talking, of course, about "hold baggage." As soon as you receive your PCS orders, take a couple of copies of them along with your stereo equipment to the hold baggage center (adjacent to Bien Hoa Air Base) and that's all there is to it. They'll have it packed and sent out that same day. Happy listening!

Note: As I mentioned in the stories about my Cu Chi days, buying stereo equipment and sending it back home was perhaps the biggest single buying experience and souvenir purchase among the vast majority of troops who served in Vietnam. We can thank, in great part, the Japanese for this phenomenon, as they were the primary producers of stereo sound systems at that time, as well as the "music renaissance" of that era (late 60s/early 70s) and the proliferation of stereo component systems that had become a very big part of United States and world culture at that point in time as well.

Dear FTHM:

I recently returned from R&R in Hong Kong. While I was there, I think I might have picked up a venereal disease. I'm not quite sure that I did, but I do get this burning sensation every time I urinate. Is there any surefire way of telling whether a person has VD or not?

P.C.P.

Dear P.C.P.:

It sounds like you've contracted a rare form of Hong Kong black venereal disease. If your hair starts falling out, and your left ear turns green, you know you're in trouble. There's only one surefire way of determining whether or not you have VD, and that's through a medical examination. It's really a painless procedure, and no one will ever even know you made the visit. It's your life, P.C.P., but it's always better to be safe than sorry.

Dear FTHM:

I understand there is a mandatory human relations program underway. I would very much like to participate in it. Is there any way?

T.T.

Dear T.T.

Yes, there is a way. According to a MACV directive, each unit is to establish a human relations council that will advise the unit commander on matters relating to this subject. See your unit commander.

We welcome any questions you may have.
Send your queries to "From the Horse's Mouth"
1st Air Cav PIO, APO In-Country.

Kind of silly, huh. But then again, our readership did have an average age of 19.

I decided to spend that afternoon mentally preparing for my series of drug articles. Essentially, they would consist of a series of interviews with division brass that might have something to say about the subject. I was going to interview the division shrink, the head chaplain, the top legal and law enforcement officers, and the CO himself. But based on the way I was feeling, I decided that the best way to prepare for all of this was to lay out in the sun for a while. The weather was absolutely spectacular. Hot, yes, but I was use to this by now. OD cots used for tanning were scattered throughout the base camp area…some on bunker rooftops. And, as I was soon to discover, laying out to get that perfect Nam tan was an even bigger past time in Phuoc Vinh than it was at Cu Chi. The lifestyle here was much more "southern California."

Tom, who wasn't driving anyone anywhere that afternoon, decided to join me to catch a few rays. We put on some music and headed for the two cots that were sitting on top of the bunker directly behind our hootch. Once on top, we stripped from our fatigue pants to our boxer shorts, which we rolled up to maximize the sun's coverage of our bodies. Some guys sunbathed in the nude to gain total coverage, but I was a little too modest for that. As soon as we had settled into place, Tom lit up a joint and passed it my way. This time there was no question about which substance we were smoking. The fragrance of burning pot from the cloud of smoke Tom had created surrounded me. I had come to love that smell. It was the first time I had smoked since the "skag incident," and my first pot-smoking experience since arriving at Phuoc Vinh, and I was looking forward to the high that I knew the con sa would provide.

Tom related that "just about everyone here smokes pot…either occasionally or all the time." As I listened to him talk, and started to get pleasantly stoned, I found myself studying his persona. He had an interesting look to him. He was Anglo, but had what appeared to be a deep natural tan, and very curly hair that was almost frizzy. He always wore multiple strands of large beads around his neck, mimicking an almost African look. And like Lieutenant Garcia, he always had a smile on his face, always seemed relaxed, had a genuinely polite southern personality, and seemed unaffected by the war and its environs.

So there I was, lying in the mesmerizing sun again, with the Stones *Gimme Shelter* playing in the background, getting stoned. And all of this occurring during a work day, at the headquarters base camp of the 1st Air Cavalry Division, in the Republic of Vietnam. But this time it was different. There was no paranoia about being busted. No hassles from NCOs or officers. It was like being in an oasis in a desert of killing fields.

My trance was broken by a familiar sound—the distinct rhythmic noise of Hueys flying overhead, a gaggle of them. Another thing very different about Phuoc Vinh was that it was the base of an air mobile division. Helicopters of all types, but mostly Hueys, were constantly in the air. And their distinct sound will always be with me. The constant drone of their activity reminded me that there was still a war going on out there, somewhere. And once again, I felt a little guilty, and a lot thankful, that I was avoiding it.

Note: To this day, when a helicopter flies nearby, I can tell immediately if it's a Huey without having to look up. Hueys are still a workhorse in the military, even to this day.

The next day I got started on the first of my drug abuse feature stories by interviewing the head base chaplain. He was a Lutheran minister and a nice-enough gentleman, a major who had been in the army since Korea. He told me that he thought drugs were being used to the extent that they were as a replacement for the spiritual. "It's a need that each of us has," he told me, "and drugs serve as a replacement when one doesn't have God in their lives. But I can certainly understand why so many young men are disillusioned in this environment," he added, in an uncharacteristically unmilitary remark. I was impressed by his candor and thanked him for his time, even though I knew I'd never be able to include that last comment in my story.

After the interview, I returned to the office to write up the story. But it was only Wednesday, and my deadline wasn't until Friday. And since it was already 1600 hours, I decided to call it a day and return to the hootch. When I got there and opened the door, I got a big surprise. There he stood—in full civilian dress—Dennis Buckman. "Dennis," I screamed, "where did you come from?" Then I remembered that he told me he had been assigned to the 1st Cav when he dropped in on me during my next-to-the-last week at Cu Chi.

As I mentioned a little earlier in my story, I met Dennis in basic training at Fort Dix, New Jersey. He was from Wilmington, Delaware, and was my peer. He was a graduate of Saint Joseph's College in Philadelphia, while I was a graduate of Saint Joseph's College in Rensselaer, Indiana. And we were also fellow political science majors. Dennis and I had some good times in basic training. In fact, he was one of the guys who helped me get through it with my sanity intact. He hated the army even more than I did, but mainly because it was a major hassle and intellectually inane. He had a deadpan sense of humor and an incredible wit. Dennis and I parted ways after basic, when I went off to Fort Leonard Wood, Missouri, and he to Fort Benning, Georgia. But there he was, standing in my hootch, waiting to visit me in all his faux-civilian glory.

He told me that he was sent to Vietnam with an infantry MOS, but when he was transferred to the 1st Cav, he was able to get a job in transportation. He was the shop foreman at the local motor pool. I smiled as I tried to picture this in my mind. You had to know Dennis to appreciate the irony. Over the next two months, before he got his ETS and went back to the world, Dennis and I would get together often. We'd catch a movie or have a couple of beers, and we'd do a lot of analyzing and commiserating about our state of affairs being in the army and being in the Nam. Dennis didn't get high, but rather, had his own ways of coping with his surroundings (but neither did he drink enough to qualify as a juicer). For example, when I first saw him in civilian clothes, I jokingly asked him where his uniform was. "I never wear it," he responded. And he didn't. Every time that I saw him over the next two months, including at work, he was wearing civilian clothes. It was his way of saying, "I'm not really here, so fuck you, Uncle Sam!" And because Phuoc Vinh was the way that it was, he got away with it. And I don't know where he got all the civies (although he always seemed to be wearing the same outfit—brown polo shirt, tan jeans, and sneakers). I mean, I had a pair of shorts and a couple of T-shirts and that was it. In fact, I was going to have to write home and have my parents ship me some clothes when it came time to go on R&R, that is if Paula didn't send me the clothes that I asked her to send.

Christmas was just three days away now, and the thought of spending it away from home was starting to hit me. Like most of us, this would be my first Christmas not celebrated with family and friends, and it certainly left an empty feeling inside me. But if it's true that misery loves company, then I'd be having plenty of company. The army tried to compensate for the absence with upgraded food, multiple turkey dinners, and a couple of days off from work, which I'm sure was greatly appreciated by the guys who came in from the bush. Most of the guys were also getting goodie packages from home, so every day during the holiday period it was "munchie heaven" at the office and back in the hootch. We all got lots of cards and letters as well. On the twenty-third, our last day of work before our three-day holiday, we had our office Christmas party…lots of food and drink, and lots of hilarity, as we had drawn names with the challenge being to see who could come up with the most gross or offensive gift. McKowen won, but I can't remember what his gift was. And for added excitement, there was a rocket attack during the party that temporarily forced us into the nearby bunker. Ten rockets hit on the other side of the base, but no casualties or damage was reported. I guess it was a "Merry Christmas" greeting from the local VC.

The "Christmas Vietnam '70" issue of the *Cavalier* came out that day as well. I had two articles in this issue, one headlined: "Chaplains Bring Alive Spirit of Christmas," which described the efforts of chaplains LTC John Borstead and Major Donald Clarkson to bring the true spirit of Christmas to the children who lived in the hamlet of Bau Ao, located just northeast of Phuoc Vinh. The hamlet was populated, in large part, by three hundred Cambodian refugees. Through his efforts, Chaplain Borstead was able to obtain a donation of seven hundred boxes of "throwaway candy" from the PX, as well as many boxes of food that had been arriving from various charitable organizations in the United States. Chaplain Clarkson, in the meantime, had coordinated donations from his hometown of Salina, Kansas, as well as with charities in and around Fort Riley, Kansas, including from families who had soldiers serving in Vietnam. They sent nine boxes of clothing for the occasion. The article ended with the sentence: "If the true Christmas spirit is one of giving, then the chaplains of the 1st Air Cav had set a fine example…the children of Bau Ao will attest to this."

The second article was more in keeping with the humor of the Nam. It was entitled: "Grunt's Christmas," and was (looking back at it) a feeble attempt at humor, as it captured the overheard conversation between two grunts at a fire support base…PFC Grumpe, and SP4 Claus. I won't burden you with the entire piece, but here's an excerpt:

> **SP4 Claus**: Ah, quit your complaining, Grumpe. Christmas in the Nam is what you make of it. For instance, George had his miniature trains with all the accessories sent from home; and Tom has painted the wings of 400 cockroaches red and green to decorate our Christmas tree.

PFC Grumpe: Speaking of the Christmas tree, you know that USARV Reg. 007-25 states that Christmas trees in bunkers will be no taller than five feet. And you've invited the whole damn company to the party when you know the fire marshal has told us that occupancy in this bunker by more than 10 people is strictly forbidden.

SP4 Claus: I know that. But I'm sure the CO will let us slide by; after all, it is the season to be jolly.

PFC Grumpe: Sure it is. How do you expect me to be jolly in 100 degree heat, knee-deep mud, and with these damn mosquitoes buzzing around my head.

SP4 Claus: Try the eggnog! At least we know we're going to have some good entertainment this year. The CO got the whole company off duty to see the Bob Hope Show.

PFC Grumpe: With seats in the 491st row, I should have brought my telescope.

SP4 Claus: What's with you anyway, Grumpe. Do you have something against Christmas or something?

PFC Grumpe: No, not really. To tell you the truth, I was kind of looking forward to it.

SP4 Claus: Then what's the problem?

PFC Grumpe: I DEROS tomorrow…

138 days. Christmas Eve, which, as it turned out, was no big deal in the Nam, started out kind of sad and lonely. I woke up late, around

1100 (still a little hung over from the office Christmas party), and decided to lie out in the sun for an hour, thinking it would revitalize me. So I set myself up and put on AFVN radio, which was playing Christmas music non-stop. I found it depressing and turned it off. After about thirty minutes in the sun, which was about all I could take (it was very hot), I got dressed and made my way over to the office. It had dawned on me while lying there, that I wanted to call one of my medic friends from the 25th, Bob Truxall, who was now working at a field hospital in Saigon. Before leaving Cu Chi, we talked about getting together there at some point before we both left the Nam. I wanted to see if a weekend in January was doable for him, as I knew I could get a weekend pass from Lieutenant Garcia and could easily hitch a ride on a chopper. January seemed like the best time for me, as I had nothing planned, and I didn't want it to interfere with my R&R, which was coming up in February.

Dennis came over later that afternoon with a bottle of vodka, and we sat around drinking and telling war stories. We then drove over to his unit and had Christmas dinner together. After dinner, we hung out at his hootch drinking and rapping with his buddies until around 2100, at which point I asked Dennis to drive me back to HQ Company. I had considered going to midnight Mass (yes, there was a midnight Christmas Eve Mass in Phuoc Vinh), but unfortunately I had CQ (Command Quarters) that night. I pulled the short straw and had to stay up all night to answer the phone if necessary (someone was on duty 24/7 at the press office). I made some coffee and hoped to God that I'd be able to stay up all night, as I was already falling asleep.

Christmas came and went on an uneventful note. The day after was just another day in paradise, with one exception—the annual Bob Hope Show was happening. I thought I would be eager to take in this much-anticipated event—the opportunity to be entertained by one of the legends of show business, a USO/military war zone tradition that dated back to World War II, an event that I had watched for many years on television. And now I had the opportunity to witness it in person, as a GI in a war zone, live and up close, the Bob Hope USO Tour. I didn't go.

I regretted it somewhat after the fact, passing up the chance to witness a piece of "military Americana" firsthand and for the stories that I wouldn't be able to tell when I got back to the world. But essentially, lying in the sun and partying with the guys who didn't go was more appealing to me than the thought of traveling to Long Bien to be lost in a huge crowd of horny, smelly guys screaming at Lola Falana and Miss World. Besides, AFVN was covering it live, so I could watch it on TV from the comfort of my hootch and still have that Vietnam experience. And I had a big event to cover the next day, so I wanted to be fresh. Believe it or not, the bishop of all Armed Forces Catholics, His Eminence Terrence Cardinal Cooke, would be paying a visit to the First Team on the twenty-seventh. In an advance statement, the cardinal said: "Our friends would not be safe at home unless you were here promoting peace." What a crock of shit. The visit marked his second year of spending the Christmas season with the troops in Vietnam, a custom begun by Francis Cardinal Spellman, the Military Ordinariate until his death in 1967. During the homily of the concelebrated Mass, Cardinal Cooke stressed the importance of remaining optimistic while in Vietnam. "Optimism," he stated, "is the key to facing reality and coping with it. It is also the Christian way." Yea, right…and I'm not sure that's the way that Christ would have seen it.

McKowen and Lieutenant Garcia covered the Bob Hope Show for the newspaper and somehow managed to get front row seats for the event alongside the brass (Garcia at work, I'm sure). So besides McKowen getting great shots (he was an excellent photographer with the best equipment) for the two- page center spread we were planning for the paper, I'd have the advantage of first-hand stories that I could relate back home as if they were mine. So we got great coverage for our story.

The headline for the *Cavalier*, which was published on January 13, 1971, read: "BOB HOPE SCORES SEVENTH WINNER… Ski-Nose Brings Galaxy of Dazzling Beauties." McKowen wrote the story, including the caption under the front-page photo of Hope on stage, which read, "After a brief introduction by Deputy MACV CG Frederick C. Weyand, Bob Hope walked onstage and said, "With all the troop withdrawals, I'm surprised to see you here. It's nice of you guys to stick around just for me." He then rifled joke after joke, like an M-16 on rock & roll. This made Hope's seventh Vietnam Christmas tour appearance, and he expressed the hope that a return engagement would not be needed next year.

Members of the tour included singers Gloria Loring and Bobbi Martin, singer-dancer Lola Falana, baseball star Johnny Bench, Less Brown and his orchestra (his "band of renown"), and the singing/dancing of the Golddiggers and the Dingalings, plus Miss World. Hope performed before an estimated twenty-two thousand GIs at the Curry Amphitheater in Long Binh. But other than the experience of witnessing this once-in-a-lifetime event firsthand, they admitted that getting there, dealing with the heat and the long lines, and then waiting to get back was a major hassle. And if there's one thing that we REMFs tried to avoid at all costs in the Nam, it was a hassle.

133 days. On December 29, we got a phone call from one of our contacts who worked at MACV in Bien Hoa. He told us not to quote him on this, but he had heard a rumor that the 1st Cav might be the next unit to be withdrawn from Vietnam. Needless to say, this created quite a furor in the office. We all sat around and theorized about the possibilities of what might happen, how it would happen, and when it might happen. If the rumor did come true, I wondered, would I go with the Cav, or be transferred to yet another unit. Who knew and, at the moment, who cared. It was still the holidays, and I was going to a hootch party at our next-door neighbors.

The next major event, which I didn't realize was a major event, was New Year's Eve. I had heard that it was quite a party night in the Nam, but I had no idea what a big night it was at Phuoc Vinh. The place went absolutely wild that night, and the celebrating began early. So by the time midnight rolled around, there were a lot of "totaled" people wandering around. The evening started with a group of us going to the EM Club, where we were entertained by yet another USO-provided Filipino rock band. After we had our fill of that, and after quite a few beers, we made our way back to the company area to take up positions on top of the bunkers. This would be the best vantage point for the light and sound show that was about to ensue. A fireworks display, you might presume. Well, sort of. Only this event featured live fire in the form of ammunition, and it wasn't sponsored by the army.

I don't know if it was out of frustration or just celebration, but all control was lost on New Year's Eve at Phuoc Vinh, and I certainly wasn't ready for what was about to happen. As soon as we took our seats on top of the bunker right behind our hootch, Tom pulled out his seasoned and now familiar ivory pipe and loaded it with con sa. We then proceeded to get our heads right for the show. There was already a lot of noise in the background—the popping and crackling sound of Chinese fire crackers, the sounds of loud music and laughter, and the sound of what appeared to be gunfire. As midnight approached, the volume and frequency of the noise increased. And then, all of a sudden, the guy sitting next to me leaned over and yelled, "Flare!" At that very instant, he popped off a flare that he had been holding in his hand, the blast and sound (swoosh) of which nearly blew me off my chair. As it skyrocketed upward, the night sky became illuminated with its bright red-colored smoke. What a rush!

It was then that I noticed the sky all around the perimeter of the base being periodically illuminated in a variety of color. Flares were going up everywhere. An occasional Roman candle also lit the sky. The sounds of gunfire were also increasing, which I found a little disturbing. It seems firing one's weapon into the air was a Vietnam New Year's tradition—of sorts. To me, it seemed kind of dangerous, not to mention a waste of precious ammunition. What if the VC decided to attack that night? But sure enough, guys were pouring out of their hootches, firing clip after clip of ammunition into the air. I began to think that it might be a good idea to move the party "inside" the bunker. As all this was happening, I noticed a couple of choppers approaching the base perimeter. They had their search lights on, moving them back and forth in a seemingly frantic manner, as if to say: "We're trying to get back onto the base, so would you please hold your fire for a goddamn minute!" The choppers kept circling, keeping a safe distance from the perimeter. Eventually, they turned around and left. Who knows where they had to go to land for the night. But wisely, they avoided the air space over Phuoc Vinh base camp.

It was a wild New Year's Eve, one I'll never forget. It ended an incredibly eventful year, one that took me halfway around the world to Vietnam. It also ushered in 1971, the year I was going to get the hell out of this place.

CHAPTER 10

How High Can You Fly

With the excitement of the holidays behind us, life returned to normal, if there is such a thing as normal in the Nam. The next couple of weeks were very laid back, yet also full of little surprises and new experiences. I had become very accustomed to the casual lifestyle in the rear at Phuoc Vinh. Other than the top brass in the NCO and officer corps, no one ever wore a full uniform unless required for work or military functions. We worked five-hour days at best. Formations, inspections, and other military games were virtually nonexistent. And the tolerance of the military establishment for this lifestyle was, well, almost unbelievable. For instance, Cassidy had sewn a "Mr. Zig Zag" patch on the shoulder of his fatigue shirt, which he wore like a jacket, while Tom sported a patch with the peace sign emblem on his. And they got away with it. Tom also nailed a large "peace symbol" that was painted in red on a piece of plywood to a tree truck directly behind our hootch.

The lifers were different too. They were not only serious soldiers, but were also consummate professionals who conducted their business with a certain class and swagger, if you will. I don't know if it's because the division's unique air mobility gave these guys a greater opportunity to take part in the war. But whatever it was, they definitely had it all over the 25th Division in terms of class and confidence. And they seemed to respect all of their soldiers, including the draftees and REMFs, which was not always the case in the Nam.

And oh yes, we got the official word today that the 1st Cav is being withdrawn from Vietnam, but they are leaving one brigade behind in Bien Hoa (the date for the withdrawal was not announced). So unless a miracle happens, I'll be going to the 3rd Brigade, 1st Air Cavalry Division's Information Office in Bien Hoa to finish my time in the Nam. I was told the office I'll be working in is about five blocks from the airport, so you might say that I'm getting closer to leaving this place all the time.

124 days, January 7. Last night we had a little unexpected excitement, as the hootch next to ours burned to the ground. No one was hurt, and with the base fire detachment only a block away, they were able to get it under control pretty quickly. And thanks to their quick action and expertise, they saved all the surrounding hootches. The guys living there, most of them from admin, lost everything, including a couple of expensive stereo systems. But all in all, we were very lucky, considering the potential for disaster living in a defoliated forest.

By mid-January I had not only completed my series of drug articles, but a thirty-nine-page Command Information Program as well. It was like writing a term paper again, and it got rave reviews from the division brass. In fact, I was notified that the division chief-of-staff had put me in for an Army Commendation Medal for my efforts (it would be my second, as Captain Becker got me one before I left Cu Chi). Colonel Rogers was a jolly, white-haired gentleman who presented the award himself at our monthly (as opposed to bi-weekly at Cu Chi) company cookout and awards ceremony.

When the festivities ended that night, a group of us decided to go to an outdoor movie on the other side of the base, which was sort of like going to a drive-in movie, but without the car. A big screen was set up at one end of a large parking lot, with tables and chairs set up on a patch of lawn at the opposite end of the lot. While sitting there watching, a distinct whistling sound followed by a loud whoosh flew over our heads. Two seconds later a rocket impacted about five hundred yards in front of us. Someone yelled, "Incoming," and we all scattered for cover. I dove under a pickup truck that was parked nearby. As I did so, another rocket came in right behind the first one and exploded a little farther away. And that was it. None of us moved for about five minutes or so, until someone yelled, "Clear." We all then reassembled on the lawn to watch the remainder of the movie. This was the closest I'd come to incoming and almost being hit. But what really surprised me was how seemingly unaffected I was by the experience. Startled, yes; scared, not really. And thus was life in the rear in Vietnam. You learned to live with whatever came your way.

During the next couple of weeks, the level of activity in and around Phuoc Vinh picked up considerably. Some of the guys think it was all a lead-up to Tet, which occurs sometime around the first of February. We were getting hit by either rockets or mortars a couple of times a week now and were under a heightened state of alert. So you can imagine my surprise when I got word that I had pulled guard duty…for only the second time since arriving in the Nam, I might add. Now even though I felt the area around Phuoc Vinh was relatively secure, it seemed to me that you were a sitting duck in one of those guard towers on the perimeter of the base, especially during a period of heavy incoming activity. And the thought of manning either a machine gun or grenade launcher didn't sit well with me either. But sometimes you gotta do what you gotta do.

Tom drove me to my assigned post at 1900 hours, a guard tower near the rear gate on the other side of the base from Headquarters Company. I thanked him for the ride, grabbed my knapsack and rifle, and started walking toward the wide ladder I'd climb to the top of the tower as he pulled away. Guard towers, with low-lying bunkers placed in between them, circled the perimeter of the base camp. It was dark, so I couldn't see anything other than the roof over the observation deck of the tower. As I reached the top of the ladder and came eye level with the observation deck platform, I noticed another soldier sitting on a chair holding what appeared to be a lighted cigarette. It turned out to be a big, fat smoking joint. As I climbed onto the deck he asked me if I wanted a hit. To my complete surprise (although in retrospect I don't know why I should have been so surprised), my tower-mate and fellow guard was stoned out of his mind.

My initial reaction, which I thought to myself, was that it might be a good idea if one of us stayed straight for the night. But out of force of habit—or some unwritten "head code of conduct"—I took a hit, not thinking (stupidly) about how stoned I might get. I then put down my gear and started looking around to get a feel for the environment of the guard tower where I'd be spending the night. My eyes were still adjusting to the darkness, and I suddenly started to become a little paranoid. But at the same time, I also started getting into the experience. There were two chairs, a 50mm machine gun and a grenade launcher with plenty of ammunition, a small table, and a starlight scope in the guard tower. As my eyes adjusted, it was the starlight scope that caught my interest. I had heard about them, but had never seen, much less used one. It was an infrared device that allowed one to see in the dark, even though all the images were a bright fluorescent green color. I picked it up (it looked like an oversized pair of binoculars) and stared into the lenses, looking out and turning the scope from side to side. It was very cool. I could see into the small village that was located just down the road from the rear gate of the base. Mama sans, wearing their traditions non la hats, were moving from hut to hut, as if feverishly working on some task. A dog walked down the middle of the dirt road that ran through the small hamlet. And a young boy raced down the road on a bicycle. Looking at all this activity through the starlight scope made the whole scene seem surreal. Of course, my state of mind might have contributed to this perspective.

Then I started seeing...or imagining that I was seeing...things. For instance, I'd think I'd see a sapper attempting to crawl through the wire. But then I'd blink, and when I'd look again, no one was there. Then it would happen again. At first, it was a little unsettling. But after a while, I just wrote these images off to a heightened sense of awareness caused by an adrenalin rush from fear...and being stoned. While all this was going on, my tower-mate pulled out a radio and tuned into AFVN, which was featuring Led Zeppelin that evening. Radios were taboo on guard duty, for obvious reasons. But we were in Phuoc Vinh, where rules were weighed on their merit—whether or not one would get caught—and usually ignored. So we spent the rest of the night listening to music and the late-night chatter of the

DJ, while watching Vietnam after dark through the lens of a starlight scope. The night ended uneventfully at 0700 hours.

Normally, I would have had the day off after guard duty. But Lieutenant Garcia was kind enough to give me a special assignment that began later that afternoon. So even though I would only get a few hours' sleep, I told him I'd be happy to do it. Besides, he was such a good guy that I would do anything for him—well, almost anything. He told me to come back to the office at 1500 hours and he'd explain the assignment to me.

A side note here. Not only was Lieutenant Garcia a great leader and a good guy, he also represented the attitude and caliber of all the men in the IO, as well as in the other functions in the rear at Phuoc Vinh. For example, with all the preparation needed to send the division home, with special publications to be produced, etc., Sergeant Seawall got the authorization to add another artist to the IO staff. But rather than put in for a trained artist with the requisite MOS, he had his buddies in admin search the files of grunts in the bush to see if one of them might have been an artist by background. When one was found, he was able to pull this guy out of the field and get him reassigned from his infantry unit to the IO. This happened quite often in the Nam, but I noticed it more with the Cav in Phuoc Vinh than I did in Cu Chi. Even though there was a sense of unity and camaraderie among the REMFs at Cu Chi, the 1st Cav at Phuoc Vinh epitomized the brotherhood that existed between the REMFs and troops in the field, a mutual respect and true sense that we were in this together and were there for each other.

I had set my alarm clock, so I made it on time to the office. Lieutenant Garcia was talking to McKowen at his desk when I arrived, and when he saw me, he stopped what he was doing and said, "Everyone, I have an announcement to make. We're going to be publishing a special 'Farewell' edition of the *Cavalier*. It will be the final edition coming out of Phuoc Vinh before we all leave. And I'm naming the Stoupman here as its editor." With that the guys broke into applause and catcalls. I was a little embarrassed and felt my face turning red. The lieutenant then asked me to follow him into his office.

BEHIND THE WIRE

As I was to learn, being named editor of the farewell edition of the *Cavalier* was not the special assignment he had for me.

The special assignment was to escort a correspondent from *Newsweek* magazine around the base and out into the field. He was in Phuoc Vinh to write a story for the magazine on the army's premiere airmobile division. It was division policy (and became policy for all units serving in Vietnam in the latter years of the war) that all civilian press had to be accompanied by a military PIO at all times, and usually by an officer. The media was *not* to be left on their own, whether in the rear or in the field. This policy was enacted after numerous articles started to appear in newspapers and magazines back in the world, about mutinies, race wars, drug use, and other sensational sidelights of the Vietnam War. It was instituted so the military could control information, and access to information, surrounding its activities. So imagine our delight when Lieutenant Garcia was selected to be responsible for the guy from *Newsweek*. And to my surprise, he delegated the task to me. I guess my reputation as a "follow the line" military writer had grown to the point where he could do this (he told me on the QT that he didn't want to waste two days of his time with this guy…and that he trusted me to "do what was right"). I got the message and could hardly wait to tell this guy what was really going on in the Nam.

I met up with the correspondent, whose name was David Graham, at the First Team Press Camp after joining the guys in the office at the mess hall for something to eat. The lieutenant took Mr. Graham to dinner at the Officer's Club, and then brought him to the office where I was waiting. After plugging our own news organization, Lieutenant Garcia turned him over to me to begin the assignment. Our two days together started the next morning with the usual shtick. With Tom as our driver, I gave him the "highlights tour" of the base camp. When that was competed, his first request was to interview a couple chopper pilots, as well as their commander. So our first stop was the 11th Aviation Group, consisting of the 227th and 229th Assault Helicopter Battalions, and the 228th Assault Support Helicopter Battalion. This is where all the Hueys, Cobras, and Chinooks were based, so we'd have no trouble finding people to interview.

After completing his interviews, we went to the division XO's office (executive officer, second in command), since the CO was out attending some kind of powwow at MACV. The XO, Colonel Bill Buxton, was more than happy to discuss the proud history of the 1st Air Cav, as well as all of its accomplishments in the Nam (with a lot of discussion of its record for "kills"). By this time, I think Mr. Graham had had enough of the "official" story. It was time to fill him in on the "unofficial" story and show him what life was really like at Phuoc Vinh. After a short break to freshen up, we went to dinner with the guys from the press office, and then we took him to the EM Club to have a couple of beers. Sitting at a table in the corner of the club, we began to spill our guts. We told him about the absence of discipline and the mutinies that were occurring throughout the military in the Nam and about the fraggings and the murders. We shared stories about the black market and how some career soldiers were getting rich from the war, coming back for second and third tours to do so. And we told him about the luxurious lifestyle that many of the lifers had carved out for themselves in the rear, especially in the metro Saigon, Bien Hoa, and Long Binh areas, as well as at other mega base camp sites.

We then traveled back to the hootch and treated David to a smorgasbord of high-quality products from the Golden Triangle. This guy couldn't believe what was laid out before him. He said he had heard stories about all the dope in Vietnam, but thought they might be exaggerated. He discovered they weren't. We got him stoned, then continued to fill his head with stories of life in the Nam.

The next morning we headed out to the field so he could see the division in action. We had a Huey assigned to us for the day and a pilot who turned out to be a real cowboy. Colonel Rogers accompanied us to the first of our three stops, FSB Dragon Head. We would leave the colonel there, let David get some photos and interview a couple of grunts, and then we'd proceed to FSB Mace, which was located at the foot of the central highlands near the village of Song Be. It sounded like a pleasant day, even though our second stop was to an active combat zone. I had heard that the Song Be area was beautiful and was looking forward to the trip. And even though I enjoyed Colonel Rogers' company, after we dropped him off (his personal chopper would fly in to return him to Phuoc Vinh) the Huey would be ours for the rest of the day. It was like getting the car from your dad for a night out on the town.

It took us over an hour to get to FSB Mace. Mace was the newest of the division's outposts, supporting two hundred of the 1st Cav's elite infantrymen, and at the moment, it was a beehive of activity. As we flew in, we could see all kinds of action in the surrounding area. Cobras were firing their rockets and 16mm guns into the hillside, while Huey's ferried troops in and out of the base. Occasionally, a Loach (a small, bubble-front helicopter used primarily for scouting and reconnaissance) would fly over the area. After landing, we walked around the base looking for officers and soldiers that David could interview without getting in the way of the action. After about ninety minutes, he said he had gotten enough, and with the Huey having been refueled, we took off for Song Be.

The ride to Song Be was amazing. Our pilot was Warrant Officer Jordan Kirk, a handsome, blond surfer- type from Newport Beach, California. As the chopper hovered, preparing to lift off the ground, WO Kirk shouted back to us that because of the activity in the area, we'd have to fly just above the tree tops for the thirty-minute ride to Song Be. He then gave us this shit-eating grin, turned forward in his seat, nosed down the aircraft and took off, as if he was putting the pedal to the metal of a V-8 Cadillac. We soared along the tree tops as fast as I think that baby could fly. And as we learned real quickly, when it came to handling his Huey, Kirk was a real cowboy.

The ground below us, which had become increasingly forested, sailed by at a rapid pace. Occasionally, we'd fly over open spaces and rice patties, and Kirk at one point dipped down and buzzed a water buffalo, causing it to run in fear, taking the papa san and his plow along with it. The land was beautiful, and the ride exhilarating. I think David was totally freaked out, yet really enjoying himself at the same time. I'd have to say I was with him on both counts.

Song Be was the picture of a lush, jungle paradise. It was located at the foothills of the central highlands, at the western edge of the 1st Cav's area of operation. Our destination was FSB Buttons, an outpost that supported combat activity in the area. When we got there, we found the place virtually empty. Apparently most of the troops based there were out on patrol, so we spent about an hour talking to the few Skytroopers who were there holding down the fort. When we were finished and about to leave, one of the guys suggested that we take a detour on the way back along the Song River. He said it was incredibly picturesque and not to be missed. "And," he said, "it was a great spot for swimming."

Since it was hot as hell that day, and since we were ahead of schedule (as there were so few soldiers at Button to interview), we decided to take his suggestion. We said good-bye to the guys and flipped them the peace sign as we scrambled toward our chopper. After checking his map, we lifted off, and Kirk pointed the Huey northwest toward the Song River. In a matter of minutes, we were there. Kirk dove down and leveled off just above the water, and like a hydrofoil, we followed the path of the river as it twisted and wound its way through the lush jungle canopy. The scenery was breathtaking, and we were transfixed as Kirk masterfully flew his Huey along the course of the river. In some places, the water was only ankle deep, with large rocks scattered throughout its bed. At other times it was filled with rapids and an occasional waterfall.

Kirk spotted a clearing with a beach area large enough for us to land and put the Huey down gently onto its surface. It must have been a popular swimming spot, as there were a few locals frolicking in the water, and a mama san was doing her laundry on one of the large rocks on the river's bank. But to my surprise, our rather dramatic arrival did nothing more than put smiles on their faces. This was definitely a mellow place, and apparently we weren't the first GIs who had paid it a visit.

After securing the chopper, we stripped down to our boxer shorts (which, thankfully, we were wearing that day) and made our way to the water's edge. I waded out to where the river was about waist deep and dove in. The water was cool and refreshing and crystal clear. It felt great to break the heat this way, an unexpected treat. David and WO Kirk came right in behind me. After a couple of minutes, as we stood around talking, a couple of the kids swam over to us. They had big smiles on their faces, and you could see that we were a real novelty to them. And, needless to say, they were real curious about the helicopter. They would point to it, look at each other, giggle, and then look back at us. Since we were sufficiently cooled off by this time, Kirk suggested that we take the kids for a ride. David and I looked at each other, shrugged our shoulders, and said, "Why not."

We gestured to the kids to follow us as we made our way back to the aircraft. Although reluctant at first, we were able to coax them into the Huey. They didn't say a word, and their eyes were as big as saucers as we strapped them into the rear seats. As we lifted off, however, their faces lit back up, and squeals of delight came out of their little bodies. Watching their reaction to this incredible experience was worth the whole trip up here, and I wondered whether or not David would include this experience in his article, or as a short story in another publication. After a few passes up and down the river, to the horror of the mama san who was taking this all in with great anxiety I'm sure, we dropped the kids off and sent them on their way, with Hershey bars in hand. I'm sure it's an experience that they'll remember for the rest of their lives.

As we lifted off from the side of the river, I noticed that the sun was beginning to set. And since we had better than an hours' ride ahead of us, that meant we wouldn't be getting back to Phuoc Vinh until after dark. That made me a little nervous. After all, the war in most parts of the Nam only came to life after nightfall, and helicopters were prime targets. But with Kirk at the controls, I wasn't too worried.

The ride back to Phuoc Vinh was unreal. This time, instead of flying along the tree tops, Kirk took us up to ten thousand feet. The bright, setting sun illuminated the landscape in an array of amazing colors. From jungle and rivers to vast open areas breaking away from the foothills of the central highlands, you could virtually see forever. Portions of the landscape were covered by bursts of white clouds, while other areas basked in a combination of shadow and setting sunlight. We saw a thunderstorm to our east, with lightning bolts coming out of its dark clouds, and then the arch of a gigantic rainbow breaking through its outer limits. The beauty and silence of it all brought tears to my eyes. The only sound to be heard was the beating drone of the Huey's rotor blade. David Graham and I would occasionally turn and just look at each other. Neither of us could believe where we were or what we were seeing. It's an experience that I'm sure will be burned into our memories for a lifetime.

We got back to the base without incident, and I said good-bye to David. We clasped hands in the Nam handshake of brotherhood, and he thanked me for an incredible experience and for having the guts to show him what was really going on behind the scenes in Vietnam. "Up until meeting you and your friends," he said. "I've only been fed official military propaganda," he went on. "Now that I've learned a few things about what's really going on and have been able to verify others, I have to figure out how I'm going to write and present all of this…and how I'm going to get my editor's OK to print it." As he walked off toward his quarters in the officer's hootch, he said he would mail me a copy of his article. I felt really good about what I had done and hoped that if the truth continued to get out, we might actually be able to wind up this fiasco a little sooner than later.

The next morning I went to the office to begin preparations for the special "Farewell" supplement to the final issue of the *Cavalier*. And then, later that afternoon, I'd be catching a ride with the division XO to Saigon, where I planned to spend the weekend, thanks to the weekend pass that accompanied my Army Commendation Medal. This time I was going to stay at the Caravelle Hotel, which was located right on the city's central plaza, adjacent to the Catholic Cathedral and across the plaza from the National Opera House. I also planned to hook up with Ed (Doc) Gilroy, my medic buddy and hootch-mate from Cu Chi, who had been reassigned to a field hospital in Bien Hoa.

Ed and I met up for dinner, then we went to the big USO Center off Tu Do Street. In addition to enjoying the entertainment and meeting and rapping with guys from all over the Nam, who were either in Saigon on R&R or military business, I was able to make an actual phone call to my girlfriend in Pennsylvania.

We were going to be married seventeen days after I returned from the Nam, so most of the call was spent listening to her tell me about the wedding plans. After leaving the USO, I made my way back to the hotel, while Ed grabbed a rickshaw back to his residence. I awoke late the next morning, had breakfast in bed (a cheese omelet), and slowly made my way to the air base to catch a ride back to Phuoc Vinh (as I often did while working in Phuoc Vinh, I would hitch a ride with any 1st Cav chopper that had room and would be heading back to base camp).

While I was at work on Monday I got an interesting invitation. Lieutenant Garcia told me that the Headquarters company commander, Captain Bill Richardson, had approached him about finding a fourth for their bridge club that evening. "His second in command was on R&R, so he asked me if I knew anyone that could fill in. You play bridge if I remember correctly, don't you, Stoupman," Garcia asked me. "Yes, I do," I responded. "Great," he said, and then proceeded to ask me to join them at the Officer's Club at 1900 hours. Normally, I would have been taken aback by the offer. But then again, this was Phuoc Vinh, where anything was possible. What a difference from the adhered-to class structure at Cu Chi, where the closest I got to the officer's club was my two-week stint serving as bartender, subbing for the guy who went home on emergency leave. The evening was a lot of fun, and you'd never have known that I wasn't an officer and one of them by the way I was welcomed and treated.

The next few weeks progressed with the usual flurry of activity and sidelights, such as: One of the guys in HQ Company came down with malaria, which was a reminder to all of us to take those large orange mothball-size anti-malaria pills we were supplied with and supposed to be taking daily. Most of us stopped taking them after a while, as diarrhea and upset stomach was one of the common side effects. Besides, if you were stationed in the rear, the bigger base camps sprayed regularly for mosquitoes. The guys in the field, on the other hand, had to be more vigilant. In this climate, they were constantly plagued by mosquitoes, so they carried mosquito repellant with them whenever they went into the field, usually in small bottles that they put under the headband on their helmets.

I got another assignment. The Military Command in Vietnam (MACV) puts out a quarterly magazine called *Tour 365*. Our division was assigned to do a feature on Vietnamization, and of course they gave it to me.

They were going to send me to Tokyo for a week to help put together what would probably be the final edition of the *First Team*, the division's quarterly magazine, but Lieutenant Garcia is going in my place, as the dates coincide with my R&R dates, which can't be changed. Oh well, you win some, you lose some.

One of the guys in admin is starting a fund to collect money to send his dog back to the states. Sometimes I think I should have done that for Sgt. Pepper…still feeling guilty about that.

I found out that I was going to be offered a 41-day drop—meaning, I could leave the Nam 41 days ahead of the 365-day schedule. But I'm going to turn it down, as I'll still have a little under a year to serve when I return, and it would mess up our wedding plans, which are set for seventeen days after my DEROS.

I ran into another guy I went to OCS with today. He's now a scout dog handler and had his German shepherd with him. His dog was beautiful, but he had a real dangerous job and I didn't envy him. I wished him well.

108 days, January 23. Phuoc Vinh got hit again last night, a little more heavily than usual. We had two attacks within thirty minutes of each other, and nine guys were injured, but again, not on our side of the base. People are starting to get tense, as Tet is next week and anything can happen. But if it does, I have a nice, big, safe bunker right behind my hootch. And speaking of things heating up, the temperature here has turned from a pleasant hot to an unbearable hot. We're moving into the peak of the dry season, and it's going to be miserably hot until I leave. Hitting 100 degrees is not unusual, and I hear it's even worse in Bien Hoa, where it can get up to 120 I've been told.

At midnight tonight I break a hundred days and become a two-digit midget. It may not sound like much, but it's a milestone in the Nam, in the ever-present tradition of counting down to DEROS. The guys got together and threw me a surprise "breaking 100" party. It lasted into the wee hours, and we cooked steak, chicken, and shrimp on our make-shift grill (we have an "in" with one of the cooks at the commanding general's mess hall). The guys here really are great, and everyone is constantly thinking of everyone else, which makes life here a lot more bearable. Work by day, party by night—what's not to like.

90 days, February 10. We just heard the latest "semi-official" rumor about our leaving here. I thought that we'd be going to Bien Hoa around the first of April. Now I hear that we might be going sooner than that. I just hope that the Cav doesn't leave Phuoc Vinh while I'm on R&R...You never know with the army.

Things are really moving fast now with lots to do. Among other things, and while I still have time, I completed my order for a stereo component system today through the PACEX catalog, a five-component system for $682 ($1,500 stateside value). Wanted to get the order in while I still had the time, not knowing from day to day what might happen to me. My parents are buying the system for me as a wedding present.

I'm feeling a little weak and have a slight sore throat today. But I think it's just from fatigue, as I've been running around a lot lately. A lot of guys have the flu and haven't gotten out of bed or eaten much in days; they're also vomiting and constantly running to the latrine. I've also heard that the milk has been bad lately, as a couple of guys in admin came down with food poisoning. And a lot of guys, especially the grunts, have bad cases of the crud. So all in all, I'm considering myself lucky just to have a slight sore throat.

87 days, February 13. I just finished writing most of the copy for the sixteen-page souvenir supplement of the paper, and all by myself I might add. Increasingly, I was being given most of the writing assignments at the IO, including preparing an outline for the fourth quarter CIP. I was paying the price for speedy writing and dependability, as I was overloaded (and kind of missing my slacker days). Lieutenant Garcia and I are off to Saigon today to set the type, and we're flying in the colonel's private chopper. He really likes my writing. While I'm down there, I also have to travel to MACV to get the information on all the 1st Cav's Medal of Honor winners for a back page feature for the final issue of the paper. Lieutenant Garcia is flying back with the colonel late this afternoon, but since I won't be finished at MACV in time, I'll have to spend the night at a hotel, which means I'll have an opportunity to have a drink at the Continental Hotel with some of the civilian press, since that's where they hang out. I'd been wanting to do that.

Well, I'm now sitting in the terminal at the Bien Hoa airport, waiting to catch a 0800 hours fixed-wing plane back to Phuoc Vinh in the morning. All the hotels were booked, so I have to spend the night in this fucking airport. Sleeping on a wooden bench was not what I had in mind for the evening. I did make it to the Continental Hotel for a drink, though, and hung out with a reporter for CBS, and of course, "we talked." I also heard from him that there had been a big earthquake in Los Angeles, centered near Northridge. I have cousins who live near there, so I hope they're all right. To kill time while waiting for the morning flight, I bought a book, *The Andromeda Strain*, which I read in a few hours. I also got to watch (and drool) as a "Freedom Bird" arrived with a load of fresh troops. The only thing I could think of as I watched the file of bright green uniforms pass me by was…eighty days…*short*!

Back at the office that day, I was a little tired and a little irritable from lack of sleep. When I got to my desk, McKowen reached over and handed me a cup of coffee. "Looks like you could use this," he remarked. I just looked at him. Then he blurted out, "When are you going to put in for your R&R, Stoup? You are long overdue, you know, and your time is running out." And it was. "I'd do it now if I were you, for when you get to Bien Hoa, they may not let you go." The thought of missing out on my R&R horrified me, and I suddenly woke up. I had my dates and location picked out for some time, but had yet to put in the paperwork. McKowen's warning prompted me to do so right away. He was planning his "third," by the way. He had an in with the admin clerk who cuts travel orders, so he was able to get away with it (apparently, Lieutenant Garcia just turned his head the other way). I don't know how he had the balls to take three R&Rs (I had heard of guys getting away with two), when only one was authorized per twelve-month tour of duty. But McKowen had balls—big ones—and was one of the most self-assured guys that I had ever met. He told me that he had mentioned to his buddy in admin that I'd be coming, and not to worry, he'd take care of me. "But you'd better get your young ass over there as soon as you can," he emphasized.

I told him I'd see to it, but it was Friday, and I had too much on my plate that had to be done to do it that day. And besides, I was feeling like shit and wanted to recover by the evening. I'd get to it tomorrow, or the next day. So right after lunch, I went back to the hootch and took a three-hour nap. When I woke up, I realized that Dennis was going to be making his way over from the motor pool to have a few beers with us to kick-off the weekend. And his presence always cheered me up. He'd be wearing his now-familiar uniform of off-white poplin pants (excuse me, trousers, as was drilled into us at basic training: "Women wear pants, men wear trousers, soldier!), a brown polo shirt, and sneakers. If the sun was shining, he would be hidden behind aviator-style sunglasses. I still don't know how he got away with wearing civilian clothes all time. And as I mentioned before, there had to be times when he was required to wear his uniform, but I had yet to see it. On this particular night, the main topic of conversation would be—you guessed it—R&R.

As I lay in my bunk waiting for Dennis to arrive, I started reflecting on my love life. Needless to say, I was horny. Believe it or not, for my age, I was surprisingly not horny most of the time. I guess all the excitement and distractions of the Nam kept my focus away from sex. In fact, in some ways, it was kind of like sex for me, as I did "get off" on the fear and thrills and beauty that I often got to experience. Also, if it's not present, or available, one doesn't dwell on it—at least I didn't. My frequent trips to Saigon did provide me with plenty of opportunities, but I just wasn't into that kind of "hit and run" activity…and its potential consequences. However, there were guys who did seem to need (or want) it all the time. These guys, for the most part, took advantage of the hootch maids that came onto the base frequently. I guess it satisfied their needs and made the girls a little extra money to boot…but I wasn't about to go there. No, my love life consisted of letters from my girlfriend (actually fiancé) and being left to my own devices. Just as I was considering doing just that, the door to the hootch swung open and in walked Dennis.

I was hungry, so we made our way to the mess hall and had a Friday fish fry. Then we headed back to the hootch, met up with the guys, and broke out the beer. The conversation, as I mentioned previously, focused on R&R. I had originally planned on meeting Paula in Hawaii for my R&R, the R&R site most often selected by married soldiers and those who wanted to see their girlfriends or families, but Paula's father wouldn't hear of it. He was an old-world Italian and wouldn't let her go because we weren't married, even though we were both twenty-three years old. So I had to come up with another location. We talked about it a lot at Cu Chi, with Doc raving about Bangkok, which did seem to be the destination of choice, with Sydney a close second. Sydney, as I mentioned during my previous discussion about R&R with the guys at Cu Chi, was primarily popular with the guys who were tired of "slant eyes" and who wanted an American-like culture, round-eyed women, and the English language. And on top of that, there was a certain intrigue about "the land down under." But Bangkok, on the other hand, epitomized all that was beautiful and exotic about the Oriental culture. From what I was told, it was a paradise, and more than any other location, it catered to the GI's every whim and desire. So I had narrowed my choice down to those two. Dennis informed us that he had changed his mind, and that he was going to Hong Kong, because it was "civilized," and he wanted to buy a camera and some equipment. Hong Kong, more than any other location, was known for its incredible shopping and buys. In addition to Sydney, Bangkok, Hong Kong, and Hawaii, we could also choose from Taipei, Singapore, Manila, and Tokyo—all amazing locations, and choosing one of them was one of the most difficult travel decisions I would ever have to make. I chose Bangkok.

BEHIND THE WIRE

The following Monday I went to the admin office to put in for my R&R. Since the travel clerk was McKowen's buddy, I knew I would get what I wanted and when I wanted it. While I was filling out the paperwork, he informed me that my promotion had come through. "What promotion?" I asked. He told me that he had heard from McKowen that Lieutenant Garcia had put me in for a direct field promotion to Specialist 5th Class. This would not only elevate me to E-5 status (same as a sergeant), with a significant pay jump (by army standards), but also guaranteed that my life and future assignment back in the world would be at a half-decent level, and my Information Specialist MOS would be guaranteed.

After signing my request for travel—I'd be leaving in a little more than a week—I hurried back to the office to find Lieutenant Garcia. I wanted to thank him for what he had done and get filled in on the details. As I was to discover, my previous promotion to Spec. 4 had been too recent for him to go through normal channels to get me another one. So he put me in for a direct field promotion for "meritorious service" and he got it. Garcia then informed me that he would be leaving for home in a little more than three weeks (I had no idea, or had forgotten, that he was that short), and that he wanted to do this for me before he left. What a guy! And on top of all that, he told me I'd be getting my promotion directly from the division commander, Major General Walter McCraw. I thanked him profusely, while he just shrugged his shoulders, shook his head, and said with a big smile, "It was nothing, Stoupman."

On Wednesday morning, Lieutenant Garcia and I made our way to the division commander's office. In preparation for the event, I had the hootch maid iron my fatigues so they almost looked starched. And I slicked back my hair so it would appear shorter than it actually was. When we arrived, the lieutenant took me right to the general's office. The division photographer was waiting outside the office, as Lieutenant Garcia had summoned him to capture the event. When we walked into the office, General McCraw was seated at his desk. The first thing I did was come to attention and salute. Lieutenant Garcia gave him a sort of side-ways casual salute, with his typical big smile on his face, then raced over and shook his hand. Apparently, the CO was also a fan of Lieutenant Garcia (his personality was infectious). Then after a few moments of small talk, MG McCraw came over (I was still frozen in the position of attention), removed the Spec. 4 insignia pin from my shirt collar, and replaced it with that of Specialist 5th Class. The general was a tall man who towered over me as he pinned on the stripes. When he was finished, we saluted each other again, then we shook hands as he handed me the certificate indicating my direct field promotion. Then, as the camera flashed, we posed for a couple of shots. "I understand you've been doing some mighty fine work for the division," he remarked. "Congratulations and keep up the outstanding work, Specialist," he continued. "Thank you, sir, I will," I replied. With that, the ceremony was over, and the photographer and I left the room. Lieutenant Garcia stayed behind for a few minutes to chat with the CO, while I waited in the outer office. I was really feeling good and suddenly in the mood to celebrate.

On the walk back to the First Team Press Camp, Lieutenant Garcia told me to take the rest of the day off.

As we bid each other farewell, he turned to me and said, "And let's have a drink tonight to celebrate."

"I think I can handle that, sir," I responded, giving him a snappy salute. But little did I know when I said this, that an event would transpire that afternoon and into the evening that would actually turn out to be a little more than I could handle.

I went to lunch early after leaving Lieutenant Garcia, then made my way back to the hootch. Cassidy and Tom were just starting to rouse, as they both had guard duty last night. Since they had the rest of the day off as well, we decided to wander around the base and try to find something interesting, or at least different, to do. Even though we had Tom's jeep at our disposal, we decided to walk.

Our first stop turned out to be our last—the division day room. The day room was like a mini-activity center, with a pool table, lounge area with a television, darts, board games, and it also had a small kitchen and eating area. To our surprise, no one was there (it was a work day), not even the special services guy who ran the place.

Upon further investigation, we found a note on the inside of the door that said he had gone to MACV for the afternoon, but would leave the door unlocked for anyone who wanted to take advantage of the facility. We thought that was real nice of him, especially considering the activity we had come up with.

Tom, who had been opening and closing cabinet doors, was staring at the oven. He put his hand to his lips and rubbed them, kind of like you do when you have an idea. He then pulled a box of brownie mix out of one of the cabinets, turned to Cassidy and me, and said, "Let's bake us some brownies." We said OK, but it took us a couple of seconds to realize what kind of brownies he was thinking about making. His shit-eating grin should have given it away.

While Cassidy and I played a game of 8-ball, Tom ran back to the hootch to secure the missing ingredient. Before long he was back, with an ounce of fine Vietnamese con sa in his pocket. As he cleaned the sticks and seeds from the pot in a strainer, Cassidy and I whipped up the brownie batter and preheated the oven. It was just like home...well, sort of.

We continued to play pool while the brownies baked and cooled. We then cut the batch into squares, wrapped them in wax paper, and placed them in a paper bag. Cassidy, who was starting to get a little paranoid about getting caught, was furiously cleaning the pan and putting the kitchen back to the condition in which we found it...minus a box of brownie mix. With our baked goods in hand, we left the day room and headed back to the hootch. Along the way, we decided to make a pit stop at the PX for some munchies, which we figured we'd need later that night. I also needed to pick up some toiletries for my R&R trip, which was coming up in a few days. With our shopping completed, we made our way back to the hootch to stash our goodies. We planned to share our bounty with the guys, but first decided it would probably be a good idea to put some food into our stomachs before indulging in our "dessert." So we made our way to the mess hall to grab some dinner.

When we got back to the hootch, I couldn't wait to dig into one of the brownies. I had heard that you really got stoned when you ate the stuff, but had never tried it. I took a bite, expecting the brownie to taste as good as it smelled. Unfortunately, it tasted horrible. Because of all the pot Tom put into the batter (way too much), the dough didn't rise very much. So what we ended up with were thick, muddy bricks of a chewy substance that was supposed to be a brownie. There was a hint of chocolate taste, but not much more. I nearly gagged as I tried to swallow the second bite, but I forced myself to consume a whole square, and it took me nearly twenty minutes to do so. Tom and Cassidy didn't seem to have the same problem, although they admitted that the brownies tasted like shit.

In addition to the three of us, we treated the finance clerks to the brownies as well. It was my way of getting back at them for my initial welcome to Phuoc Vinh. We also saved a square for John, who was working late on a sketch for the cover of the division yearbook. And I planned to offer one to McKowen and Lieutenant Garcia as well, although I wasn't sure they would take me up on the offer. They preferred the hops over the weed.

An hour later…nothing. I couldn't believe that I had yet to feel anything. Neither had any of the other guys, although Cassidy was complaining about an upset stomach. The Moody Blues was playing in the background. I guess the music had been playing for a while, but I hadn't really noticed it. But now, all of a sudden, it had become the perfect accompaniment to our evening of camaraderie and celebration.

And then, without warning, it hit me. I turned my head to the side to react to a joke Tom had just told, and what seemed like five minutes later, my head completed the turn. Suddenly, everything was happening in slow motion. I tried to get up off the bed where I had been reclining, and couldn't. I was drugged. If I hadn't done it to myself, I'd swear someone had slipped me a Mickey Finn. I had this shit-eating grin on my face that I couldn't erase. And looking around the room, I noticed that everyone else was wearing the same grin. The music was still playing, but sounded like it was coming from far, far away. And that's the last thing I remember.

The next morning, at 1100 hours, my eyes opened. The first thing that hit me was that my mouth was extremely dry. As I got out of bed to get some water, I noticed that everyone else was still sleeping…in the same positions that they were in when I was last conscious. I also noticed that I was still high. Four squares of the brownies were lying on an ammo box next to Tom's bed. I wrapped them in paper and tossed them into the trash can. I decided against offering a sample to McKowen and Lieutenant Garcia and didn't feel anyone else in the hootch needed any more either. Enough damage had already been done from our little experiment.

After satisfying my thirst, I made my way over to the office. I wanted to see if I was in any trouble for sleeping in. McKowen greeted me as I walked through the door with "Well, look at who has arisen from the dead." Everyone in the office laughed. McKowen went on to tell me that he and Lieutenant Garcia had come over to the hootch around 2230 to take me out for a celebration drink. He said the scene they walked in on reminded them of a mass suicide. He said they just laughed and figured we had all partied a bit too much and decided to let us be. I'm sure they had to have seen the brownies sitting on the ammo box, but he didn't say a word about it. Phuoc Vinh…you had to love the place.

CHAPTER 11

R&R in Bangkok

As soon as I finalized my plans for R&R, Lieutenant Garcia and I hopped a ride to Saigon to start the typesetting for the souvenir issue of the paper. While I was there, I went over to the USO and made an emergency phone call to my parents, to make sure that they had sent me a package of civilian clothes. I couldn't get ahold of them. But I figured that if I didn't get the package in time, I'd just borrow some clothes from the guys who had them from their R&Rs and buy whatever else I needed when I got to Bangkok.

You see, we lowly EMs had to ship all of our civilian clothes home before departing for Vietnam. And you could only travel in civilian clothes on R&R—no military attire was allowed. So it was kind of a catch 22, and very typical of the military. I'm not sure why this was, but who would want to travel in their uniform anyway. Maybe the army wanted to give us a genuine break from the thought and reality of the war and military duty. Then again, maybe they didn't want us to disgrace the uniform when we got into the kind of trouble and situations that many GIs got into when on R&R. But whatever the reason, we were leaving the Nam in civilian clothes and wouldn't have to wear our jungle fatigues for eight glorious days.

The package with my clothes arrived the day before I was to leave, thank God. I spent the day in furious activity, nailing down things at the office and gathering all my personal shit to pack in my duffle bag. Colonel Rogers was flying to Bien Hoa the next morning for a meeting at MACV and offered me a ride in his chopper. He said that he'd have his driver take me to Ton Son Nhut Airport after he dropped him off at his meeting. I figured that Lieutenant Garcia set this all up for me. The guy really knew how to operate. It was like traveling first class.

When I got to Ton Son Nhut (the civilian airport for Saigon), I checked in at the U.S. military desk for R&R and overseas travel, where I got my travel orders processed, and was given my ticket for Pam Am flight 232 to Bangkok. The flight was supposed to depart at 1300 hours, but in true "hurry up and wait" military fashion, we didn't board until 1530. So I wandered around for a while and then took a seat on one of the wooden benches in the terminal. While sitting there, I struck up a conversation with the two guys sitting next to me, who were also headed to Bangkok on R&R. One was a sergeant from Chicago, Bob Workowski, who worked at the U.S. Embassy in Saigon. The other, Gil Brown, was a brother from Harlem who was a signal corps motion picture photographer assigned to MACV. We immediately hit it off, and as the conversation ensued, covering everything from the army to our likes and dislikes and so on, we decided it would be fun to do things together during our week in Thailand.

The three of us managed to get seats together on the relatively short flight to Bangkok (under ninety minutes). It felt good to take off in the relative luxury of our 707 and to be leaving the Nam, even though we knew it to be a temporary respite. It also felt good to be in civilian clothes again. We had a lot of laughs on the flight, and by the time we arrived, I could already tell that we were going to have quite an adventure together.

As soon as we landed and deplaned, they herded us onto three blue Mercedes Benz buses. We didn't even have to hassle with our bags, which were loaded onto the buses for us by airport personnel. It was difficult to get a feel for the city on the bus ride from the airport, but I had a feeling I was going to like it here. It was hot, there were palm trees swaying in the wind, and I wasn't in the Nam any more. What more could a GI ask for.

The buses were air conditioned and had PA systems that were manned by our guide for the thirty-minute ride from the airport to the welcome center in central Bangkok. The welcome center was operated by the U.S. government and was the drop off and pick up location for all GIs on R&R in Bangkok. It was also the place to come if you needed help or got into trouble, if you got sick, or if you wanted permission to get married.

On the ride into the city, our military guide (in civilian clothes) gave us an "unofficial" briefing on some of the things we should know before being set loose for our R&R. He informed us—in a tour guide rather than a military voice—that because of its tolerance and the many temptations that this tropical paradise had to offer, Bangkok was by far the most popular of the R&R destinations. Hundreds of thousands of GIs had already enjoyed the pleasures of the city, and because of this, the local economy was thriving. "Everyone caters to the GIs in Bangkok," he pointed out. "But if you're not careful, you might bring back something that you hadn't planned on."

That last point led to a discussion of the art and science of acquiring women in the country. It was assumed, even by the military, that everyone came to Bangkok to get laid. After all, it had gained the reputation of being the land of beautiful and abundant women. And when you add to that the fact that GIs were there to take a break from the war and that many, if not most of them, hadn't been with a woman for a considerable period of time, it was a given that hooking up with a woman was the primary reason for making the trip to this paradise. But the whole notion still blew my little Catholic mind, as it was contrary to my upbringing and my somewhat naïve and yet-to-be-developed moral sense. But then again, as I had already come to learn, there was a whole different moral code surrounding war.

It didn't matter if you were married or single, Catholic, Protestant, or Jewish. If you wanted a woman, you got one. It was considered acceptable because it was the war, and in the war, you did what you had to do to get by. If that meant smoking a joint, downing a six-pack, taking speed, or snorting skag, you did it. If it meant blessing the troops in a religious service before sending them off to kill or be slaughtered, you did it. And in the case of the Nam, if it meant refusing duty because you didn't believe in what you were doing, or because you were too short to risk another mission, you did that too. Why should it have been any different when many of our supposed role models—the career military—were either involved in graft and corruption on some level, or were primarily interested in earning more combat time and pay, more battle ribbons, and more promotions to bolster their careers. I mean, when your intended purpose for invading a country is to decimate the land and eliminate the enemy (and a huge portion of the civilian population) for the trumped up objective of "stopping communism" before it spreads throughout the world, then everything else kind of breaks down from there.

Since the beginning of warfare, men have always interpreted morality. They've always taken matters into their own hands, especially when it came to satisfying their needs, wants, and desires. It comes with the territory. And so is the case with the Nam. That's not to say that morality doesn't exist in the military, even considering the circumstances. It does, with the vast majority of the troops and their leaders. But considering the amount of immorality that surrounds everyone in this war, going to Bangkok to spend some time with a woman—and in other guilty pleasures—seemed not only normal but almost a just reward. But enough rambling. Bottom line, guys just want to get laid!

We were told that the city of Bangkok had over twelve thousand registered prostitutes between the ages of eighteen and twenty-four (obviously, there were younger and older women—and men—available as well). Each girl was required to carry a pink government card that had to be stamped every ten days following a physical examination for venereal disease. We were strongly advised to ask for and inspect this card before sampling the merchandise. The procedure for acquiring these girls was as follows: There were basically two types of prostitutes that catered to the GIs…bar girls and sauna girls. Bar girls went for $15 to $20 per night, while sauna girls, of a supposedly higher social level, went for $25 to $35. And this was for the night—and sometimes into the next day! We were told not to pay even a dollar more, as these were set prices. As was common in many societies, you dealt with the madam, or in the case of Southeast Asia, the mama san. For the most part, you found the bar girls in the many bars and clubs that Bangkok was famous for. You found the sauna girls in the numerous baths and sauna establishments that could be found throughout the city.

Twelve thousand girls…it was hard to believe. But then I remembered the stories that Doc and the guys in Cu Chi used to tell after returning from R&R in Bangkok…about how they found their girls and stayed with them all week, as if they were steady dates. And how they would give them extra money to go shopping or get their hair done and how many of the girls would even take them home to meet their families. The whole scene sounded incredible to me—and a bit bizarre.

Unfortunately, many of these girls had come to Bangkok from small cities and rural areas to make the first real income of their lives for them and their families. Many were also looking for a husband, so they could realize that difficult-to-achieve dream of making it to America. But more often than not, their lives ended up in jeopardy. Prostitution was counter to their culture and religious beliefs, and most of these girls were eventually ostracized from their families and villages, never able to return. The mixed-race children that often resulted from these liaisons became social outcasts, even more so in Vietnam than in Thailand. And the girls themselves often ended up on the street, surrounded by crime and desperation.

We arrived at the welcome center right on time. We were led inside and taken to a briefing room that had bench seating. It was here that we were given our final instructions and told when to report back to the center. Then they handed out a booklet that contained information about hotels, restaurants, tours, shopping and the like. The booklet also provided tips about bartering, local customs, and enlightened us to certain cultural taboos, like never touching anyone on the top of the head. From there we were taken to the currency exchange room, where we formed three lines to change all our MPC into baht, the Thai currency (although many of us had also brought along our own personal stashes of greenbacks). And that was it. After we exchanged our money, Bob, Gil, and I walked out of the center and we were free—for a week—in the exotic paradise that is Bangkok, Thailand.

By this time it was early evening and we were tired, so we decided to find a hotel, have a good meal, and call it a day. We would start fresh in the morning, pursuing pleasure and exploring all the sites and treasures that Bangkok had to offer. We did, however, vacillate back and forth as to whether or not we would get girls that night, but we decided to wait.

We hopped into one of the many taxis that were waiting outside the welcome center and asked the driver for his recommendation for a good, but reasonable, hotel. The driver, who spoke very broken English, repeated the word *hotel*, and said, "I take you to the King's Diamond Hotel." I quickly looked up the King's Diamond Hotel in the booklet they gave us to see if it was listed. It was in there, among the list of recommended lodgings. "OK," I said, and we took off heading into the heart of the city.

As we pulled up in front of the hotel, which was slightly off the beaten track, we were immediately greeted by a doorman who acted as if he knew we were coming. He opened the door for us, bowed in greeting, and grabbed our luggage. The hotel was relatively small, about five stories, with a swimming pool off to one side. It was located in a semi-commercial/residential neighborhood, about a quarter mile from the main business district. The evening was warm and pleasant, and there were many incredible smells in the air, with two that were recognizable—honeysuckle and curry.

We checked in and got three separate rooms on the top floor of the hotel. The rate was $5 a night. After they settled in, Bob and Gil came over to my room to discuss our plans for the week. I pretty much had a game plan in mind as to what I wanted to do, which I shared with my two new buddies. Since they had nothing other than the obvious in mind, they said my plans sounded good to them and deemed me "the tour organizer" for the week.

By this time we were starving and decided to discuss the rest of our plans over dinner. Rather than taking a cab and making an evening out of it, we opted for familiarizing ourselves with the area and sampling some of the local cuisine. Besides, we wanted to stretch our legs, so we decided to walk around the neighborhood until we found a place that looked appealing. But as soon as we hit the hotel lobby, we were surrounded by taxi drivers and others who wanted to take us, show us, and sell to us. Fortunately, the hotel manager intervened and asked us what our pleasure was for the evening. I told him that we just wanted to take a walk and find some good Thai food. He recommended a restaurant two blocks down the street. But before he let us go, he introduced us to John, who he said would be honored to be our "driver" for the week.

He proceeded to tell us that the best way to get around and see all the sights was by auto and that most GIs took advantage of a car service. Then he added, "John would be happy to serve you." We looked at each other and decided that it sounded like a pretty good idea. Then I asked the inevitable question, "How much?" The manager said it would cost each of us $10 for the week. "OK," I told him, trying not to let on that I thought the price was a real bargain. And I'm sure the hotel got a cut of his fee, which was hard to fathom at only $30 for the week. So for the rest of the week, John hung around the hotel lobby waiting to take us wherever we wanted, whenever we wanted. He also served as our tour guide, and ultimately, our friend. But tonight, we didn't need him.

After an interesting and delicious Thai dinner, we took a leisurely stroll before heading back to the hotel. It was a beautiful evening, and the sights, sounds, and images were all captivating—from the displays in the shop windows, the variety and diversity of the people who were out and about, and the neon lights that were reflected on the wet streets (it had rained while we dined, as it often does without warning in the tropics), to the hustle and bustle of a variety of vehicles, scooters, bicycles, and the like…it all was fascinating to take in. Our plan was to spend the next three days looking for girls, shopping, and seeing as much of Bangkok as possible. After that, we decided to head to the resort town of Pattaya Beach, which was located on the Gulf of Siam. I had heard from the guys that this was a real tropical paradise, with large, white sand beaches and warm, crystal clear water as well as beautiful women. And after the beach, we'd come back for one final night of adventure in Bangkok.

After returning to the hotel, we hung out in my room for a while, being entertained by local TV programming. But before long, there was a knock on the door. It was the hotel manager, accompanied by three young Thai women. Upon asking permission, he stepped inside the room, while the girls remained in the corridor. "I thought you might like some companionship for the evening," he said in perfect English, directing his statement to me. I thanked him for his thoughtfulness, but told him that we were tired and planned to look for girls tomorrow. He looked back at me with a puzzled expression on his face, then smiled, bowed, and backed out of the room. Bob and Gil just stared at me, as if to say, "What the fuck."

A short time later, there was another knock at the door. It was the hotel manager again, this time with three different and even more attractive girls. One of them was carrying a small shopping bag. He motioned for me to come out into the hallway. As I did, he directed the girl holding the bag to open it, revealing an ample quantity of marijuana, with a water pipe resting on top of it. I couldn't believe my eyes. This guy apparently wasn't going to give up until he found something that satisfied us…and he certainly knew what the GIs liked. Again, I said thanks, but no thanks (although the sight and smell of the pot made it very tempting). And again, he walked away with a perplexed look on his face. The girls lowered their heads and giggled softly as they followed him down the corridor. When I stepped back into the room and told the guys what had just happened, I could see them weakening, so I said, "You guys can do whatever you want, but I'm going to get some sleep. Let's meet in the restaurant for breakfast at eight so we can get an early start," I continued. And with that they left, with Gil muttering something under his breath. And thus, ended my first day in Bangkok.

The next morning I was awakened by the warmth of the sun streaming in the window onto my face. I could tell that the day was going to be a hot one, and now rested, I couldn't wait to get out and begin the adventure. I met Bob and Gil for breakfast right on time, so I assume they followed my lead and got some sleep. After a breakfast of papaya juice, an exotic array of fresh fruit, and a variety of Thai pastries, we were ready to go. John was waiting for us in the lobby, and we told him that today we wanted to see some of the city's famous Buddhist temples and landmarks, and do a little shopping. And that's exactly what we did.

As we pulled up to our first stop, I couldn't believe my eyes. It was the city's main temple complex and Presidential Palace. The exterior of the temples were incredible—the most ornate and beautiful structures that I had ever seen. We visited the Grand Palace and its surrounding grounds and bell towers, as well as the Temple of the Emerald Buddha. Inside this temple, seated on the floor chanting in prayer, were bald-headed monks in their bright saffron robes. Tourists weren't allowed in this temple, but peering through the massive open doors we could see, on an ornate alter at the other end of the cavernous room, a six-foot tall Buddha that was carved out of pure green jade. It was spectacular and obviously the crown jewel of Thai Buddhism. Most of the other Buddhas were covered in gold leaf (some were made of pure gold from what we were told) and were either standing, sitting, or reclining. Our final stop, in fact, was at the Temple of the Reclining Buddha (Wat Pho), the oldest and largest wat (temple) in Bangkok. The Buddha is 150 feet long and 49 feet high and is covered in gold leaf. Its eyes and foot soles are inlaid with mother-of-pearl. Bob and I were amazed by everything we had seen. But it was Gil, who had never left Harlem before coming to the Nam, who was really blown away. He walked from temple to temple as if he had gone to heaven, and he kept having me photograph him as he posed in front of everything of interest, especially the statues of the giant monkey gods.

After touring the temples, John took us to the main commercial district for a little shopping. I was in the market for jewels and Thai silk, a suit and some clothes for myself, and of course, another Buddha statue for my collection (I acquired my first one in Saigon). I not only purchased a custom-made suit and some shirts, but got a pair of knee-high leather boots as well. All they did was trace the outline of my feet onto paper, and then told me to stop back in two days to pick them up. The boots were only $25; the suit, $40. Then I found a cocktail ring for Paula containing twenty-six small rubies. And to my delight, a stunning bracelet, earrings, and dress wedding band set all in 18-carat sculpted Thai gold (this was going to be my weeding present to her). I also bought a cocktail ring with multi-colored precious stones for my mother and a 10-carat topaz ring for my sister. And I bought myself a uniquely designed ring in 14-carat gold with a large black star sapphire in the center. I think, all in all, I only paid $150 for the lot. Incredible. This verified everything I had heard about shopping for gems in Bangkok. After purchasing the jewelry, it was on to find the "piece de resistance." I found the perfect Buddha statue in a store that featured an amazing variety of statuary in all sizes, variations, and materials. After a long deliberation (which irritated Bob and Gil a bit), I chose a 15-inch tall standing Buddha made of a bronze material that shined like gold. I was thrilled. Now all I had to do was carry it around with me until I returned to Phuoc Vinh.

After we had our fill of shopping—and the incredible heat—we headed back to the hotel. It was now late afternoon, and we decided to take a swim and lie around the pool for a while, then grab an early bite before heading out for our evening of adventure. Tonight we definitely planned to find female companionship. As we were sitting around the pool discussing what we had been told about the art and science of "acquiring" women in Bangkok, we were paid another visit by the hotel manager. This time he came bearing a gift—a plastic bag containing what looked to be an ounce of finely graded Thai marijuana and a pack of rolling papers. He told us it was "compliments of the house," and if we wanted more, to come to his office anytime. I couldn't believe it (I know, I've been saying that A LOT in the past nine months). This was all happening in public—in broad daylight and in front of the other guests at the pool. No one even seemed to notice, as if this was an acceptable thing that happens every day. And I guess it was…in Bangkok…during the time period of the Vietnam War.

Apparently, if he couldn't sell us women, he would try to sell us drugs, giving us a sample to whet our appetite. I guess it was a "full service" hotel, providing not only rooms and food, but a call girl service, a car service, and who knows what else. The three of us were mind-boggled. It was a paradise version of Nam, minus the lifers and the war. It appeared that there were no rules or laws against the many forms of pleasure the GIs indulged in while on R&R. And if there were, heads were certainly turned the other way. And it appeared that everyone in Bangkok was in on the hustle. The pleasure money being brought into Bangkok by the GIs on R&R was fueling a robust economy and was making this city a boom town, if not a modern-day Sodom and Gomorra.

We thanked him for his gift and rolled ourselves a couple of joints—right at poolside, like we did this every day. Even though I was enjoying the experience, I have to admit that I found myself looking over my shoulder on occasion to see who might be watching us or if the MPs were going to rush in at any moment and bust us. But it never happened. And as I sat there, with the sun beating down on my body, I looked up to the heavens and whispered the words, "Thank you."

(Note: There were MPs stationed at all R&R sites to handle any situation with GIs that might get out of control. But because of the importance of GI dollars to their economies, when there was an incident, local authorities would usually turn over any GI arrested by the local police to the MPs, who would usually just put them on the next plane back to Vietnam, unless the incursion was serious, as in the case of rape and murder.)

On our way back to our rooms to change, we asked John's recommendation for dinner and also asked him to join us. He was reluctant at first, but we finally convinced him to come. He took us to a little place in the center of the business district that he said was a favorite spot among locals, which is always a good sign. And once again, we had an incredible Thai dining experience.

During dinner we finalized our plans for finding girls. Bob and I decided to go first class and get sauna girls, while Gil said he preferred the bar scene. So after dinner, John dropped Gil off at one of the city's bigger and more popular pick-up bars, then took Bob and me to a sauna bath tucked away in one of the city's nicer districts. The neighborhood was actually quite toney, with up-scale shops, residences, and even an embassy or two. We turned off the main drag onto one of the side streets, then pulled up to a three-story building in the middle of the block that had a small neon sign hanging over the door that read: "Sauna." The street was black and shiny from the rain that had recently fallen, reflecting the lights of nearby buildings in an out-of-focus abstract pattern. The atmosphere was very surreal…very much out of a 1930's movie. I didn't know if I was more nervous or excited.

We thanked John as we got out of the car and told him we would see him in the morning. We then walked up to the building's handsomely carved door, which was locked. I rang the doorbell, and after a moment, we were let in by a gentleman wearing a black business suit. He greeted us warmly and led us down a long entrance hallway and into a large room that was located at the end of the corridor. As we entered the room, we couldn't believe what we were seeing. Right there, in front of us, was one of the most bizarre sights that I had ever seen. Before we could even react, our escort seated us at a table in a centrally located booth.

The room was large and dark, with restaurant-style booths lining three of the room's four walls. A small, dimly lit lamp on each table provided the only lighting. Smaller café tables and chairs also circled the room's center piece—a large glass structure, a gigantic cube—brightly lit and fully furnished. It was a glass-walled "living room" with plush carpeting, chairs and sofas, a big-screen television, end-tables with lamps, and so on. And sitting, standing, and playing in this glass box living room were thirty-five beautiful young women…all wearing identical white uniforms.

The uniforms consisted of white socks, shorts, and polo-style shirts, with each girl sporting a large red number on the front and back of their tops, ranging from 1 to 35. The girls were laughing and talking with each other, watching TV, and reading popular magazines—acting as if they were at a slumber party, and seemingly oblivious to our presence. It was as if the girls were in a glass sorority house, and we (voyeurs) were watching them from our private tables in what appeared to be a night club rather than a sauna bath setting. It was incredible.

After a few minutes of staring in disbelief had passed, with neither of us saying a word to each other, the mama san (i.e. madam) of the establishment joined us at our table. She was an elegant, late-middle-aged woman, dressed in a gorgeous silk dress and totally bejeweled. She sat down next to me and summoned a waiter to take our drink order. Then she engaged us in small talk, asking us where we were from and how we liked Bangkok. After our drinks arrived, she asked us which of the girls struck our fancy. Looking right at us, she suggested numbers 14 and 27. I couldn't tell if she had assessed our personalities and was trying to match us up with girls based on her assessment of our "type," or if she was pushing certain girls that she wanted to rent for the evening, or if she was just making a friendly suggestion. But whatever her reason, she said, "You'll like these girls…They are very nice."

Bob and I just looked at each other. We were in a mild state of culture shock and were still rubbing our eyes in disbelief. To be honest, as much as I wanted a woman, I was having a little bit of difficulty dealing with this very strange scene and all its implications. But it didn't take me long to get over that.

We didn't respond immediately to the mama san's suggestions, but rather spent more time studying the girls. Finally, I said, "How about number 11?" Then Bob made his selection. As soon as we had spoken, she snapped her fingers and summoned an assistant, who in turn went to the door of the glass room and called out the girl's numbers. In a matter of minutes they were at our table.

The girls appeared to be shy and seemed as uncomfortable with the whole scene as we were. That actually put me at ease. The mama san temporarily left us alone with the girls, as we exchanged names and engaged in small talk. After a few minutes she reappeared and asked us if we were satisfied with our selections. Bob and I looked at each other and nodded in agreement. With that, she asked if we wanted a sauna and massage, or if we just wanted to pay for the girls and leave. The rather abrupt manner in which she asked the questions caught me off guard and made me feel a little uneasy. I looked at Bob and asked him what he wanted to do. He said he was ready to get out of there and paid the mama san his $35. I hesitated and decided to have a massage before leaving. After all, that's what you came to a sauna for, right?

We got up from the table and I said good-bye to Bob, telling him that I'd meet up with him and Gil in the morning. Then Nok (which she told me means bird) led me by the hand out of the room and down the corridor to a stairway leading to the second-floor sauna area. We entered a private room that was about the size of your average small bedroom. It had a bathtub against the far wall and a large platform table in the center. There were also a couple of chairs and a small table stacked with towels and massage oils. The room was dimly lit and smelled of oils and incense. While she drew me a bath, Nok started to undress me. Once naked, I stepped into the tub and she bathed me. After she was finished, I wrapped a towel around my waist and made my way to the massage table. I lay on my stomach while Nok lightly pounded her open hands up and down my back. And then, all of a sudden, she started giggling. "What's so funny?" I asked her. She put her hands up to her face, partially covering it, and whispered, "I don't know how to give massage."

The mama san was waiting for us by the front door as we were about to leave. Nok had her overnight bag in hand. I paid her the $35, and she told me that if I wanted to be with her for the week, Nok would take care of collecting the rest of the money. And with that, we were off. We grabbed a cab and made our way back to the hotel. The remainder of the night was spent remembering what it was like to be with a woman.

The next day we met up for breakfast late in the morning. Bob, Gil, myself and our three lady friends. It was a sight to behold. Gil, who was dressed in a silk robe and smoking a cigarette in an elongated cigarette holder, just sat there nodding his head with this shit-eating grin on his face as we all chatted. We told the girls that we planned to spend two more nights in Bangkok, and that we'd love to have them stay with us. They said (surprise) that they would like that. We planned to continue our touring during the day, while the girls went to the salon or shopping with the money we gave them (as we had learned was SOP from those who had come before us). We also had to pay the additional $70 each for two more days upfront (not a bad deal for a forty-eight–hour period), as the girls had to take the money to the mama san right away. Strictly business, you know.

At my suggestion, we decided that today we were going to tour Bangkok by boat, working our way through the city's many canals (as I learned, Bangkok is known as the Venice of the East). The sights along the waterways were amazing, encompassing all the images of the Orient that I had stored in my memory from books, travelogues, and movies. We passed temples constructed of colorful inlaid tile and gold that glistened in the sun. We passed villas and walled estates. We motored along beautifully landscaped parks where people were playing and relaxing. But most often, we passed through poor neighborhoods and shanty towns, with houses on stilts and women doing their wash on rocks alongside the waterways.

The canal system covers a great portion of the city. And like Venice, there are also a number of major waterways that are active with commerce. From water buses and tankers to boats and barges of all sizes and shapes, these vessels carried goods from the land and sea to marketplaces located throughout the city. It was a sight to behold, as there was nothing like it in our part of the world that I was aware of. We stopped on occasion to shop for souvenirs, or to sample some of the vast variety of local food that was being prepared and sold in the open air and even on some of the boats. Then we had a late lunch at an outdoor restaurant along the main canal and got a little drunk sipping Thai beer as we watched the parade of vessels float by.

That night, we took the girls out on the town for a dinner and floor show. We went to a place they selected, a dinner club that's popular with tourists. I guess it was a big deal for them to be seen at a place like this, especially with GIs on their arms. But I found the place to be somewhat tacky and a bit too "Western" to my liking. And after the great food that we'd been eating since arriving, I found the dinner to be mediocre at best. The show consisted of a dance orchestra and a presentation of traditional Thai dancing. A tuxedoed "Thai Jerry Lewis" served as MC.

The next day, while the girls again did their own thing, we did a final round of shopping and picked up the custom-made clothes that each of us had ordered. We then had John drive us to a dock at the main canal, where we picked up a water taxi to the city's recreational island park. We had reservations for lunch at one of the more popular tourist spots in all of Bangkok, an upscale outdoor café theater.

Large, brightly colored umbrellas covered each table at the café to shade patrons from the intense tropical sun and to protect against the rain when an occasional downpour occurred. The food was really good at this place, and while we ate, we enjoyed a show that consisted of Thai kick-boxing, traditional Thai dancing, and a cockfight.

After lunch, we strolled through the park, which also contained a small zoo. It was almost like a petting zoo, as many of the animals and birds had been domesticated and roamed freely within the confines of the park. Incredibly beautiful parrots and exotic birds in every imaginable color filled the trees, screeching in delight. A variety of species of monkeys were also frolicking in the trees and on the grounds. As we were walking down a pathway, an albino spider monkey swung down from a low-lying branch of a nearby tree right into my arms. He wanted me to swing him around as I grabbed his long, outstretched arms, just like a two-year-old would enjoy. His all-black, tiny leathery hands were a stark contrast to the long, pure white fur that covered his body. The experience was a real rush and endeared me even more to the charm and beauty of this land.

That night, which was our next to the last in Bangkok, was our last night with the girls before leaving for Pattaya Beach. We would have been content just going out to dinner and then going back to the hotel. But the girls wanted to go out again, because it was such a big deal to be seen with us. This time, they wanted to go to a movie. Gil, who was all dressed up in his new duds, and sporting his now trademark cigarette holder, wanted to go back to the nightclub where he had met his girl. So Bob and I and our girls piled into John's small car and headed to a movie theater, while Gil and Lan took a taxi to their destination.

John took us to a very residential section of the city, about a fifteen-minute drive from the hotel. The main attraction of this neighborhood was a large, three-screen theater complex situated on a square. The theater had a huge, wrap-around billboard promoting the three films being featured. The billboard was dominated by large painted faces of the stars and promotional copy written in Thai. All of the films were Thai productions, but they were subtitled in English. John dropped us off and said he would come back to the same spot in two hours.

As we were standing in a long line waiting to buy our tickets, a strange sensation came over me. I had the feeling that people were staring at us. I looked around, and sure enough, Bob and I were being stared down, not so much by the Thai women but by the men and mostly men our age. They were looking at us as if to say, "What are you doing with our women, you ugly Americans? You are ruining their lives and helping to destroy our culture. Go away…get the hell out of here." I suddenly became very self-conscious and a little paranoid. I had never had the feeling of not belonging before, at least not in a cultural sense. The girls were giggling and whispering to each other, apparently enjoying flaunting us in front of their men. Bob and I looked at each other. I could tell that he was uncomfortable as well. The movie was terrible…and so was the entire evening.

The next morning we said good-bye to the girls. We told them we'd look them up when we got back to Bangkok in three days, although we had no intention of doing so. We were off to a new location and new adventures and couldn't wait for our next tropical high (and thanks to the gift from the hotel manager, we had enough pot left to help get us there). We crammed our things into John's small trunk, put what didn't fit in between us in the backseat, and then headed south for Thailand's famous beaches along the Gulf of Siam.

The countryside on the drive south was spectacular in its beauty and diversity. We passed a Buddhist university with classic temple architecture not far outside the city limits and then drove for hours through lush farmland. From temples and villas to rice patties and small villages, we stayed glued to the windows for the five-hour drive to the beach. Along the way, John told us about Thai history and culture and gave us little tidbits of information as it related to what we were seeing. We stopped in a small village for a delicious lunch at a quaint little restaurant that John said was one of his favorites. He told us he always stopped here on his way to the beach, which was obvious by the way he was warmly greeted by the owner and staff. Drinks were on the house.

As we neared the resort area, the vistas became breathtaking. The foothills of nearby mountains gradually descended toward the sea. In their path were wide, sweeping beaches of pure white sand, lined with palm trees and other exotic flora. It was the most beautiful scenery I had ever laid eyes on, and I thought for sure that I had died and gone to heaven.

It was close to four by the time we arrived at our destination. The resort town of Pattaya Beach was relatively small and very charming (a friend who visits there frequently today tells me that it is now a large and booming metropolis). It reminded me of resort towns along the French and Italian Riviera that I had seen in travel brochures. We drove along the main street of the town until we came to a modern, all-white, tiered hotel that was built into the hillside. It looked like a villa that you would see overlooking the Mediterranean at Monte Carlo. We each got a room at the resort-inflated rate of $15 per night. After settling in, we took a long walk along the beach, occasionally mingling with some of the wealthy vacationers that had come to this paradise from around the world. Then we returned to the hotel, showered, and made our way out for dinner. John took us to a lively little place on the beach where we spent the rest of the evening—eating, drinking, gazing at the beautiful people, and soaking up the local culture. It was very pleasant, and we got very drunk.

The next morning I woke to the sound of surf, and to the sunlight that was streaming into the room. A gentle breeze was blowing the sheer white curtains that were filtering the warmth of the sun. I looked at my watch. It was eleven. I don't know what time we got back to our rooms, but we had apparently been sleeping off our hangovers. I was the first one to arise, and not wanting to waste any more of the day, I roused the troops. It was time to hit the beach for a day of sun and clear tropical waters.

Speaking of clear tropical waters, Bob and I definitely wanted to go snorkeling. Gil was afraid of the water, mostly because of the fish and anything else that might swim up to his legs. "I've never stepped foot in an ocean, and I certainly don't intend to start now," he told us. So Bob and I spent the afternoon laying in the sun, snorkeling in the warm waters of the Gulf of Siam, and walking the beach gazing at the array of beautiful natives and tourists who were there to worship this wonderland of nature. Gil went off "to do his own thing," whatever that might have been. That evening, we explored the village and shopped for souvenirs. Then we had a great dinner at a chic little restaurant, sampling more Thai food and making comparisons to its Vietnamese counterparts.

The next day we decided to charter a boat and cruise the sea and explore some of the small islands that dotted the horizon south of Pattaya Beach. As we were driving to the dock to meet up with our boat, I noticed a sign that read, "Scuba Gear - $5.00 A Day." Bob turned to me and said, "Let's do it." I thought about it for a second and then nodded in agreement. I asked John to take us back to the building where the sign was posted. Gil just kept shaking his head, saying, "I ain't gonna put no scuba gear on and jump into any damn water." Bob and I just laughed and told him he could stay in the boat and let us know if a man-eating shark was approaching us. At that point he asked John to take him back to the hotel, but we convinced him to come along, as the trip would be an adventure he could tell his friends about when he got back to Harlem.

As part of the rental agreement and waiver we had to sign, we got a five-minute demonstration on how to strap on the gear and use the oxygen. After that we were off, with gear in hand—and for only $5 each for the day. When we got to the dock, the boat was waiting. It was smaller than I had imagined, an elongated, wooden rowboat shaped sort of like a crescent moon, with a motor at one end. Sitting in the boat was our "captain," a pleasant-looking middle-aged man, and his eight-year-old son. Also in the boat was a gas can, a food basket, a few bottles of water, and various and sundry fishing gear. I presumed that while we were diving and doing our thing that papa san and his boy were going to do a little fishing. Gil looked very hesitant. We loaded the scuba gear and our backpacks into the back of the boat and then made our way out into the gulf. Before leaving, we told John to meet us back here at five, the time we were due back.

The day was really quite memorable. We brought our cameras and took quite a few pictures of our captain, Han, and his son, Nhut. They we as intrigued with us as we were with them, so we had a great day together. We spent a lot of time just cruising around, letting our hands fall into the warm water as we laid there soaking up the sun. After about an hour or so out on the water, we decided it was time to try a little scuba diving and asked Han if this was a good place to drop anchor. He nodded yes. As we put on the gear, Gil broke into giggles (he was a giggler rather than a laugher), pointing out how silly we looked. With our breathing apparatus in place, Bob and I jumped off the side of the boat into the water. Gil watched in amazement, while entertaining the boatman's young son by putting on some ridiculous hat that he had purchased in town. Gil loved to hold court.

We treaded water for a minute or so, until we got accustomed to breathing through the mouthpiece, then we dove under the water. Unfortunately (or fortunately, depending on how you look at it), we didn't get down very deep, as we had not learned how to de-pressurize ourselves for the descent. Even though we were wearing weight belts, we could only go down about ten feet before our ears started feeling the pressure. So that was the extent of the depth of our dive. I guess at the time we didn't realize how stupid we were to attempt scuba diving without instruction. But at the moment, it didn't seem to matter, for we were surrounded by incredible beauty…and sea life of all kinds. Maybe it was only glorified snorkeling, but it was still a trip.

After about forty-five minutes of playing in the water, Han took us to a nearby island for a late lunch. There were a couple of buildings on the island, including a modest open-air restaurant. So we sat in lounge chairs and enjoyed the view while our lunch was being "caught" and prepared. This must have been a regular routine for Han (and other boatmen like him, I would imagine), as he almost immediately caught us a large fish, which he gave to the cook at the restaurant to prepare for us. It was one of the most beautiful fish I had even seen. Its silver body was covered with florescent sky blue spots and was trimmed with electric yellow pin stripes. The fish was cleaned and cooked before our eyes on a rock fire pit on the beach. And it tasted wonderful. The cook served it with Thai vegetables, rice, and some incredible sauce. We washed it all down with warm Thai beer. After eating, we reclined on our lounge chairs for a while, held captive by the hot tropical sun and the lush island environment.

Before we knew it, it was four fifteen and time to go if we were going to make it back to the dock by five. So we put our towels and gear into our backpacks and made our way to the boat. It took us almost an hour to get back, for the sea was getting increasingly choppy, as the wind had been progressively picking up during the day. We said good-bye to Han and Nhut and thanked them for a great day. We gave an extra $10 to Han (the boat was $35 for the day) and put a $5 bill into Nhut's hand. His face lit up as he bowed and gave us this huge smile. It really made me feel good. And by the way, neither of them spoke English, but that didn't stop us from communicating with them with ease all day long.

Since this was our last night in Pattaya Beach, we really wanted to go out and party with the locals. And we were ready to meet some girls from the town as well (which I think Gil had already done the afternoon he went off on his own). John suggested the hottest bar and restaurant on the beach, a little spot on the outskirts of town that sat out over the water on stilts. The restaurant was open air, and the roof was made of bamboo, giving the whole place a real tropical look and feel. Attached to the restaurant was a large, circular bar favored by the locals. We got a table overlooking the water and started drinking Thai beer and rice wine. It was hot that night, and between the alcohol and the heat, I was sweating like a pig. But at least they had ceiling fans cranking away overhead.

As usual, we had a great dinner and again took advantage of the incredible seafood that was literally within our reach. After dinner, we made our way over to the bar, carved out a spot, and continued drinking Thai beer. After a few minutes, Gil excused himself to go to the men's room, and a short while later returned with three gorgeous women on his arm. I don't know how he does it, but he certainly has a way with women. I think part of it is that there aren't too many African-Americans in Thailand, especially outside of Bangkok. At any rate, we bought them a drink, and after a lot of laughter and merriment, we all went back to the hotel for one last fling in the exotic locale that is Pattaya Beach.

The next day, as soon as we could drag ourselves out of bed (the girls didn't spend the night, at least mine didn't), we checked out of the hotel and made our way back to Bangkok. We didn't feel much like eating when we got up, but about mid-way into the trip we started getting hungry and decided to stop for a bite. After a quick but tasty lunch, we headed back to the city for one last night on the town.

To avoid the girls we "left behind" tracking us down (they knew we were returning to Bangkok today), we checked into a different hotel for our last night in the city. The Siam Palace was a little closer to the center of the city…and to the action…and a little more upscale than our previous haunt. It was also at the inflated rate of $15 per night. After checking in and taking a quick shower, I ran out to do some last-minute shopping. I wanted to buy gifts for the guys who were going to be in my wedding party. The choices were endless, but I ended up buying brass beer mugs with handles shaped like dragons, and carved teak jewelry boxes. Fortunately, I had packed an empty duffle bag in my suitcase, anticipating that I might be bringing back a treasure trove of stuff. And by the time I left Bangkok, the duffle bag was stuffed.

That night we had a "farewell to Bangkok" dinner at one of the city's fanciest restaurants (jackets required, fortunately supplied by the restaurant). And afterward, we went to Gil's favorite—and only—night spot for a few drinks. We weren't there long before we noticed a group of young ladies eyeballing us. Bob and I toyed with the idea of scoring girls for the night, but decided against it when we looked at our watches, knowing what time we had to be up in the morning. Gil couldn't make up his mind, but wanted to hang around and hold court for a while longer, or as Bob and I saw it, to see what kind of trouble he could get himself into. So we wished him well and got up to leave. As we were walking out of the bar, I turned around to look at him one more time. The sight of Gil, cigarette holder in hand, surrounded by women, brought a smile to my face. Little did I know, but that would be the last time that I would see him—perhaps ever—so it's an image that's forever etched in my mind.

Getting up the next morning was tough. We had to be at the welcome center by ten to sign in and catch the bus to the airport, so Bob and I had arranged to meet for breakfast at eight. Before leaving my room to join him, I called Gil's room to see if he wanted to join us. There was no answer. At eight forty-five, we checked out and left the hotel. We had John drive us to the center, figuring Gil would show up there at some point. We said a very sad good-bye to John, and thanked him for a great week. We told him our Thailand experience wouldn't have been the same without him and gave him a generous tip that we had prearranged with each other. We also exchanged contact information, but I knew I would never see or hear from him again.

We reluctantly walked inside the welcome center, signed in, and waited to be called to the buses. We looked around, but still no Gil. Before long, we were on the road to the airport. Unlike the trip into the city, which was alive with conversation and unofficial briefings, the ride to the airport was deadly silent. You could tell everyone was depressed at the thought of leaving this paradise, especially with our destination being Vietnam. It was already like the whole thing never happened, like it was some sort of amazing dream. I felt especially bad for the guys who had to go back into combat.

We weren't at the airport more than fifteen minutes before they called our flight. We all trudged on board and, within minutes, were airborne for the short trip back to Ton Son Nhut. Gil never made the flight, but I'm sure he managed to talk his way out of whatever trouble he had gotten himself into. Even though I probably wouldn't run into him again in the Nam, I did have his address back in Harlem and planned to get in touch with him when I got back to the world.

After we landed, I said good-bye to Bob and promised to keep in touch and look him up when I moved to Bien Hoa. From there, I caught a ride over to the 1st Cav's 3rd Brigade Headquarters in Bien Hoa, to see if I could hitch a ride in a chopper back to Phuoc Vinh. It was either that or spend the night in Bien Hoa and wait for the next morning's C-130 shuttle flight to the base camp. As luck would have it, I was told that a warrant officer was flying a Loach back to Phuoc Vinh in one hour and that he had room for a passenger. So I hung around the airstrip and waited for my ride, sitting on my suitcase, watching the air mobile division come and go in a flurry of activity. And then, like a thunderbolt, it hit me. The familiar sound of a low-flying Huey overhead broke my reverie, catapulting me back to reality. I was back in the Nam. Fuck.

CHAPTER 12

Farewell to Phuoc Vinh

Just about an hour to the minute, a Loach approached and landed just in front of where I was sitting. I suppose the pilot knew I was the guy looking for a ride, as I was the only one around, and was sitting on the hard-sided suitcase that Cassidy had lent me, with a duffle bag at my side. He exited the aircraft and came over to help me with my bags. Even though he was a warrant officer, we greeted each other with a handshake and introduction rather than a salute. I asked him if he had room for me and the bags, and after looking them over, he responded, "Barely."

"What's inside that one?" he asked, pointing to the hard-sided suitcase. I looked down and noticed what had caught his eye. Apparently, sitting on the suitcase had caused the bronze Buddha statue that I had packed on top to create a protruding image of itself on the vinyl. Not wanting to explain my passion for Buddha art (as opposed to religious icons), I told him it was a metal sculpture that I had purchased on R&R. He gave me a strange look, then helped me load my bags behind the two seats of the small aircraft.

The ride back to Phuoc Vinh was exhilarating (I know…enough already with the superlatives about flying). Being the passenger in the small, bubble-front Loach (my first time riding in this particular helicopter), you really got the sensation that you were flying. The pilot kept the chopper fairly low, so we had great visuals of the terrain along the way. It was both beautiful and disturbing, flying over land that vacillated from beautiful countryside to bomb-cratered and defoliated areas that bore the scars of the war.

As we were landing, I noticed Tom waiting for me in his jeep. The pilot must have radioed ahead that I was onboard, and word must have made it to Headquarters Company. As soon as we landed, Tom pulled the jeep up to the chopper. I grabbed my bags and thanked the pilot for the ride. Tom helped me put my stuff into the jeep, then reached across the seat and gave me the now traditional handshake and a big "Welcome back!" I didn't say much on the short drive to the company area, as I was still in reverse culture shock.

As Tom and I walked into the hootch, we were greeted by Cassidy, who immediately descended upon me wanting to know every detail of my trip. As I unpacked, I started to fill them in. And then, later that night, as we did some partying to celebrate my return—the excuse du jour—I continued telling stories about my R&R experiences in Bangkok.

I didn't wake up the next morning until 0900 hours. Since I had been gone for more than a week, I didn't want to be too late for work. So I hurriedly took care of my bodily functions and got dressed. But before leaving for the office, I still had one more important thing to do. I had to update my short-time calendar for the days that I had missed while on R&R. My short-time calendar, which officially began at 100 days, was now down to **72 days** and a wake up. For the first time, I actually got the feeling that I was getting short.

As I walked through the door of the First Team Press Camp, I received a round of applause from the guys…and quite a bit of teasing about the satisfied look on my face. Then McKowen, who only had a week left in the Nam, came over and told me that Lieutenant Garcia wanted to see us. We went into his office and got the usual big Chicano smile from the lieutenant. Then he said, "Stoupman, I have some good news for you. You've just been named editor of the *Cavalier*." Even though there would only be one or two more issues before the division was withdrawn, it was Lieutenant Garcia's parting gift to me, as he was also leaving the Nam five days after McKowen. At this point, McKowen extended his hand and said, "Congratulations." I was caught off guard and didn't know what to say, so I just thanked them both and promised to continue the proud tradition of the press corps that they had made me a part of.

The place just wasn't going to be the same without those two guys. And to be honest, I wasn't looking forward to either of them leaving. McKowen had taught me just about everything I knew about journalism, and his were going to be some pretty big shoes to fill. And who knows what kind of person would be replacing the lieutenant. The fact of the matter was…there was no one who could replace him. He was one of a kind. But life had to go on, and at least the editor's position had a little prestige attached to it. And besides, I was getting short as well.

I left the lieutenant's office to another round of applause. I blushed…then quickly called everyone on the staff over to my desk. "There's going to be some new rules around here," I told everyone, with their facial expressions changing from smiles to "what the fuck." "Just kidding," I quickly retorted. "The real reason I called you all over was for an important assignment." Before anyone could say anything, I continued, "We have a *major* party to plan." And that, of course, was the joint going away party for Spec 5 McKowen and Lieutenant Garcia. And they were not only going home, but were getting out of the army as well. It was ETS for the both of them— the most beautiful acronym in the English language. Normally, we wouldn't be able to combine a party for an officer and a low-status NCO (E-5). But this was Phuoc Vinh, where rules were open to interpretation…at least most of the time. And we planned on interpreting this one our way.

The party was a blast—the biggest one I had been to yet, with more food and drink than I'd ever seen in the Nam. About two hundred people showed up…from a full bird colonel to hootch maids. It was a real tribute to Lieutenant Garcia, who was extremely well liked throughout the division. He had a way of making a lot of friends, and I think almost every one of them showed up for his farewell. Needless to say, as the evening progressed, a lot of people got pretty messed up but none more than Lieutenant Garcia. At one point, I thought we were going to get busted, because a couple of jeeps full of MPs pulled up. But as it turned out, they were sent to watch over us so no one got hurt or into serious trouble. I think Colonel Rogers sent them over (he was like a father to Joe Garcia). Imagine…being protected, rather than busted…by the MPs at a wild party. Only in Phuoc Vinh…and only for Lieutenant Garcia.

I stayed up all night with a group of hardcore partiers from the First Team Press Camp. After most of the outsiders left, we all got stoned while we watched Lieutenant Garcia fade into oblivion. He had really gotten wasted on Jack Daniels, his favorite beverage. Eventually, we carried him off to bed. And then, two hours later, it was time to put him in the shower and start pumping him with coffee. It was time to get him ready for his trip back to the world. The party was over.

63 days. March 10. I'm sitting here in my room, with my fan blowing on my face, listening to the Moody Blues *To Our Children's Children's Children* album. It's a very hot day here. And by the way, I hit eighteen months in the army today—that's halfway, unless I get an early out. And this Friday night we're going to have a big (twenty-second) birthday party for my roommate Cassidy, who's DEROSing in five days.

Two days into my new position, I had to fly to Lai Khe to do a story on an orphanage near there. Lai Khe was an old 1st Division (Big Red One) base camp, and just outside the old base camp was the Ben Cat Orphanage that housed nearly eighty children. The orphanage was supported by the Cav's 11th Aviation Group. And then, two days later, I got what would turn out to be my last field assignment in the Nam. I was given the opportunity to travel into the Central Highlands with one of the Cav's elite air mobile infantry units to write a story about the Montagnard. This group of indigenous people was gradually being wiped off the map thanks, in great part, to the war. Both the U.S. and South Vietnamese military used them almost like mercenaries, as scouts, and for front-line (in first) combat activity. Like Native Americans in our country, they were not part of mainstream society in Vietnam. Yet because their homeland was in the Central Highlands of South Vietnam, they were forced to participate in the war. And they had a reputation for being fierce and cunning fighters. But in reality, they were a gentle people who lived a primitive lifestyle, primarily working the land that they loved so much. The near destruction of their culture and homeland is another of the many tragedies of the Vietnam War.

SOME BACKGROUND (from Wikipedia): The Montagnard, also known as Degar, are the indigenous peoples of the Central Highlands of Vietnam. The term *Montagnard* means "mountain people" in French and is a carryover from the French colonial period in Vietnam. Originally inhabitants of the coastal areas of the region, they were driven to the uninhabited mountainous areas by invading Vietnamese and Cambodians beginning prior to the ninth century. In the mid-1950s, the once-isolated Montagnard began experiencing more contact with outsiders after the Vietnamese government launched efforts to gain better control of the Central Highlands. And following the 1954 Geneva Accord, new ethnic minorities from North Vietnam moved into the area as well. As a result of these changes, Montagnard communities (which at one time were comprised of thirty different tribes, with more than six ethnic groups, speaking a number of different languages) felt a need to strengthen some of their own social structures and to develop a more formal shared identity.

The Montagnard has a long history of tensions with the Vietnamese majority. While the Vietnamese are themselves heterogeneous, they generally share a common language and culture and have developed and maintained the dominant social institutions of Vietnam. The Montagnard does not share that heritage. There have been conflicts between the two groups over many issues, including land ownership, language and cultural preservation, as well as access to education, resources, and political representation.

As the Vietnam War began to loom on the horizon, both South Vietnamese and American policy makers sought to begin training troops from minority groups in the Vietnamese populace. The U.S. Mission to Saigon sponsored the training of the Montagnard in unconventional warfare by American Special Forces. These newly trained Montagnard were seen as a potential ally in the Central Highlands area to stop Viet Cong activity in the region. Later, their participation would become much more important as the Ho Chi Minh trail, the North Vietnamese supply line for Viet Cong forces in the south, grew. The U.S. military, particularly the U.S. Army Special Forces, developed base camps in the area and recruited the Montagnard, roughly forty thousand of whom fought alongside American soldiers and became a major part of the U.S. military effort in the Central Highlands. In 1967, the Viet Cong slaughtered 252 Montagnard in the village of Dak Son, home to some 2,000 highlanders. Known as the Dak Son Massacre, it was in revenge for the Montagnard's support and allegiance with the Republic of Vietnam.

Thousands of Montagnard fled to Cambodia after the fall of Saigon to the North Vietnamese Army, fearing that the new government would launch reprisals against them because they had aided the U.S. Army. The U.S. military resettled some Montagnard in the United States, but these evacuees numbered less than two thousand. In addition, the Vietnamese government has steadily displaced thousands of villagers from Vietnam's central highlands, to use the fertile land for coffee plantations. Outside of Southeast Asia, the largest community of Montagnard in the world is located in Greensboro, North Carolina.

The day trip to the Central Highlands (I avoided overnight trips to the field if at all possible) was exciting. There was combat activity in the area, but we were going to a supposedly "neutral zone," which was home to the country's largest concentration of Montagnard people. Like the trip to Song Be, we flew over mostly heavily wooded mountainous terrain. We also flew at a fairly high altitude to avoid the chance of catching enemy fire. When we arrived, we met up with an infantry company that was working in an area just outside the neutral zone. After a security briefing, they lead us toward the largest Montagnard village in the region, which was only meters away.

The village was located in a partial clearing inside a wooded area. As we entered, people stopped what they were doing and gave us big smiles. Many of them had mouths full of shiny gold teeth. The village itself was quite primitive—actually the most primitive sight I had seen in either Vietnam or Cambodia. Their dwellings were little more than grass huts, and their dress made them look more like natives of Africa or remote regions of South America than indigenous Vietnamese. They did their cooking on open fires in a common area and carried water from a nearby stream in buckets balanced on their heads. It was an amazing sight to behold.

Their agricultural skills, coupled with the fertile land, made them practically self-sufficient. But watching them farm, one had to wonder how they managed to thrive. Their tools and implements were crude, and everything was made and done by hand. They forged their own metal, constructed their own tools, and wove their own cloth. But they still needed some contact and trade with the outside world in order to survive. Through Vietnamese interpreters who knew their language, I interviewed a number of them. They were extremely friendly and happy to talk. Mostly, I asked them about the land or their families. But occasionally, I'd slip in a question about the war, just to get their response. The questions often went unanswered.

We didn't hang around the village very long. The infantry major that I rode along with needed to get back to Phuoc Vinh. He only brought me with him because Colonel Rogers made him do it. But at least he got to check in on his men; that I'm sure thrilled them. Before leaving, I purchased—for $2 in MPC—a beautiful, hand-woven bag from one of the Montagnard women. She was bare-breasted, deeply tanned, with glistening black hair and a large gold front tooth. She apparently made these bags for trade and found me an easy mark. It was a nicely designed woman's shoulder bag in bright yellow, red, and black colors. It would be another gift for Paula and a real keepsake. I then asked a young boy, who was standing nearby watching our interaction, to take a picture of me and the Montagnard woman. I made sure the bag was in the picture so that I could prove, someday in the future, that this bag did, indeed, come from a remote tribe of people known as the Montagnard from the Central Highlands of Vietnam.

52 days. March 21. The Montagnard story appeared in the *Cavalier* the following week. It was also picked up by the *Pacific Stars & Stripes*, which was another notch in my journalistic belt. Yes, life was good in Phuoc Vinh, and I was getting short. But then, just as I was getting complacent again, we got a bulletin from division headquarters. The 1st Air Cavalry Division would be vacating Phuoc Vinh by the end of the month—going home—except for the 3rd Brigade, which had already started the move to Bien Hoa. And the division was preparing a big stand down ceremony for March 27, which included a visit and speech from the Vietnam commanding general, General Creighton W. Abrams. CBS was supposedly going to be covering the ceremony, but thankfully, I have no role and nothing to do with it. Colonel Rogers told me that the IO was one of two critical posts that had to stay behind until the end.

He also informed me that he wanted the farewell issue of the *Cavalier* to be ready and into the hands of departing troops in eight days. The final regular edition, with the cover headline of "Skies Up," was already completed and at the printer. Completing the "Souvenir" issue on time was going to be tight, but everything was ready to go except for the cover. Tom, Cassidy, and most of the other guys were all going home. So it was going to be quite a full ten days, between completing the souvenir issue of the paper and a rash of going-away parties. And after that, I'd be packing my bags (again) and heading for Bien Hoa—to the real rear—where we would have hot showers, flushing toilets, and concrete buildings to live in. War is hell!

The next day, Colonel Rogers sent me to see Master Sergeant Will Haupt, who was in charge of the admin section. He would assure that my orders were cut to reflect the position I was promised by Lieutenant Garcia. When I got there, he informed me that the IO office in Bien Hoa would be staffed by three officers and 10 EMs, and that I would be the ranking enlisted man, as all the other E-5s and above were either going home, or were being reassigned in-country.

A new artist who had just been pulled in from the field helped me design a new front cover for the paper's commemorative issue. I wasn't happy with the one McKowen had come up with, and since he was gone, he'd never know that I changed it (until I mailed him a copy, that is). The newspaper was tabloid size, and we decided to use a full-page color photograph for the background. And what else would you put on the cover of an air mobile division's final edition other than a gaggle of Hueys flying in formation at sunset. Colonel Rogers loved the idea and gave me permission to arrange for it.

The next day, about thirty minutes prior to sunset, we had five Hueys fly overhead so we could do a series of test shots. One of the division's photographers, a guy named Jack Fish, was doing the photography honors. He was thrilled, as all he usually did was shoot award ceremonies and promotions. With our test shots completed and looking good, and with the sun in just about the right position on the horizon, I signaled for the Hueys to fly over us one more time. I was communicating with the lead chopper by radio. After all, I was a radio operator when I arrived at Phuoc Vinh, right? Then, precisely at the peak moment of sunset, the gaggle of choppers flew in our direction one more time. We got our shot, and the Hueys headed off…into the sunset. The whole experience was another mind blower…summoning a gaggle of Hueys to fly for a photograph. The next day I thanked the company commander of the aviation unit and asked him how much he figured it cost in time, manpower, and fuel for us to get our shot. He said about $20,000.

"Souvenir Issue" read the banner headline placed over the dramatic red color photo on the cover of the final edition of the *Cavalier*, which made it into the hands of the troops going home right on schedule. And that's where most of them were going, but not me. I was packing my bags for Bien Hoa. Within a week, most of the remaining troops would be airlifted to either Bien Hoa Air Base or to the air base at Cam Rahn Bay. The remaining troops would travel with what could be salvaged from the base camp in convoys. The Army of South Vietnam would probably take over much of Phuoc Vinh Base Camp, which I imagine meant their families would be moving in as well. And oh yes, the big stand down ceremony with General Abrams was cancelled at the last minute…hours before it was to happen. They decided, for security reasons, to move it to Bien Hoa. In its place, we had smaller stand down ceremonies, unit by unit, where each of us was awarded an Army Commendation Medal—my third.

The night before the airlift began, we—what else—partied. It was our last night to do so in Phuoc Vinh, and we were very melancholy about it. Those of us remaining knew that we would never experience a place like this again. And even though most of the guys were going home, it was a more retrospective than joyous occasion. We had formed close friendships here, and we had been through a war together…well, sort of. And we had experienced and shared a form of nirvana in the tropical setting of Southeast Asia. It was similar to the way I felt when I left Cu Chi, only a lot more intense. Because then it was only the relationships that I was going to miss. But now, it seemed that life in the Nam—at the best it could possibly be—was coming to an end. And I still had forty-two days left in the country.

41 days. April 1. We said our good-byes, promising to keep in touch, and went our separate ways. I was sitting outside my hootch, my bags next to me, in full uniform, waiting for the bus to pick me up. The heat was almost unbearable, hitting 100 degrees almost every day this week. And the humidity was almost as high. And the heat in Bien Hoa is even worse, I was told. Even though I'd been there many times, I wondered what life stationed in Bien Hoa would really be like. At that moment, the bus pulled up to where I was sitting and opened its doors. I would soon find out.

CHAPTER 13

Bien Hoa Sucks!

When the group of us who had been reassigned to the 3rd Brigade arrived in Bien Hoa, they were ready for us. No waiting, no paperwork, no replacement company. Our hootches were ready, our assignments were ready, and our "new rules" were posted in plain view. It was as if the lifers had nothing better to do than prepare for our arrival. They were salivating, as if we were fresh meat coming in for a feast. I was assigned to Detachment 5, CSSB, 3rd Brigade (Separate), 1st Air Cavalry Division (Air Mobile). It was an administrative unit that served what remained of the 1st Air Cavalry Division in Vietnam.

The first thing they had us do was line up in formation for roll call. Then Command Sergeant Major Robert Walker walked back and forth between each row, berating us as slobs and wimps. "I've never seen such a sorry lot of REMFs in my life," he barked. "You bastards had a party in Phuoc Vinh," he continued, "but the party's over. This is Bien Hoa. You're back in the rear now, gentlemen, and your life has just gone from bad to worse." Little did we realize at that moment just how true his words would ring.

He and the Headquarters Company commander, the soon-to-be infamous Captain Jim Stein, then proceeded to read us the riot act. One by one, we were told what we'd have to do to shape up. We were told to get haircuts, to starch our fatigues, and to polish our boots. Unofficial badges, pins, or whatever were literally ripped off our fatigue shirts and boonie hats. We were told that there would be a formation every morning at 0600 hours. And we were told to check the company bulletin board daily for detail and guard duty assignments.

My stomach began to churn, and I had this sinking feeling. Sure, I was getting short and would only have to tolerate this abuse for a relatively brief period of time. But after Phuoc Vinh, this was not only depressing—it was scary. Those of us who had just come from paradise kept looking at each other. We were in shock. How were we going to endure this? I had a feeling it was going to be worse than Cu Chi had ever been.

We were then dismissed to settle into our hootches. I was assigned to an admin hootch right in the center of the company area. Fortunately, I ended up with a great bunch of guys—compatriots who would help me get through these final days and all this bullshit. There was Mike Dillenger, an admin clerk who would become my best friend. Chuck Colby, a scout dog handler (working with the MPs) from Arizona. There were also two legal clerks, Randy Gerard and Bill Reilly, and an assortment of others, including a cook, two intelligence clerks, and another admin clerk who worked with Mike. The hootches were larger than the ones at Cu Chi and Phuoc Vinh. They were almost like state-side barracks, but with that personalized Vietnam ambiance. Like most hootches in the Nam, they had dividers for privacy, most with two-man compartments. Decoration and personalization was still permitted, but only within the realm of a hard-to-define military acceptability.

I was to share a two-man compartment in the hootch with Mike, who was from East Lansing, Michigan. He had been with the 3rd Brigade since coming to the Nam five months ago and had been stuck in Bien Hoa the whole time. This was good (for me), as he knew the ropes and the personalities. His knowledge and experience would not only be invaluable in helping to guide me through the bullshit, but also for letting me know who and what to avoid.

They gave us the rest of the afternoon off to unpack and settle into our hootches, but they expected us to report to work the next day at 0700 hours, giving us an hour to eat and get ourselves together after the 0600 hours formation. Mike had the afternoon off as well, so we got to know each other while I unpacked. He was also a college graduate and shared my opinions about the war and the military. He filled me in on life in Bien Hoa and how it had become increasingly intolerable since he arrived. He said that ever since the troop reduction had been announced, the lifers had become "ungodly miserable." From the perspective of many of the lifers, it was bad enough that they were stuck in the rear. But now they also had to put up with an increasing number of short-timers from the field, and these guys were coming to Bien Hoa with an attitude. They were either coming from places where they had been able to do their own thing (like Phuoc Vinh), or they were coming in from the stress of combat. In either case, these guys were short, and they didn't want to deal with any army bullshit. Obviously, this irritated the lifers, who felt it was their mission to whip these guys back into line. And this, in turn, pissed off the troops who felt it was their due to spend their last days in the Nam in a hassle-free environment. The entire situation was explosive, which made my final days in the Nam interesting, to say the least.

After I finished unpacking, I asked Mike to walk me over to the PIO office to show me where I would be working. It was in a barracks building that had been converted into offices. I walked in and introduced myself and learned that I would be working with a number of admin people, as the information function for the division was considerably smaller at brigade level. I also met my boss, Captain Len Aulen, the brigade information officer. He appeared to be harmless enough, a noncareer officer who was content biding his time in the rear. I was assigned a desk and a typewriter and was told that I'd be responsible for putting out a bi-monthly newspaper called *Gary Owen* (the nickname of the 3rd Brigade), as well as continuing my work producing Command Information Programs. As I looked around at the sullen faces of my co-workers, the windowless office building suddenly took on a prison-like persona. The whole scene was depressing, especially when compared to the First Team Press Camp.

Mike then walked me around the brigade area to orient me to the place. It was large and totally "urban." There was row after row of barracks buildings, a number of office buildings, and a myriad of other structures housing motor pools, flight operations, supply, and the like. There were also clubs and restaurants nearby, many of which I was familiar with. But unlike Cu Chi and Phuoc Vinh, there were no outdoor, hole-in-the-ground urinals or latrines. Instead, there were indoor showers and toilets. Now one would think that after coming in from the field that this would be an improvement. Theoretically, yes. But unfortunately, there was seldom any hot water. And most of the plumbing was in a constant state of disrepair, which meant that quite often the toilets didn't flush. Needless to say, this made entering these facilities almost unbearable. In fact, the situation had become so bad, according to Mike, that they were considering digging some outdoor latrines.

Dinner in the mess hall that night was also an experience. We didn't get there until almost 1800 hours (dinner was from 1630 to 1830), and by the time we arrived there was little left to choose from. It looked like a typical state-side mess hall, with a lot of stainless steel and attitude. I made the mistake of commenting about the lack of selection, after which the cook proceeded to tell me that if I wanted selection I should have showed up earlier, and that if I didn't like what I saw, I could get the hell out of his kitchen. I could see that my final forty days in this hell-hole were going to be less than pleasant. Mike also cautioned me to be selective about what I ate, as a number of guys had come down with stomach problems from the food. He said they had complained to the CO about it, but to no avail. The CO said the problem wasn't the food, but the weak stomachs of a bunch of spoiled, wimpy soldiers.

That night, a bunch of Mike's friends came over to the hootch to hang out and listen to music. The camaraderie was a pleasant respite from an otherwise scary day. I got to know the guys in the hootch, as well as Mike's friends who congregated with us. They were a good bunch of men…all caught up in the same miserable situation. And, as they say, misery loves company. But there was something different about this gathering. I knew from my Nam experiences that most of these guys were probably heads, yet no one had pulled out a joint or a bowl. I turned to Mike and asked him what was up with that, and he confirmed my suspicions. Indeed, most of the guys were heads or, worse, junkies. But he told me we had to wait until the lifers had either gone to bed or were sufficiently sloshed at the NCO or Officer's Clubs before we could openly do our thing.

Bien Hoa had become a real (military) police state, and one had to exhibit extreme caution, I was told. Like the rest of the Nam, a lot of dope was smoked in Bien Hoa. But it generally couldn't be done in the open, and scoring the stuff was getting more and more difficult. The military was accelerating its crack down on drugs (after all, I had just completed a three-part series on drug abuse for the 1st Cav). And, of course, pot was the easiest target. It was bulky, and it had a distinct smell when burning. Heroin, on the other hand, was cheap and easily smuggled in. And unfortunately, more and more guys were getting hooked. Between the trauma of combat for those who had experienced it, the frustration and the bullshit of the rear for those who had to endure it…and the easy access and low prices…heroin was becoming the drug of choice…and escape…for many. And this was not only a bad situation, it was also a very sad, sad situation.

At approximately 2300 hours it was determined that it was safe to partake. One by one, the guys in the hootch went for their stashes, which were hidden in some pretty ingenious places. As the smorgasbord of pot and paraphernalia was laid out, Chuck told the story about the time he had his stash hidden under a loose floor board in the hootch and how one day, when he went to retrieve it, he saw that his bag was nearly empty, with a big hole at one end. Next to the bag was a large rat laying on its side, breathing heavily, with teeth exposed in what appeared to be a grin on its face. Needless to say, he changed the location of his hiding place and put the rat out of its "misery."

I had brought an ounce of some dynamite pot with me from Phuoc Vinh, but it didn't seem to be needed that night, as everyone else seemed to have at least that much. The guys helped me brainstorm as to where I might hide my stash, and we agreed on a dry spot in one of the ammunition boxes outside of the hootch. We then proceeded to party into the wee hours, grooving on the music and enjoying each other's company. We forgot about the bullshit of Bien Hoa for a little while as we laughed and got silly on the weed. But we were also very cognizant of where we were, and where we could have ended up. Even with all the bullshit of Bien Hoa, we were thankful that we were assigned to the rear.

The next day, after our 0600 formation and my new morning rituals, I found myself back behind a typewriter. Only this time it had the feeling of being a real nine-to-five (actually a seven-to-four) job. Rather than a lot of story and feature writing, which was the mainstay of my existence at Phuoc Vinh, I now spent most of my time chronicling 3rd Brigade activity, which entailed compiling combat and military statistics, making withdrawal announcements, and writing army propaganda from directives. *Stoup's Scoop* and other light features were gone, as there was no place for humor in any of these publications. Occasionally, I'd get to report on the infrequent activity that was going on in the field. And then there were the always-optimistic reports on Vietnamization, and the success we were having turning the war over to the South Vietnamese, which was more army propaganda, as we would learn long before the fall of Saigon in 1975.

But one evening, an out-of-the-ordinary Nam-routine experience did occur. After dinner and a couple of beers at the EM club, Randy, Bill, Mike, and I went back to the hootch to determine if it was safe to indulge in our favorite pastime. When we got there, however, Randy said he had a surprise for the four of us. It seems that a friend of his back in the world had mailed him a little treat, and he wanted to share it with us. It was four tabs of blotter acid. Well, needless to say, this put an entirely different slant on the evening! It was the first time I had come across LSD in the Nam, and I had never taken, or should I say tripped, on acid…and neither had Mike. The two of us looked at each other, shrugged our shoulders, and said, "What the fuck." But I was cautious, and a little nervous, so I said I only wanted to take a half a tab. Mike agreed.

We put on some Janis Joplin (which we thought was appropriate for the occasion) and "dropped." Then we sat around and told stories about our lives and exploits while we waited for it to kick in. Randy also lit a joint and passed it around. Before long, our stories became increasingly amusing, or so it seemed. We began laughing at just about anything that anyone said. Then we became silly…telling silly jokes…and relating silly stories. And then everything became hysterically funny. We were laughing so hard that we were crying. I pulled a small American flag out of my pocket that I carried with me to dry my eyes. And for what seemed like at least an hour, we laughed at each other's stories, almost to the point of exhaustion. But then, almost as suddenly as it had started, our moods changed direction. We became quiet and introspective. The music and our conversation became "significant." And at one point, we just looked at each other, as if to say, "Where the hell are we? And how the fuck did we get here?"

I got up after a while and walked outside. I sat on top of the ammunition boxes that formed a small wall around the hootch. It was a beautiful evening, and the stars in the sky seemed brighter and clearer than I had ever seen them. As I sat there, I contemplated the mysteries of the universe, and thought about all the problems facing people everywhere. The solutions for solving these problems seemed so simple in my mind. And then, out of the corner of my eye, I noticed one of the company dogs, a medium-size collie mix, walking toward me. I got down off of the wall and crouched down to pet him. As I did so, he sat down and looked up at me, as if with knowing eyes. I started talking to him about the problems of the world, and the craziness of the Nam. And he responded to me by making the kind of sound that a dog makes when it tries to talk back to you. Not a bark or a whine, but the kind of sound a dog makes when it tries to talk. You know the sound. Anyway, at that moment I felt as if this dog understood what I was saying, and that we were actually communicating with each other. I felt a real spiritual bond with this animal, as if our two species were united. It was unlike anything I had ever experienced.

I eventually went back into the hootch. By this time, everyone was in their own space, so I laied down on my bunk and closed my eyes. Pinwheels of vibrant colors entertained me until I fell asleep.

33 days. April 9. I just learned from Captain Aulen that the Command Information Program for the quarter that I had been laboring on for quite some time had been "shelved" by LTC Wise, the battalion commander, and wouldn't be distributed to the troops. It appears he had some issues with the content, which had been determined by Colonel Rogers before the withdrawal from Phuoc Vinh. Some of that content pertained to the root causes of drug abuse in the army (most of which I pulled from the series of interviews I conducted with 1st Cav brass at Phuoc Vinh, and my subsequent series of articles in the *Cavalier*). I guess he was a little uncomfortable with some of the findings, such as low morale being one of the root causes of drug use among the troops, since the morale in his AO was extremely low. Oh well, at least I won't have any CIP's to write again before I leave the Nam.

I just looked at my calendar. It's Good Friday. I didn't even know it was Holy Week, or that this Sunday is Easter, so you can see how religious the scene is over here. And there was a little excitement in the brigade area today, as an NBC camera crew was here filming soldier's reactions to Nixon's recent announcement about more troop reductions. I got to accompany them, but didn't get a chance to "talk" to them as I had with the CBS crew in Phuoc Vinh, as Captain Aulen also came along. And you can imagine the kinds of comments the troops were making—about Nixon, the war, and the army. Let's put it this way, most of the comments would never see the light of day or make the news back home.

Essentially, I didn't leave Bien Hoa, except for occasional trips to MACV headquarters in Long Binh to interview the brass or deliver IO paperwork for approval. On one trip to MACV, I had an interesting and somewhat enlightening experience. One of the admin clerks who accompanied me (he was delivering a 3rd Brigade personnel report to the chief of administration), asked me if I wanted to see something that would blow my mind. "Of course," I responded, asking him what it was. After we had completed our tasks, he said, "Follow me." He led me to the building's elevators and pushed the button for the top floor. Since we were already cleared to be in the building, we had no problem going to an otherwise restricted area. As the doors opened, he led me down a hallway and through an open door that led to the general's private dining room. Since it was well before noon, the room was empty, except for one staff person preparing the tables for lunch. I couldn't believe my eyes. I might as well have entered the main dining room at the Plaza Hotel in New York. Fine linens, crystal glassware, silver flatware, and fine china were placed on each of the ten round tables in the room. Silk drapery covered the windows, and plush carpeting in red and gold covered the floor. Upon closer examination, we noticed that each piece of china was not only trimmed in gold, but featured a red flag emblem with two gold stars, indicating that the service that day was for a two-star (major) general. (Ironically, the current flag of the Republic of Vietnam features a gold star on a solid red background.) I can't say that I was totally surprised, but this sight, in my estimation, reinforced the notion of an out-of-control military command living like kings in the fiefdom they had created for themselves over the course of the war in Vietnam. I grabbed a small dish (presumably that held pats of butter) as a souvenir, put it in my fatigues trousers, and we high-tailed it out of there. (And incidentally, that piece of military "memorabilia" sits on my desk to this very day.)

Like my latter days at Cu Chi, and to some extent, Phuoc Vinh, I was fortunate enough to make it to Saigon periodically to put together the paper. But otherwise, my daily routine was predictable and seldom veered from the norm. I'd get up in the morning and drag myself to formation. Then I'd put up with the stench in the latrine and take a cold shower. Then it was off to the mess hall for a breakfast that usually consisted of cold cereal (safe) and whatever fruit was available and edible. Then I'd arrive at the office by 0715, do a little writing, read whatever magazines and newspapers I could get my hands on, and shoot the shit with my fellow desk jockeys. When work ended at 1600 hours, I'd go back to the hootch to relax, write letters, and listen to music. After a dinner that ranged from "OK" to stomach turning, it was back to the hootch to spend the evening with the guys. Except for the details and guard duty that were occasionally thrown into the mix, that's how we spent most of our days in Bien Hoa.

30 days. April 12. Thirty days has September, April, June and…*me*! Eleven months down…one to go.

Here is an excerpt from a letter home written on this day:

> After tonight, no more months left, only 29 days. It is finally coming, and believe me, it's driving me up a fucking wall. I am going nuts. I can't eat, which is nothing new for me over here. I can't smoke (cigarettes), because I promised myself I wouldn't anymore. I'm pissed off because I haven't heard from you for so many days. But I'm not really pissed off at you, just at the fucking situation. I mean, I'm so sick of letters that I can hardly sit down to write one anymore. I've had it with romance on paper. Thirty days is so damn long, yet it's so short. You are so damn close, yet so far away. This is a really horrible period…

There was one incident that occurred a few weeks after my arrival that did cause some excitement outside the norm. In just about every war, the Red Cross, in addition to its presence at USOs, has sent volunteers to the field to help boost morale among the troops. Most of these volunteers were women known as Donut Dollies. I think they got that nickname during World War II, because they were best known for bringing coffee and donuts to the troops in the field. And that was primarily what they did in Vietnam as well. The Red Cross would send them into the field to bring newspapers, magazines, refreshments, and "conversation" to the troops. They would fly them into outlying base camp areas to be with the troops for a few hours, then would fly then back to the rear. But with very little action occurring in the field these days, most of the remaining Donut Dollies worked the big base camps in the rear.

Even though the efforts and intentions of these (mostly young) women were appreciated, many of the troops considered them a tease. I mean, imagine what went on in the minds of guys out in the field who'd been dealing with the war and military bullshit for months without seeing a woman (other than the locals). Then, as an intended morale builder, the army flies in two or three young lovelies—in little striped uniforms—to bring them goodies and conversation. Even though the troops considered this a nice diversion, many of the guys just looked at them with lust in their eyes. It was only normal.

But working with the troops in the rear was a little different. For one thing, these girls also lived in the rear—in Red Cross compounds—which means they also occasionally mingled with, and in some cases even dated, some of the guys. To make a long story short, one of these girls was raped and murdered in Bien Hoa not too long after my arrival. Based on initial evidence gathered at the crime scene by military and civilian investigators working on the case, a profile of a suspect was drawn up. The man they were looking for was a Caucasian, in his early twenties, approximately 5'9" tall, and weighing about 150 lbs. Well, I fit that description to a tee, and therefore became a "general suspect" in the case (along with hundreds of others). I had to go to MP headquarters to be photographed, palm printed (they found a palm print at the murder site), and interviewed. But that was the extent of it. A few weeks later they caught the guy, convicted him in a general court martial, and sent him to prison for life. The incident provided a little added excitement in an otherwise mundane rear echelon existence.

Even though the lifers attempted to maintain control and keep the upper hand through their formations, haircut and uniform inspections, and the like, the troops in Bien Hoa were as testy and independent as any that I'd seen. There was a lot of insubordination and attitude, a lot of sick calls, and a lot of goofing off. A good deal of this behavior was basically ignored, because the lifers just didn't know how to handle it. For example, a lot of guys would just take off on weekends for Saigon or for the beach at Vung Tau, the popular and beautiful beach resort town just to our east. Coincidentally, the next-to-the last issue of the *Cavalier* featured a cover story on Vung Tau, which, along with China Beach near Da Nang, was the most popular in-country R&R spot throughout the Vietnam War period. And these guys would stay for days, even though they knew they'd be counted as AWOL. Or they would extend their overnight or weekend passes by a day or two, also making them AWOL. They just didn't give a shit, and they knew that chances were they'd only get a reprimand, or extra details, when they returned, if that. And so many guys did this that many of the lifers just turned their heads the other way, for it would have made them look bad if they actually reported the number of AWOLS of men in their charge. Most guys could have cared less what their military records looked like, just as long as they got that honorable discharge. The lifers, on the other hand, cared a great deal about their military records.

Yes, just as the lifers told us the day we arrived, our lives at Bien Hoa base camp were, indeed, progressing from bad to worse. For a while, with morale near rock bottom, some of us tried to improve base conditions and communications with the lifers by establishing an "Enlisted Men's Council." But they cancelled the council after less than a month without giving us a reason, which just amplified the morale problem. We knew the lifers were an unhappy lot, but it pissed us off that they were taking it out on us.

On top of the military's frustration at having to withdrawal from a war that they knew they were probably going to lose, they also had to deal with another situation they couldn't control, a major drug problem among the troops. Drug use, primarily in the form of marijuana (for relaxation) and speed (to stay alert and awake on combat missions, not to mention the buzz), had always been a part of the Vietnam War culture. But now there was also a rapidly growing problem with hard drug use, and the military's ineptitude in handling the situation only made it worse.

The big "crackdown" started after a documentary about drug use in Vietnam appeared on network television in 1970. The program exposed the extent of drug use among the troops in Vietnam to the American public, which in turn created an outcry in Congress. And as a result, the military was forced to move into action to combat the problem, which is one reason why the 1st Cav had me write that series of articles for the *Cavalier* and a Command Information Program on the subject. It was another war they thought they could win, but ultimately did not, because the fundamental problem wasn't just drugs. Rather, it was a complex set of issues around "just cause" and morale, cause and effect. It was the folly of forcing hundreds of thousands of men, through conscription, to participate in a war that they not only didn't want to fight, but more fundamentally, that they didn't believe in. And drugs, as we all know, provide a means to escape from reality.

Even though the military experienced some success in their crack down on the use of pot, they were having a harder time dealing with the heroin problem. For one, it was flooding through base camp gates at an alarming rate. Even though they were inspecting people and packages coming in and going out, small vials of skag were easy to smuggle. The price was also dirt—about $10 per vial—and the addiction was quick and strong. GIs who couldn't fight its grip succumbed easily, and more and more addicts were being created. It should also be pointed out that North Vietnam and the Viet Cong had become increasing aware of the GIs affinity for drugs as the war years progressed, and thus were supplying drugs to the South in increasing quantities, especially heroin, as a tactic to incapacitate U.S. troops.

In the final years of the war, the more frustrated (some of) the lifers became, the more they took it out on the troops. And the more they took it out on the troops, the more the troops fought back by means of insubordination, AWOLs, drug use, or worse (i.e., fraggings and outright murder). It was a no-win situation. And toward the end, it caused a near collapse of esprit de corps among the troops remaining in Vietnam.

So as the crackdown ensued, and those of us who basically did our jobs and played the game as directed, only wanting to smoke a little pot every now and then, suffered. For the first time since arriving in Vietnam, getting pot was actually becoming difficult. We still scored, of course, but we had to be crafty and ingenious in order to succeed undetected. The lifers constantly tried to "get" the heads, and those who were suspected of being pot heads were constantly harassed. They'd use tactics like moving guys from hootch to hootch in an attempt to separate those who were suspect of being heads from the "good soldiers." I can remember the irony, as we'd walk through the company area at night in search of someone with a joint, practically tripping over the empty vials or skag that were strewn all over the ground.

Then, one night, something happened that really got our goat. I can remember it vividly, as I had just reached **25 days** on my short time calendar. At 0200 hours, all the lights in our hootch were thrown on, and we were invaded by a band of do-good lifers—led by our company commander. They got everyone out of bed and made us empty the contents of our trunks, drawers, duffle bags, and anything else we had containing our possessions, onto the floor of the hootch. Under the guise of a "health and welfare" inspection, they went through all of our possessions. It was quite obvious that they were looking for drugs, even though they wouldn't admit it. Of course, we were ready for them, as we suspected something like this might happen one of these days. Our small supplies of pot were well hidden, and they didn't find anything, which pissed them off even more.

The next morning at formation, the "straw that broke the camel's back" was dropped. We were told that we had to spend the rest of the day taking down all dividers and partitions in the hootches, turning them back into big, open spaces. "You assholes just lost all your privacy," Captain Stein barked. "From now on, every move you bastards make is going to be out in the open. And anyone who gets caught breaking any regulation is going to have hell to pay."

We all just turned and looked at each other. Nobody said a word, but the look of shock and frustration was written on everyone's face. I didn't know about anyone else, but I was pissed, and I wasn't going to let Stein and his cronies get away with this. If he wanted to play games, then we'd play games right back. As far as I was concerned, this was war. And unlike the Vietnam Conflict, this was a war that we were going to win. I had a plan and couldn't wait to get back to the hootch to discuss it with the guys.

CHAPTER 14

Article 138, Uniform Code of Military Justice

There were essentially two people that I wanted to go after: Lieutenant Colonel John Wise, the CSSB battalion commander, and Captain Jim Stein, the Detachment 5 commanding officer. Even though we were also constantly hassled by Command Sergeant Major Bob Walker, we had no real beef with him. Basically, he was a harmless lifer who was just doing his job the only way he knew how to do it. It was his job to keep us all in line, sort of like a father does with his kids when they misbehave—strong discipline with a lot of caring. He didn't initiate policy, but rather followed the orders given to him by Wise and Stein. It was Stein who really made our lives miserable, and it was Wise who was the unenlightened man at the top of the chain-of-command who let it all happen.

Captain Jim Stein was a real bastard, the kind of lifer you loved to hate. He was tall, with fine blond hair that he had cut into the quintessential military buzz. His face was pock-marked from childhood acne, and he was built like a brick shithouse. He was less than highly intelligent, which probably explains why he was only a captain at this stage of his ten-year career. And he had a real nasty disposition. You could tell that he was bitter about being assigned to the rear and frustrated as hell that he had to deal with the caliber of REMFs that were under his command.

Maybe at this stage of my tour, after having made three moves, I was also frustrated—and a little more than irritated at having to serve under the likes of this asshole. But whatever the reason, I decided to take it upon myself to get back at this guy. It became my personal mission and, I hoped, would be my parting shot at the military before exiting Nam. We had tried to communicate with the lifers, but were ignored. We complained about the lousy conditions, but to no avail. So now it was time to take matters into our own hands, and I had an "ace in the hole" to help us do just that.

When I got back to the hootch after formation to begin the task of dismantling our partitions and privacy walls, I pulled Mike aside and told him I had a plan to get back at Captain Stein and his cronies. I reached for my wallet and took out a folded piece of paper that I had kept there since arriving in the Nam. I read it to him:

Article 138, Uniform Code of Military Justice

> Any member of the Armed Forces who believes himself wronged by his commanding officer, and who, upon due application to that commanding officer, is refused redress, may complain to any superior commissioned officer, who shall forward the complaint to the officer exercising general court-martial jurisdiction over the officer against who it is made. The officer exercising general court-martial jurisdiction shall examine into the complaint and take proper measures for redressing the wrong complained of; and he shall, as soon as possible, send to the Secretary concerned a true statement of that complaint, with the proceedings had thereon.

Mike wasn't quite sure what it meant, or what I had in mind, so I explained it to him. I reminded him that we had registered our complaints and unhappiness with base conditions to the company commander and had been ignored. That we had attempted to communicate our concerns through the Enlisted Men's Council, and Stein's response was to disband it. So now, through Article 138, we had the means to go over his head—right to the brigade commander.

Mike still wasn't sure what I had in mind, so I continued. "I want to submit a formal complaint against this guy, but I don't want to do it alone. There's strength in numbers, and I'd like to get the whole company to initiate proceedings." He just looked at me like I was crazy. "I want you to help me organize a meeting of all the guys in the company. We'll have it tonight, after the lifers come through the company area for the last time."

"But won't a gathering of the whole company attract the kind of attention we don't want?" Mike asked. "It sounds too risky to me, especially the way they've been on us lately," he continued. I thought about it for a minute and decided he was right. "Then what we'll do is go from hootch to hootch. Just let the guys know that something's up, and that we'll be around to tell them about it later tonight."

Of course, this whole conversation was taking place while we were dismantling what little privacy and civility we had left. As each wall and partition in the hootch came down, my resolve to get back at the lifers intensified. When we were finished, Mike went off to start spreading the word about the "secret meetings" we'd be having that night, while I went over to talk to Randy Gerard, one of the legal clerks who lived in the hootch. I recalled a conversation I had with Randy shortly after arriving in Bien Hoa. He told me that one of the brigade lawyers, a Captain Richard Feldesman, hated the army as much as we did, mostly because he resented the fact that he got a gig in the Nam rather than a cushy stateside position. He told me during that conversation that Feldesman would be a good person to go to if any of us ever got into trouble. So I briefly explained to him what I was up to and asked him if he thought Captain Feldesman would be sympathetic to our cause and give me some unofficial counsel. He said he thought he would, which brought a smile to my face. I told him that if I— or rather we— were going to pull this off, that we definitely were going to need some legal advice.

I left Randy and made my way to the adjutant general's office to look up Captain Feldesman. Fortunately, when I got there, he was the only one in the office. He was sitting with his feet up on his desk, reading a copy of *Playboy*. "Captain Feldesman," I said, as I saluted him. "I'm Specialist Jim Stoup, and I was wondering if I could have a minute of your time." He waved off my salute as being unnecessary and said, "Sure...what's on your mind." I proceeded to tell him about the lawyer I had met when I first got to Vietnam, and how he had given me a copy of Article 138 from the UCMJ to hold onto for future reference. I explained to him what he had told me about Article 138 and how to use it if necessary. I then proceeded to tell him about the unbearable conditions we were living under (which he was well aware of) and about the official and unofficial harassment we were being subjected to on an almost daily basis. I told him how Stein had ignored our complaints and attempts at communication and how he had disbanded the Enlisted Men's Council. In short, I told him we felt that we had the grounds to initiate a formal complaint, using Article 138. For what seemed like an eternity, Captain Feldesman just sat there looking at me, but it felt as though he was staring right through me. He was obviously deep in thought. And then a big grin came across his face, and he said, "Specialist...I think you're on to something."

Feldesman said it wouldn't be safe talking in the office, as someone could walk in and ask what I was doing there. So we went outside and got into the AG's jeep and drove around the base while we conversed. I explained my plan—the list of grievances I had compiled and how I thought it would be more effective to have the entire company (or as many as possible) initiate the proceedings. He agreed, but pointed out that it is illegal to "petition" in the military. And by having everyone sign a document, it would be considered the same as a petition. But he advised that by having an individual signature page for each member of the company, it would be interpreted legally that each person was individually initiating the proceeding.

That was exactly what I needed to know and wanted to hear, and I thanked him profusely for the information. As we pulled back into the company area and alongside the AG office building, he went on to say that he would be happy to review what I put together to assure that it would be legally viable. But he said that we'd have to be very clandestine about it and cautioned that we should not be seen together. It would also be critical to our success, he pointed out, that his "touch" be undetectable. And, of course, if questioned, he'd deny any knowledge or involvement. As I got out of the jeep, I gave him a snappy salute and said, "Yes, sir!" Then I yelled over my shoulder that I'd be back in touch as I practically ran the entire way back to the hootch. I could barely contain my excitement, and couldn't wait to tell the guys.

Late that night, Mike and I paid a visit to the various hootches within Detachment 5. I explained to the guys in each hootch what Article 138 was all about and how it provided us with a vehicle, not only to air our grievances, but to get back at Captain Stein and Lieutenant Colonel Wise for all the bullshit they've been putting us through. As Mike took notes, we gave everyone the opportunity to tell us about any injustices they might have experienced and to list any complaints they had about base camp conditions. We then took an informal poll to see how many guys were willing to sign a document initiating a formal complaint against our leaders. We wanted to gauge our support at this point in the process to see if we were, indeed, going to have strength in numbers. We asked those who were hesitant to think about it, as it was going to take us a couple of days to get the document ready. But with only one or two exceptions, our initial support was almost total.

Feeling good about what we had just accomplished, Mike and I made our way back to the hootch to party with the guys. As we walked through the company area, Mike commented on the alarming number of guys we had just visited that were nodding off, one of the tale-tell signs of one being "high" on heroin. I had been too focused on my mission to pay much attention, but it was true. These guys were like zombies, and the whole atmosphere around them was a downer. It wasn't like the good old days in Cu Chi or Phuoc Vinh, where most guys experienced the "happy high" of pot as music flowed from the hootches. No, skag had become a real problem. And as far as I was concerned, its use was exacerbated by the misery and low morale brought on by the lifers and a stagnated war.

The next day after work, Mike and I began compiling the information we received from the guys in the company. We then wrote out a first draft of the document so I could bounce it off Captain Feldesman. When we were finished, I went to my office and used my typewriter to prepare the draft, since I could cover my tracks by using the excuse that I was working late on an IO project if I had to. Once approved, Randy and two more of the clerks who worked in the office offered to help me crank out the necessary number of copies. To make copies of documents in those days, one had to use carbon paper (using the mimeograph machine would have been much too risky).

By the end of the second evening after the initial meetings, the whole detachment was buzzing with excitement. Mike and I were concerned about leaks—or troops loyal to the lifers revealing our plan. But Stein and Wise were disliked so much that we didn't think that was going to happen. Before going to bed that night, Mike, Randy, and I reviewed our plan of action. I still couldn't believe we were actually going to do this.

17 days. April 25. When I awoke early the next morning, the adrenalin was already pumping through my veins. The first thing I did was cross another day off my short-time calendar. I was down to sixteen days and a wake-up. Then I took a quick shower and headed off to morning formation, after which I went to the mess hall to wolf down some breakfast. Before going to work, I made my way to the AG's office to see if Captain Feldesman was in. I had the draft of our document hidden in my fatigue shirt. As good fortune would have it, again, he was there…and alone. He told me that since he was the low man on the totem pole, he always had to open the office. He said the senior officers never got there early (of course they didn't, I thought to myself). In short order, he scanned what we had written and nodded his head in approval. "This looks pretty good," he murmured, "but you need to make a few format revisions for it to fly." I furiously took notes on the document as he told me what to change. We were both paranoid as hell that someone was going to walk in on us, but luckily no one did. I thanked him again for his assistance and told him that I hoped we could meet up in the world someday to reminisce about this whole incredible experience.

Before I left, he told me the person I needed to deliver the document to was the company XO, Lieutenant Mike Greenly. Since we were going after the company commander, he was the next in line in the chain of command. Lieutenant Greenly, he pointed out, was legally obligated to deliver the document to the brigade commander, Brigadier General Marvin Zink. With that final piece of information, I shook his hand and stared into his eyes. I almost didn't want to leave, for I knew that when I walked out that door, I'd be on my own. I felt like a little bird about to leave the nest for the first time to try my wings. I was either going to fly, or I was going to crash and sustain unknown injuries.

I made my way to the office, where I had three stories waiting to be finished. I had to get them completed today or I was going to miss my deadline for the upcoming issue of the newspaper. And I also had to find some time to make the revisions to the document that Captain Feldesman had recommended. I wasn't sure how I was going to accomplish all this, but I was speeding from the adrenalin flowing through my veins and was confident that I could get it all done.

As I walked through the door of the office I was greeted by Captain Aulen, who reminded me that I had three stories due that day. "No sweat, sir," I responded. "You'll have them on your desk by 1600 hours." Captain Aulen was a decent guy, just biding his time like the rest of us and content with doing his job and not bothering anyone (paper-pushers generally fit into that mold). I grabbed a cup of coffee, then sat at my typewriter and began cranking out story number one. It was another Vietnamization story, this one about a ceremony that I had covered yesterday. With brass from both the U.S. military and South Vietnam present, the 1st Cav turned a recently-vacated section of the Bien Hoa base camp over to an ARVN unit. And after the ceremony, true to their culture, the soldiers and their families moved in. Slowly but surely, we were winding down our presence in Vietnam. And slowly but surely, the North Vietnamese military and the Viet Cong were encroaching on the south. I'm not sure the U.S. military and its crack intelligence knew the full extent of this encroachment. And at this stage of the game, if they did, I'm not sure they really cared. We were withdrawing and turning the war over to the south. Getting out with the least amount of collateral damage was the new name of the game.

As I was writing, I overheard Captain Aulen on the phone, talking to one of his buddies up in admin. They were conversing about a big Hail and Farewell party that was going to take place at the Officer's Club this evening. It appears there was going to be quite an exodus of lifers this week—both officers and NCOs—and that they were going to have a combined bash tonight to celebrate. The timing of this news was almost too good to be true. Tonight, then, would be the night for the company meeting that I'd been planning. And with all the lifers off partying and getting drunk, the circumstances would be ideal. I'd pass the word at lunch, after getting some advice from Mike on the best location for the gathering. Now I would definitely have to revise the document by nightfall, and make enough copies to pass around to the guys for their review.

After huddling with Mike at lunch, we decided that it would be best to have the company meeting in two waves, as we were paranoid that a gathering of the entire company might attract the attention of the officer on duty. So we decided to break the company into two groups alphabetically, with A to L coming at 2200 hours, and M to Z at 2300 hours. We picked the chapel as the location, for it was always open and seldom used or patrolled. And besides, what we were about to do could definitely be considered a spiritual experience...not to mention the fact that we could also use some divine intervention. We divulged our plan to Randy and our two buddies from admin, then went our separate ways to spread the word. I told as many guys as I could on my way back to work. But my time was limited, as I still had two stories to complete and the document to prepare for tonight's meetings.

At 2145, Mike, Randy, and I made our way to the chapel. We could see our comrades starting to emerge from their hootches as we walked, taking various circumvented routes to avoid detection. After all, we were just following military protocol in regard to "cluster fucks" (to avoid suffering a large number of casualties during rocket or mortar attacks, we were advised never to gather or stand together in large groups—or clusters—in open spaces).

At 2205 we began the meeting, and I again described what Article 138 was all about and what our plan of action would be.

We then passed around the ten copies of the document that I had prepared, giving each guy enough time to read it before passing it on to others. Mike and I then did our best to answer questions and concerns, the biggest of which was the fear of it backfiring and our getting busted or having permanent records marred. I assured them that what we were doing was totally legal and "by the book," and that I had sought military legal counsel in this regard (obviously, I couldn't mention Captain Feldesman by name). I told them that because what we were doing was legal, there was nothing the lifers could officially do to get back at us. And that if everyone participated, there was little they could do unofficially either. And besides, our lives were already miserable, and we were already being harassed to the max. Our explanation seemed to satisfy the troops, for when we asked for a show of hands of those who supported us, it was unanimous.

We repeated the proceedings at 2300 hours with much the same result. Only when we asked for a show of hands this time, there were two guys who decided not to participate. They were young career soldiers, and even though they sympathized with our mission, they just weren't willing to risk their careers in the event the plan backfired. But they promised to support us with their silence.

The execution plan was as follows. Mike and I would spend the next two days preparing the final draft of the document and the eighty-seven individual signature pages that would accompany it. Then, on Monday night, May 3, 1971, one by one, the men in Detachment 5, CSSB, 3rd Brigade (Sep), 1st Air Cavalry Division (AM), would make their way to one of three separate hootches to sign their names. After that, it was in my hands to deliver the document to the XO.

9 days. May 3. I woke up early that morning, anticipating the significance of the day. As was now ritual, I crossed another day off my short-time calendar. But today was special. Today I became a "single digit midget." I was down to nine days and a wake-up. After formation, I skipped breakfast and went back to the hootch to think. All the guys were at breakfast—which was good—as I wanted to be alone for a few moments to contemplate, one last time, what I was about to do. I'll have to admit, I was nervous and began to question why I was doing what I was about to do. Self-doubt was beginning to rear its head. Was my anger and frustration with the lifers so determined that I was prepared to take on the U.S. Army—in a war zone—to get back at them? Was I out of my fucking mind? After all, without proceeding with this action, I'd be on my way home in less than ten days, with little chance of anything happening to me from the dangers of the war to, well, anything else. Was I out of my fucking mind!

I contemplated the possible ramifications, like my orders being frozen if the legal process I was initiating got too involved or backfired. I mean, I was getting married seventeen days after I got back to the world. I can only imagine how my fiancé would take the news: "I'm sorry, honey, but we're going to have to postpone the wedding, and the party for 250 people, because my orders for DEROS were frozen because I decided to sue the army before I left." There's no way she could possibly understand this…and now I'm not sure that I fully understand it either. Self-doubt was now staring me in the face. All of this crossed my mind as I mentally prepared for the conclusion of my grand scheme to get back at the lifers and perhaps, subconsciously, the army and the U.S. government…for drafting me to serve in this fucking waste of a war.

They had told us at formation that we only had to work a half day today, as most of the officers and high-ranking NCOs had to attend an IV Corp update meeting at MACV headquarters in Long Binh. That worked into my plans perfectly, as we would now be able to collect our signatures at a more leisurely, and hopefully less likely to be detected, pace. I also wanted to catch some rays, as it had been a few weeks since I had actually laid out in the sun, and it was imperative that I go home with a deep Nam tan.

After work, I met Mike for lunch to nail down the final details of our plan. Then I went back to the hootch to prepare myself for a few hours in the sun. As I was selecting some music to accompany my respite (would it be the Moody Blues, The Who, or Ten Years After…I loved their hit "I'd Love to Change the World"), a couple of guys from admin came into the hootch. They were on their way to

Vung Tau for the rest of the day and asked me if I wanted to go along. I thanked them for the invitation, but knowing they'd be getting back real late—if at all that night—I declined, telling them I didn't want to risk getting caught with only nine days left in the Nam (like I wasn't taking a risk by suing the army). "But you guys aren't going anywhere until you sign the document," I emphatically reminded them before they took off. "We weren't planning to," they laughed, sheepishly, as I went to find their signature pages.

That night after dinner, Mike and I took the signature pages to the three designated hootches (ours wasn't one of them) and waited for our comrades to file in to sign their names. By 2300 hours, our mission was accomplished. We had all eighty-five signatures and felt a great sense of relief and satisfaction. Now it was up to me to deliver the completed document to Lieutenant Greenly. As he was the officer on duty tomorrow, I'd take it up to him at HQ after breakfast. But for now, it was time to release a little pressure.

There was a USO show at the EM Club that night, so Mike and I headed over to join Randy and a few other guys from our hootch. We closed the place down and then went over to one of the admin hootches where we heard a party was going on. On the walk over, the number of empty vials of skag that littered the company walkways sparkled like little jewels in the moonlight. When we got there, most of the guys had either already passed out or were nodding off in their heroin oblivion. We decided that this wasn't the scene we wanted to end our evening with, so we made our way back to our hootch to party in a more upbeat fashion. We put on the Beatles *Magical Mystery Tour* and proceeded to trip the light fantastic on some of Southeast Asia's finest. It was the perfect way to cap off an exciting day…and celebrate the end of phase one of our mission.

I had Tuesday off, so I slept until 0900, missing breakfast. As I sat up in bed, I realized just how hard we had partied the night before, and how thankful I was that I didn't have to get up for formation. As I sat there, trying to wake up, the first thing I did was cross another day off my short-time calendar—**8 days** and a wake up. Then I put on my fatigue shirt and pants (damn, the civilian in me keeps rearing its head), slipped on a pair of flip-flops, and took a walk in search of a cup of coffee. Since Mike was working, I made my way over to his office to see if I could score a cup. And sure enough, there was a little stale brew still cooking, so I was able to get my required dose of caffeine. As I drank my coffee, we talked about my mission for the day until I felt human enough to face it, and then I departed to take a shower and get ready for my visit to the XO. On the way out the door, Mike wished me luck and told me to make sure that I filled him in immediately after leaving HQ. I assured him that I would, as the acids in my empty stomach began to churn in anticipation of the task I had ahead of me.

After showering, I put on my only pair of starched fatigues and spit-shined my boots. I wanted to look my military best for my visit to HQ. Then I retrieved the document from the bottom of my laundry bag where I had been hiding it and looked it over one last time. Everything appeared to be in order. And just in case the lifers tried to destroy or sabotage it, I had made a copy, including a copy of each signature page, for safe keeping. Mike had it hidden in a place that even I didn't know about. I placed the document into a manila envelope, looked at myself one last time in a broken fragment of mirror hanging on the wall by the door, and made my way to Detachment 5 Headquarters.

By this time it was 1130 hours, and I was hoping that Lieutenant Greenly hadn't already gone to lunch. But as I walked up to the door of his office, which was open, he was standing at his desk, talking to someone on the phone. When he saw me he waved me in. Because of the informality of his gesture, I didn't bother to salute. From the little I knew about Greenly, he appeared to be a really nice guy. He was fairly new—ROTC from Princeton—and appeared to have a lot of class. We had talked once before, when I was researching information for the CIP, about both being from the Delaware Valley, and the fact that we had both gone through basic at Fort Dix.

When he got off the phone, he greeted me with: "Specialist Stoup, what brings you to these parts? Are you going to write a story about me for the brigade newspaper?"

"No, sir," I replied. "I have another matter that I need to discuss with you." He asked me to have a seat as he took his behind his desk. As I sat down in a chair directly across from him, I noticed him looking at the manila envelope that I was carrying under my arm. But he quickly looked up as I proceeded to tell him about Article 138 and the grievance procedure that I, and eighty-four of my fellow soldiers in Detachment 5, were about to initiate against LTC Wise and Captain Stein.

He listened intently as I described our frustration with unacceptable base camp conditions, the harassment we faced on an almost daily basis, and the loss of our privacy. I told him about our attempts to express our views and complaints, all of which had only led to a worsening of conditions. And I pointed out that Captain Stein had disbanded the Enlisted Men's Council, which was our official vehicle for trying to communicate our concerns to our superiors. This move, in our estimation, was the final blow. I knew that Lieutenant Greenly was well aware of most of the situations I had described and could tell that he was at least somewhat sympathetic by his facial expressions and body language. He and I also knew, without having to say it, that there was nothing he could do to change things. "You know the army's budget has been cut way back," he said, "and with the withdrawal of troops from Bien Hoa in progress, that there's little chance for upgrades to be made at this base camp," he continued.

"I'm aware of that, sir," I responded. "But we're talking about basic sanitary conditions, enough food to eat, and unjustified harassment."

"So what is Article 138?" he asked, with a perplexed look on his face.

"Well, sir," I responded, "it's kind of like a tool provided to us in the UCMJ to help soldiers deal with situations like this." I then read Article 138 to him, explaining what it meant and how it worked. I told him that I had received legal counsel "outside of the brigade," and that the document we had prepared for submission was legal, and was within our rights under the UCMJ. Then I gave him the bad news. I sat up straight in my chair, cleared my throat, and said, "Unfortunately, sir, since Captain Stein is one of the people we're initiating proceedings against, as next in command, it's your legal responsibility under Section 938, Article 138, of the UCMJ, to deliver the document to General Zink."

When I finished speaking, we both just sat there in silence. Lieutenant Greenly looked like he had just lost his best friend, but maintained his composure. He didn't question me further. I really felt bad for him and even started feeling guilty for having to put him in this situation. But at this point there was no turning back, and I could tell he realized this. He was an intelligent man, and with everything I had just presented, he knew that this was something he was going to have to do.

I spoke first, in an attempt to break the uneasy silence. "Perhaps you should take a look at the document, sir," I said, pulling it out of the envelope and placing it on the desk in front of him. He picked it up and starting reading. The document read as follows:

The enlisted men of Detachment 5, CSSB, 3rd Brigade, 1st Cavalry Division (AM), who are initiating proceedings under Section 938, Article 138, of the Uniform Code of Military justice, in order to show the respect that is due a commanding general, and to prove our sincerity in seeking justice through Section 938, Article 138, of the Uniform Code of Military Justice, have agreed to withhold, for 48 hours, all out-of-command forwarding of copies of the attached "Complaint of Wrongs."

We are sure that you will acknowledge the injustices and lack of leadership that exist in Detachment 5, CSSB, and that you will notify us at your earliest possible convenience that positive steps are being taken to remedy our "Complaint of Wrongs" as expressed in the attached document.

JAMES STOUP

DEPARTMENT OF THE ARMY
Detachment 5, CSSB, 3rd Brigade (Separate)
1st Cavalry Division (Airmobile)
APO San Francisco 96490

SUBJECT: Filing of "Complaint of Wrongs" under Section 938, Article 138, of the Uniform Code of Military Justice

TO: MICHAEL P. GREENLY
1st Lieutenant, Infantry
Executive Officer, Detachment 5, CSSB

1. The morale of the troops in Detachment 5 is at its lowest possible point. Numerous attempts have been made by the enlisted men of Detachment 5 to present their grievances and suggestions to their superiors through the chain-of-command. All of these attempts have either failed or have been ignored.

2. Because of the appalling conditions and procedures that currently exist in Detachment 5, as well as in the entire composite service support battalion, we, the enlisted men of Detachment 5, feel it our duty and obligation to present a formal redress of our complaints to the highest Army authorities through Section 938, Article 138, of the Uniform Code of Military Justice. We have taken this step only because all other means available to us have failed.

3. For your convenience, let us quote Section 938, Article 138, of the Uniform Code of Military Justice:

    Any member of the armed forces who believes himself wronged by his commanding officer, and who, upon due application to that commanding officer, is refused redress, may complain to any superior commissioned officer, who shall forward the complaint to the officer exercising general court-martial jurisdiction over the officer against who it is made. The officer exercising general court-martial jurisdiction shall examine into the complaint and take proper measures for redressing the wrong complained of; and he shall, as soon as possible, send to the Secretary concerned a true statement of that complaint, with the proceedings had thereon.

4. This formal complaint is being made against Lieutenant Colonel John W. Wise, Commanding Officer, CSSB, 3rd Brigade (Sep), 1st Cavalry Division (AM), and Captain James D. Stein, Commanding Officer, Detachment 5, CSSB, 3rd Brigade (Sep), 1st Cavalry Division (AM).

5. The following is a list of the major complaints and grievances that exist and have existed in Detachment 5:

   A. Our walls and privacy partitions have been removed. Numerous attempts were made to remedy this situation, including the enlisted men meeting and drawing up a remodeling plan for the barracks, with the enlisted men volunteering to do the work themselves. Our request was formally presented to our commanding officer. We never even received the courtesy of a response, and therefore assume our attempts have failed.

   B. More concern was expressed for the walls coming down than for fixing the roofs and outer walls of the barracks. This, most obviously, will now cause extremely unbearable conditions for the residents of these barracks with the now present monsoon season.

   C. Enlisted men have been forced to make numerous barracks moves, without direction or plan, with many men having made as many as four different moves. We realize that our unit is in the process of changing from a company to a detachment, yet no definite plan has been presented to alleviate these unnecessary moves, moves that most obviously have no scheme or plan to them.

D. Shallow understanding of the causes and nature of the drug problem, and questionable tactics used to combat this problem.
E. Unannounced "Health and Welfare" inspection(s) during normal hours of sleep (e.g. 2230 hours to 0230 hours).
F. Superior officers barging into the enlisted men's barracks at all hours of the day and night for no practical purpose other than harassment.
G. Selecting only "certain" barracks for the "Health and Welfare" inspections.
H. The various "Health and Welfare" inspections have succeeded in troop harassment, yet have overlooked what should be the primary reason for these inspections; namely, the personal health and hygiene of the troops. Examples: total neglect of the plumbing facilities without providing alternate portable latrines, thereby causing extremely unsanitary conditions; failure to provide an adequate amount of toilet paper for these facilities; and refusal to maintain hot water facilities.

Failure of this unit to provide proper lighting (we have no lights at all) on the perimeter green line.
I. Continuous mismanagement of the mess hall:
   1. Running out of food at almost every meal
   2. Having to sign two rosters at meals for the supposed purpose of obtaining additional rations, but with the result seeming to be even less food
   3. Cold and/or uncooked food at almost every meal
   4. Obvious discrimination between enlisted men and the senior ranks in quantity, quality and conditions of the food and mess facilities
J. Unannounced cancellation of the Enlisted Men's Council. This was a forum for effective communication, and its cancellation has resulted in a vast communication gap, which is the major reason for the presentation of this complaint of wrongs.

K. Failure of this unit (CSSB) to follow regulations in its failure to provide the mandatory quarterly Command Information Program to the troops.
L. Failure of this unit (CSSB) to follow regulations in its failure to have organized a Human Relations Council.
M. Apparent total disregard for the changes in regulations and implementation of plans that have resulted from the All-Volunteer Army Project. In other words, the wishes of the Army's Chief-of-Staff, General William C. Westmoreland, and his special assistant for the All-Volunteer Army Project, Lieutenant General Forrester, are being ignored by this unit (CSSB). To document our thesis in this regard, allow us to quote the following excerpt from a speech given by General Westmoreland to the AUSA (Association of the United States Army) on October 13, 1970:

"To ignore the social mores of this younger group is to blind ourselves to reality. Their values and attitudes need not necessarily be endorsed by Army leadership...yet we must recognize they do exist. We must make service life better understood by those who fill our ranks. We will leave no stone unturned. We are willing to part from past practices where such practices no longer serve a productive and useful end."

This unit (CSSB) is most obviously acting directly contrary to the wishes of the "new" Army as stated above by General Westmoreland.

Our conclusions should be apparent. As we have stated previously, morale is at its lowest possible point, and the channels of communication have been seriously impaired. Now we ask you to draw your own conclusions and present us with an adequate response.

To assure that justice will be realized for all parties concerned, copies of this "Complaint of Wrongs" under Section 938, Article 138, of the Uniform Code of Military Justice, are being forwarded to the following individuals:

- President Richard M. Nixon, Commander-in-Chief
- General William C. Westmoreland, Army Chief-of-Staff
- General Creighton W. Abrams, Commander, US Forces, Vietnam
- Lieutenant General Forrester, Special Assistant, VOLAR Project
- LTC John Mitchell, Staff Judge Advocate, 3rd Brigade (Sep), 1st Cavalry Division (AM)
- LTC John W. Wise, Commanding Officer, CSSB, 3rd Brigade (Sep), 1st Cavalry Division (AM)
- CPT James D. Stein, Commanding Officer, Detachment 5, CSSB, 3rd Brigade (Sep), 1st Cavalry Division (AM)
- Senator Margaret Chase Smith
- Senator George McGovern
- Senator Edward M. Kennedy
- Senator Edmund Muskie
- Senator Mark O. Hatfield
- Senator William Proxmire
- Representative Robert McClosky
- Representative Bella Abzug
- Senator Phillip Hart
- Senator Walter Mondale
- Senator James Buckley
- Representative Edward Hebert
- Senator Barry Goldwater
- Senator Henry Jackson
- Senator John Stennis
- Senator Harry Byrd, Jr.
- Senator Gale McGee
- Representative Roman Pucinski
- Senator Harold Hughes
- Senator Birch Bayh

CHAPTER 15

How It Came Down, Shortness Is, Saying Good-Bye

With the last part of my mission accomplished, I made my way back to the hootch to begin sorting through my stuff in preparation for my departure, which was only a week away. I kept thinking about Lieutenant Greenly and how I didn't envy the position I had put him in. But I was sure that he wouldn't get into trouble. After all, he was only the messenger, and hopefully General Zink isn't a "shoot the messenger" kind of guy. Before I left him, he told me he would take the document to brigade HQ by 1600 hours. He was going to a meeting there anyway and would try to get some time with the general as soon as the meeting was over. I was hoping the document would get the general's immediate attention, and that whatever he was going to do, he would do quickly. Because I was real short and didn't want to get stuck in this hellhole one day longer than I had to.

I packed a box with the items I wanted to ship home, which included another poncho liner. Then I pulled out my scrapbook to begin the process of preparing it for its journey back to the world. As I learned from the guys at Cu Chi, it was tradition—if not ritual—to bring some pot back from the Nam. In preparation for the trip, I had purchased three packs of prerolled "Cambodian Red" joints on my last trip to Saigon. They sold them on the street, twenty prerolled "cigarettes," with filters, in a regular-looking cigarette pack for five bucks a pack. They were expensive, but the pot was amazing.

Using a razor blade, I carefully opened the seams on the front cover of the scrapbook and removed the padding and cardboard liner. I then carefully glued sixty joints to the cardboard in three rows of twenty. Then I sprinkled some after-shave lotion on the back side of the cardboard, and along with the padding, placed it back inside the cover. The last step was regluing the seams on the cover, and that was it—my scrapbook of Nam memorabilia was ready to go. But I'll have to admit, the thought of carrying the scrapbook with me made me nervous. After making it through an entire year without incident, I didn't want to get busted now and run the risk of not making it home on time…or worse. Perhaps I should ship it. Or should I carry it with me? I couldn't decide. But I did decide to stop worrying about it for now and enjoy my final days in the sun.

With that task completed, it was time to catch some rays. Even though the monsoon season was back, the sun was still quite intense for most of the day. And I only had a few days left to deepen that trademark Nam tan. So I spent the remainder of the afternoon absorbing the sounds of music and helicopters flying overhead while basking in the warmth of the Vietnam sun.

A bunch of us were able to secure a company jeep that evening and went to a Chinese restaurant located on the massive Long Binh base camp. After a tasty Chinese dinner, we went to one of the base EM Clubs to catch a USO show. I figured that it was appropriate to take in one more of the now classic Filipino rock & roll shows. Later that night, back at the hootch, we put on some Crosby, Stills & Nash, and elevated ourselves to another dimension. Until the wee hours of the morning, we exchanged war stories about our experiences in the Nam and theorized about what might happen as a result of Article 138. My mind was racing, and I was filled with emotion at the thought of leaving this place. At one point, the intensity of our camaraderie was so strong that it brought tears to my eyes. There truly was a brotherhood in the Nam that was unlike anything I had ever experienced. Being joined together for survival—looking out for each other—there was nothing you could compare it to. I flashed back to Cu Chi and Phuoc Vinh and reminisced in my mind about the close relationships I had developed at those two places. The whole atmosphere—from rapping and smoking pot, to listening to the incredible music of the times together—had become trademark Vietnam, and I was going to miss spending nights like these with the guys.

On Wednesday, I finished packing and took a box of stuff to the brigade mailroom to be shipped. Then I went to the office to finish the last of my stories for this week's paper, which would be my last. I also had to brief the guy that brigade had assigned to replace me. With the brigade itself being so short, they didn't bother trying to find another information specialist. So they were filling my slot with a clerk named Les Runzler, whose last assignment was working as a speech writer for the generals at MACV. Basically, I told him that if you can write speeches you can write this shit. As I reviewed past issues of the paper with him, as well as the last two Command Information Programs (the last of which still hadn't been released), we both laughed and marveled at the way army propaganda was presented. Who were they trying to kid with this stuff? We agreed—certainly not us.

Later that afternoon, when I was back at the hootch, Randy came running through the door. He was working that day and came over on his break. "Something's going on at brigade HQ," he hurriedly blurted out. "Officers and NCOs have been coming and going all day, and the place is buzzing. I'm sure it's Article 138," he remarked.

Word spread like wildfire that something was going on up at brigade HQ, and guys started coming and going from the hootch in a steady stream. They all wanted to know if I had heard anything. I told them I hadn't, but it wasn't long before I did. Shortly after dinner, Lieutenant Greenly came into the hootch. I stood up and saluted, as did the other guys in the hootch. He snapped a quick one back and told us all to be at ease. Then he walked over to where I was standing, and in a low voice told me that General Zink wanted to see me in his office tomorrow morning at 0800 hours. "Am I the only one he wants to see?" I asked. "As far as I know, yes," he answered. "At least you're the only one he asked me to summon."

"Why just me?" I wondered out loud.

"Because I gave him your name," he continued. "He asked me who had brought me the document, and I told him it was you. So I suppose he thinks you're the ringleader. You are the ringleader, aren't you, Specialist?" he then remarked, with a knowing smile on his face.

I asked the lieutenant what he thought the general was going to do. He said he didn't know, but informed me that General Zink's direct reports had been filing in one by one all day long. "It appears there's a major shake-up going on," he continued. "I think that document of yours has stirred up a lot of dust. And I think you're going to be surprised at how he responds to it."

Mike, Randy, and I spent the rest of the evening reviewing the document—line by line. I wanted to make sure I knew how to respond and elaborate on each issue we had raised. They both offered to accompany me to brigade HQ in the morning, which I took them up on. I didn't know if they'd be able to get into the meeting, but at least they'd be close by for moral support. When we considered ourselves sufficiently rehearsed, we went to the EM Club for a couple of beers. We didn't get stoned that night, though, and were in bed my midnight, as we wanted to make sure that our heads were clear in the morning.

4 days. May 8. The three of us got up around 0530, bleary eyed, and dragged ourselves to the mess hall for some coffee before formation. We decided when we got there that it probably would be a good idea to eat breakfast as well. After consuming the best breakfast we had ever been served (strange how this seemed to happen literally overnight…and the day after the general received our document complaining about the food), we went back to the hootch to shower and get dressed for the big meeting. Considering the nature of the event I had been summoned to, starched fatigues and polished boots were definitely in order. Then I crossed another day off my short-time calendar. I was down to four days and a wake-up.

At 0750 we made our way up the company street to brigade headquarters. I had butterflies in my stomach, and sweat was dripping from my armpits. Noticing my condition, Mike started telling lifer jokes in an attempt to loosen me up. As we approached the main entrance to the office building, I took a deep breath, and then I walked into the building. Mike and Randy followed. The brigade XO, Major Chuck Coleman, was waiting for me. As I saluted him, Major Coleman saluted back and said, "Specialist Stoup, we've been waiting for you. Please follow me. You men have a seat here," he said to Mike and Randy, rather pointedly.

As we proceeded down a corridor to the right of the visitor lobby, Major Coleman started chitchatting with me as if I was a long lost nephew. "I hope you're enjoying your last week in Bien Hoa," he commented. "I understand you're going home in a few days." As I responded to him with short yet polite answers, I looked over my shoulder at Mike and Randy. They were sitting, with their legs crossed, in two large lounge chairs. They both smiled and flipped me the peace sign. As we continued walking down the corridor, Major Coleman quickly briefed me on what was about to happen. "We're going to the conference room, Specialist, where General Zink has lined up a few of the officers and NCOs in his command. We want to respond to the document you presented to us," he continued.

With that we arrived at the door, which he held open for me. The room we entered was huge. It must have doubled as General Zink's office as well as a conference room, for there was a large and ornate desk at one end of the room. An oval conference table that looked like it could seat at least twenty people dominated the middle of the room. And along the side of the room opposite the corridor entrance, was a wall of chalk boards and pull-down maps of Vietnam and IV Corps, with little flags stuck all over them.

General Zink was at his desk, talking to the brigade adjutant general, who was standing next to him. And seated in silence on one side of the table with their backs to the maps were eight officers and NCOs from Detachment 5, CSSB. LTC Wise and Captain Stein were among them.

As Major Coleman and I walked through the door, everyone stood up. The eight lifers on the opposite side of the table froze at attention, while General Zink practically bounded around his desk to get to me. We exchanged quick salutes as he came forward with an outstretched hand to greet me. "Specialist Stoup, we've been waiting for you," he exclaimed while shaking my hand, almost mimicking exactly what Major Coleman had said to me when I arrived. "Please have a seat," he said, pointing to a grouping of four plush chairs at the table across from the "gang of eight."

He took the chair in the middle of the conference table and gestured for me to sit next to him. Major Coleman took the seat to my right, and LTC John Mitchell, the brigade Staff Judge Advocate, sat next to him on his left. As he took his seat, General Zink barked "at ease" to the lifers standing across from him. He then poured himself a glass of water and asked me if I wanted one. "That would be nice, sir," I responded. As he was pouring, he began to address everyone in the room. The lifers continued to stand, but in an "at ease" position, with their legs slightly apart and their hands crossed behind their backs. "Specialist Stoup and the troops in Detachment 5 have brought some matters to our attention, gentlemen," he began, as I turned uncomfortably in my seat and looked at him. "They've done so via a document pertaining to Article 138 of the Uniform Code of Military Justice," he continued, "which Lieutenant Colonel Mitchell tells me is a valid form of complaint when the chain of command isn't doing its job." With that he peered at the eight men across from him. "Well, gentlemen," he glowered, aiming his comments directly at them, "you're about to answer for your shortcomings."

With that, he asked LTC Mitchell to read the document out loud. Mitchell opened a file folder, pulled out the document, handed a copy to the general, and proceeded to read it. As soon as he finished reading the first complaint under item #5 he stopped and the general asked Captain Stein to take one step forward (the first item dealt with our privacy walls being removed). "Why did you take down the troop's divider walls, Captain?" he inquired of Stein.

"Because there was drug use going on in those barracks, General," he responded.

"You have any hard evidence to that effect, Captain," he asked.

"No, sir, I don't," Stein replied.

"Then that's a hell of a way to deal with suspicion, Captain, and a hell of a way to deal with any drug problem. I want those walls put back up, and I want that to happen within forty-eight hours," he practically yelled at him. "And no more Health and Welfare inspections during sleeping hours either, Captain…do you read me?"

"Yes, sir," Stein barked back. His face was crimson red, and his eyes were pinned to the floor.

General Zink next asked LTC Wise to take one step forward. He then proceeded to berate him for not keeping closer tabs on what was going on in his AO, as Major Coleman read all of the items and issues in the complaint that pertained to the drug problem, communications, morale, and harassment. The general raked Wise and Stein over the coals for their lack of leadership and asked for a plan to correct each and every situation by the end of the week. "I also want the Enlisted Men's Council reestablished immediately," he continued, "and I want both of you to work with Major Coleman on a plan for implementing a Human Relations Council. And, Colonel, I want that damn Command Information Program reestablished." He then turned toward the major and mumbled, "I thought we had a damn command information program," not knowing that Wise had refused to release it.

Whether intentionally or not, they ignored the item dealing with the All-Volunteer Army Project and the quote we put in there from General Westmoreland. It was really irrelevant to the complaint anyway and was only added, in a sense, to rub salt in their wounds. We had enough ammunition as it was and certainly didn't need a response to its insertion…and we didn't get one.

When he was finished with Wise and Stein, he told them to step back. Then he had Major Coleman read the complaints dealing with the mess hall and had Captain Herbert North, the brigade officer in charge of food services, and Staff Sergeant Tony Wilson, the mess sergeant, step forward. His anger was unrestrained as he reviewed each item in the complaint. "An army operates on its stomach, sergeant," he bellowed in Wilson's direction. "Running out of food is inexcusable," he continued, "and the overall state of your operation stinks from what I've been told. I want this situation corrected immediately. And Captain North," he said, turning his attention to the frail-looking lifer, "I want to know what's going on with this double signing of rosters. It sounds like there's something rotten in Denmark."

He continued in the same manner with the officers and NCOs responsible for base camp facilities, berating them for the condition of the showers, latrines, and plumbing. "LTC Wise should have been directing his Health and Welfare inspections at you, gentlemen," he told them, in a sarcastic tone. "I want those facilities shaped up and in working order by the end of the week," he continued, in a now hoarse and irritated voice.

The general then turned to Major Coleman and said, "All of this shit is unbelievable. Why am I hearing about these conditions for the first time in this complaint, major?" he asked, waving our document in the air above his head. It was obviously a rhetorical question for which the major had no answer. General Zink sensed this, and turned to LTC Mitchell and asked him to continue.

When LTC Mitchell finished reading the document, General Zink asked the group of eight if they understood their marching orders. In unison, they answered with a resounding "Yes, sir!" With that, he dismissed them, and they left the room. Now it was just the four of us in the large conference room. Major Coleman, who was still taking notes, looked up as the general turned and spoke to me. "Now Specialist Stoup, I hope the meeting we just had here demonstrates our commitment to respond to the issues you pointed out in your petition." There was a hint of smugness in his remark, but rather than challenge him, I decided to play along. "Initially, it seems very positive, sir," I responded. "But we'll have to wait until we see actual change and improvement before we'll be convinced."

I think my comment surprised him a bit, as it prompted him to turn and look at LTC Mitchell. They stared at each other for a couple of seconds, which seemed a lot longer, then he turned back to me and continued. "You're not planning to send those copies that you listed on the last page of your document, now are you, specialist?" he asked rather pointedly.

"It all depends on the actions taken, sir," I said.

"Then the action we took today should satisfy you, specialist," he continued.

"It's a good start, sir," I answered, not giving an inch. Again, I could tell that it wasn't the response he was looking for.

With that he abruptly stood up, with the other two officers quickly following suit. As I started rising to my feel, General Zink announced, "Well, I've got to go out and visit some of the troops in the field today. Would you like to go with me, specialist?" he asked, taking me by surprise. "You still have time to write one last story for the brigade paper, don't you?" he added, now back in his grandfatherly tone. I hesitated for a moment, as I was a little taken aback by his offer. But I quickly thought to myself, *What do I have to lose?* I mean, how often does a low-ranking soldier get asked by a general to accompany him in his personal helicopter to visit troops in the field. Besides, I love to fly, and this would definitely be my last chance to ride in a chopper before leaving Nam. And I didn't want to piss him off by refusing. I also thought to myself, perhaps the better I get to know this guy, the more he'll like me. And if he likes me, the more likely it will be that he'll follow through on the actions he ordered and the more likely it will be that he won't freeze my orders so I can get the hell out of this place. So I looked at him and responded, "I'd love to, sir!"

As we walked out of brigade headquarters, I noticed that Mike and Randy were gone. I guess they were told to leave, or just felt uncomfortable in that environment and decided to go back to the hootch.

When we got outside, the general's jeep was waiting to take us to his chopper. As it turned out, General Zink was also a trained pilot and always co-piloted his helicopter. I found that to be kind of cool. Here he was, the leader of an airmobile brigade, actually getting behind the wheel instead of being chauffeured in typical regal military fashion. It was impressive.

The pilot had the aircraft churning as we pulled up, and General Zink immediately took his position next to him. It was a Huey, of course, my favorite aircraft. As soon as Major Coleman and I climbed into the back and were strapped in, they closed the doors, and in a moment we were airborne. Major Coleman pointed and yelled for me to put on the helmet that was hanging on the back wall over my shoulder. Wearing the helmet would enable me to hear the chatter between the pilot and General Zink, as well as any communications from the ground. This would be a first for me, as I had never been invited to "wear the helmet" before.

Our first destination was Xuan Tam, a small hamlet not too far from Bien Hoa. Two companies from the 2nd Battalion, 7th Cavalry, were securing the area after reported sightings of VC in the region the previous day. As soon as we landed after the short twenty-minute flight, General Zink was immediately greeted by the two company commanders. As he strode into the area occupied by the troops, he was briefed by the two captains on the results of the operation. Major Coleman and I followed a number of steps behind. Along the way, the general would occasionally stop to shake hands or briefly talk with the troops. The soldiers seemed unimpressed by his presence, and I was surprised that no one saluted him as he approached. Maybe it was because they were on a combat mission, or maybe it was 3rd Brigade policy that you didn't have to salute when you were in the field, or maybe they just didn't give a shit. At any rate, after a quick fifteen-minute stop, we headed back to the Huey and were airborne moments later.

Our second destination was a little farther away—FSB Noble—at the perimeter of IV Corps. It took us about forty-five minutes to get there, and for one last time, I marveled at both the beauty and the destruction of the countryside as we flew along the land at an altitude of about five thousand feet. When we landed, a jeep was waiting to take us to the main operations bunker, which we really could have walked to. When we got there, General Zink and Major Coleman were greeted by the major in charge of the base. As we were about to enter the bunker, Major Coleman asked me to wait outside, indicating that they wouldn't be long. I guess they didn't want "a reporter" listening in on a sensitive operations briefing. "Go on over and visit with some of our fine troops while you're waiting," he added, trying to make me feel like a part of the group.

So I walked over to a group of guys who were standing outside the mess tent. One of them must have recognized me as a reporter for the division newspaper, for he yelled out, "Hey, Stoup, you doing another story on us for the brigade newspaper?" I must have met him on a previous trip to the field, I figured. "Not really," I responded.

"I'm just out here accompanying General Zink on his operations visits."

"You're doing what?" he said, with a surprised look on his face. "What are you...his new personal ass-kissing assistant?"

"I'm too short for that," I responded. "I've only got four days and a wake-up until I'm out of here. When you get back to Bien Hoa, ask the guys in admin why I'm traveling with the general. I think you'll find the reason pretty interesting. But I really can't get into it right now...You might not believe me anyway," I told him.

I then had a warm soft drink with the guys and listened to them complain about all the bullshit they were going through while I waited for the brass to finish their briefing. About fifteen minutes later they emerged, at which point General Zink started mingling with the troops. Their lack of enthusiasm for his presence was readily apparent, but the general ignored the obvious and continued glad-handing his soldiers as he walked toward the waiting jeep. As we made our way to the landing pad, I turned and flipped a peace sign to the guys, who just stood there and stared as we pulled away. I knew this would be my last visit to the field, and a strange feeling of sadness fell over me.

On the flight back to Bien Hoa something rather amazing happened. About mid-flight, General Zink turned and asked me, through the microphone in his helmet, if I wanted to co-pilot the chopper for a while. I just looked at him, not fully understanding what he meant and not knowing how to respond. "Come on up," he then motioned, as the pilot left his seat and moved to the back of the chopper. So I took off my helmet and moved to the pilot's seat. As I did so, the pilot helped me get situated, securing my seatbelt and helping me put on his helmet. At that point, through the headset, General Zink instructed me to hold onto the wheel—actually I guess you call it a throttle. And then, a minute or so later, he put control of the chopper into my hands. As soon as he relinquished control, I immediately felt the sensation of flying the Huey, with the ability to change direction or altitude with a simple movement of the hand. It was a trip! I looked over at the general, who was watching my every move with a big grin on his face. His facial expression said "now I got him where I want him" without having to say a word. I just played along by flashing him a great big smile back. But then I turned my attention back to the windshield and to the land called "the Nam" that filled its view. I knew this would be the last time I'd be gazing at this landscape for a long, long time—if ever again. And once more, a feeling of melancholy swept over me.

The general's jeep was waiting for us when we got back to Bien Hoa. His driver immediately whisked us off to HQ, getting us there in a matter of minutes. We all got out of the jeep and stood in front of the building. After a couple of seconds of awkward silence, General Zink asked me if I enjoyed the tour, to which I responded, "Very much, sir."

"Then I hope you'll act favorably to this command in your future actions, specialist," he continued, now back in his stern commander persona.

"You can count on it, sir," I replied. With that, he turned and headed into the building, with Major Coleman following close behind.

I practically ran back to the hootch, not wanting to wait even a minute more to fill the guys in on my day. I'll bet they wondered what the hell had happened to me, as I was gone for a very long time. I looked at my watch as I was running. It was 1600 hours. When I got there, Mike and Randy ran out to greet me, quickly informing me that a small crowd was gathered in the hootch to hear what had happened. They also told me not to worry, as there wasn't a lifer in sight. They had all gone off to some Hail and Farewell.

As I entered the hootch, the room broke out into cheers. Mike quickly motioned to the guys to pipe down, as I took my position center stage. I felt a little uneasy in the "conquering hero" role and didn't want to make any more of this than was necessary. But we had won the battle—if not the war—and I couldn't wait to tell the guys what had happened—in complete and utter detail—and I spent the next hour or so doing just that.

When I finished my story, there was jubilation in the air. The guys wanted to party, and since just about all the lifers were gone, and those who were on duty wouldn't dare fuck with us tonight—not after the kind of day we just had—we decided to do just that. Mike and Randy broke out a couple of cases of beer they had secured that afternoon and put on ice, and declared the evening to be my "Hail and Farewell." Before long, joints and bowls were also being passed around, and I suddenly realized that this would probably be my last party in the Nam and perhaps the sweetest, considering the day I just had and the fact that I was surrounded by all the best that Vietnam could offer.

3 days. May 9. The next morning, I woke up and almost instinctively grabbed a pen and crossed another day off my short-time calendar—three days and a wake-up. I thought to myself, am I short or what. But then a discomforting thought entered my mind. What if the lifers considered the Article 138 case unresolved? And there still was the issue as to whether or not we were going to mail copies to the twenty-four individuals listed in the document. What if they froze my orders until the case was closed and I missed my DEROS? What if I had to postpone the wedding? These were gloomy thoughts, indeed, but I decided that I wasn't going to let them get me down. I was confident that a successful closure had been brought to the case. And besides, I was too short to be gloomy. I had three days with nothing to do but pack my bags, deepen my tan, and say good-bye to my friends. And I intended to take full advantage of these moments and savor my final days in Vietnam.

I suppose this would be a good place to tell a few short-time jokes. Ever since arriving in the Nam, we were constantly bombarded with short-time jokes and sayings by soldiers who were, well, short. Army publications often included blurbs on short-time jokes and sayings, so here are a few:

- Shortness is when your change jingles instead of crumbles.
- Shortness is getting your last issue of a year's subscription to *Playboy*.

- Shortness is when you can take a bath in your helmet.
- Shortness is digging in at any noise louder than a cricket's chirp.
- Shortness is a ration card that looks like Swiss cheese.
- Shortness is when your letters arrive home after you do.
- Shortness is when your bed is a stake in a poker game and you don't care.
- Shortness is giving away a full tube of suntan lotion.
- Shortness is straining to find white space on your short-time calendar.
- Shortness is hesitating to start a long conversation because you may not be able to finish it.
- Shortness is telling a "two-digit midget" that if you had that long you'd shoot yourself.

It had pretty much become tradition in the Nam that when you got down to a few days, they pretty much let you do your own thing without being hassled. So there would be no morning formations for me again—perhaps ever. I spent the next morning sorting through the rest of my things and trying to decide whether to carry or ship my scrapbook. While I did this, I watched AFVN on the black-and-white television we had in the hootch. *The Price is Right* was on, followed by other mindless daytime shows. The only other channel we could get was the Vietnamese station that was broadcast out of Saigon. Every now and then I'd watch it just to get a feel for Vietnamese culture as they tried to depict it on this station. The Vietnamese really hadn't grasped the concept of television. It was very strange, and very amusing, to watch.

As 1200 hours approached, I finally got dressed so I could go over to the mess hall and join Mike and Randy for lunch. In addition to meeting the guys, I wanted to take advantage of the "new and improved" chow that we were finally being served. When I got there, they were waiting for me outside the entrance. As we walked through the chow line, Mike asked me if there was anything new with the case. "Nothing that I've heard," I told him. "This morning was deadly quiet."

"Did you get your orders?" Randy then asked.

"Not yet," I replied, "but I'm going to company HQ right after lunch to see if they've been cut."

With all the excitement surrounding the Article 138 case, I hadn't been focusing on what my destiny might be after departing Nam. Since I had that extra year attached to my service time because of the OCS debacle, I still had about fifteen months of active duty after my Vietnam tour ended. I was hoping to get assigned to Germany for the opportunity to live and travel in Europe. Outside of stateside duty, which was still the most likely, Germany and Korea were the two big reassignment destinations. But then again, stateside duty at Fort Ord (near San Francisco) or Fort Devon (near Boston) wouldn't be bad either. The way I figured it, with my Information Specialist MOS, the remainder of my army life would probably be fairly easy, regardless of where I ended up. But with my luck, I could end up at some lifer hell-hole, like Fort Benning, Georgia, or Fort Polk, Louisiana.

As we sat having lunch, Mike asked me the inevitable question: "So are we going to mail the copies?" He and Randy stared at me intently as they waited for my answer, as if I was about to deliver some great edict. But actually, I think it was more of a rhetorical question, so I replied in kind by saying, "Did you say…when are we going to mail the copies?" My response was met with smiles all around. "Of course we're going to mail the copies," I continued. "A ride in General Zink's chopper didn't make it all better. I want to nail those two lifer bastards and the only way to do it is to turn up the heat." Mike said he had anticipated this and had made enough copies for the mailing. He also had a plan as to how to do it, since he didn't trust sending them through the brigade's mailroom. He was going to Long Binh this afternoon on company business and would mail them from there on his way back. With the last step in the plan now in place, the two of them went back to work, and I decided to catch a little sun before going up to HQ to see if my orders had been cut.

After spending an hour or so working on my tan, I decided I couldn't wait any longer to find out what was in the cards for my future. So I got dressed and made my way to D5 headquarters to see

Lieutenant Greenly. I hadn't seen him since my day with General Zink and his staff and was hoping to get the opportunity to tell him what had come down…from my perspective. When I got there, I found that he was alone—meaning, Captain Stein wasn't around. So I got to spend about thirty minutes filling him in on the details. I could tell by his questions and facial expressions that he was enjoying what he heard. It was also pretty obvious that there was no love lost between him and the captain.

When I was finished, I finally asked him if my orders were in, and he said that they were. "In fact, they've been here for two days," he told me, expressing surprise that I hadn't come for them before now. "But then again, specialist, I know that you've been busy," he added rather coyly. With that he went to a file cabinet and retrieved my personnel file. He then pulled out a copy of my orders and handed them to me. My heart pounded as my eyes scanned the document until they came to the assignment section toward the bottom of the page. It wasn't like waiting for my orders at Fort Benning to see if I was going to Vietnam, mind you. But it was still intense. My curiosity quickly came to an end as I read the words "Assignment: Fort Jackson, South Carolina."

2 days. May 10. My next to the last day in the Nam was relatively uneventful—almost serene. After sleeping in and grabbing an early lunch, I continued working on my tan while listening to the incredible British and American rock & roll music of the late '60s and early '70s that had become the soundtrack of my Nam experience. To get into the right frame of mind, I pulled out the last of the prerolled Cambodian Red joints that I had saved for my final days and indulged. All it took was a hit or two of that stuff to elevate my mood and senses. As I lay there, in the mesmerizing sun, absorbing its power one last time, I reminisced about all that had transpired during the past year. As I did so, all of my senses seemed to converge in a powerful, total mind-body experience. It probably was a combination of the pot, the sun, and my mind racing to sort through the whole adventure. But all of a sudden, the totality of the Nam experience hit me like a ton of bricks. The sound of choppers flying overhead became eerie and deafening. The familiar sound of a jeep driving by seemed to harmonize with the sound of the music. The smells of Vietnamese food being cooked by the hootch maids sent me back to the beginning. And for a moment, in my mind's eye, I actually could smell the odor of kerosene and burning shit that first hit my senses when I stepped off the plane and into the Vietnamese atmosphere for the first time on May 13, 1970. Lifers shouting orders to the troops…Jimi Hendrix pounding out *The Star Spangled Banner*…It all seemed to converge in a powerful sensory finale to this bizarre experience called "the Nam" that was, for me, rapidly coming to an end.

That night I didn't leave the hootch. I was still numb from my afternoon reverie…but rejuvenated by my comrades as they came to say their final farewells. So I spent the evening drinking, rapping, listening to music, and getting high with the guys I had gotten to know in Bien Hoa. One by one, and in small groups, they all stopped by to wish me well. I was filled with emotion, but too overwhelmed to cry, although I often found myself wiping tears from my eyes with the sleeve of my T-shirt. As one of the medics who came by shook my hand, he slipped a little plastic bag into my hands. He then covered my hands with his and whispered, "This is for the trip home. It's a long ride over the Pacific, and these will come in handy."

With that he and his buddies patted me on the back and left. The bag contained six Valium tablets.

1 day. May 11. My last full day in the Nam was much like the day before, only now I was down to an ominous "and a wake-up." After sleeping in, my big task of the day was going to company and brigade headquarters to fill out paperwork and go through the required de-briefing and de-processing in order to DEROS on time. Among the tasks, they had to verify that my shot record was up-to-date, as well as my 201 personnel file. Then there was the records review and pick-up station, the medical records station, the awards and decorations station, a personnel actions and management station, the I.D. card and tags station; and a postal locator station. If a soldier had a problem in any of these areas, I was told, they usually could be resolved in one day. I sure as hell hoped so.

The hardest part of the day, as it turned out, was that last night in the hootch with Mike, Randy, and the guys. We had grown really close in the two short months that I had been in Bien Hoa and had gone through a lot together. I felt especially close to Mike, as we were peers, and had become soul mates. Even though I couldn't wait to get the hell out of the Nam and back to the world, I was really going to miss these guys. So as I packed my duffle bag for the last time, we enjoyed one last evening of camaraderie and one last evening of sharing the Vietnamese herb that was as much a part of the Vietnam experience as USO shows and monsoon rains.

CHAPTER 16

DEROS and Back to the World

I woke up before anyone in the hootch on *Wednesday, May 12, 1971,* and with a feeling of both elation and melancholy, crossed the last day off my short-time calendar. Then I carefully removed it from its place on the wall next to my bunk and put it into my scrapbook, which was lying on top of my packed duffle bag. It was with great trepidation that I had decided to carry it with me, rather than ship it. The last day, and the longest day, of my Vietnam tour was about to begin.

I was too excited to eat, so I skipped breakfast and went right to the showers. By the time I got back, Mike and Randy were up. Randy had secured a jeep from the AG's office, and he and Mike were going to drive me to the air base. It wouldn't be much of a drive, though, as I was departing from Bien Hoa, rather than Ton Son Nhut, where I arrived exactly one year ago tomorrow. The plane was scheduled to depart at 1100 hours, but my orders indicated that I was to report to the terminal two hours prior to departure. But since I was so close, and didn't want to "hurry up and wait" at the terminal longer than necessary, I planned to fudge that by at least thirty minutes. I mean, what were they going to do if I was late…send me to Vietnam?

Mike and Randy sat on my bunk staring at me as I placed my shaving gear and a few final items into my duffle bag. "Come on, guys…cheer up," I told them. "I mean, you'll be out of here in a few weeks yourself."

"Yea," Randy responded, "but the place just won't be the same without you."

"Yea," Mike added, "there'll be no one to stir up dirt and kick it in the lifer's faces." We all laughed. And with that, I was packed and ready to go.

As I walked out of the hootch and looked around at the company area for the last time, tears came to my eyes. It wasn't because I was sad to leave this place, mind you. It was more like all the emotions of an entire year—fear, exhilaration, sadness, and happiness—had converged in my mind at the same time. I didn't want the tears to start flowing—not now, and not in front on Mike and Randy. So I turned and started walking toward the jeep, avoiding eye contact with my two buddies.

Silence prevailed on the short drive to the other side of the base. As we pulled up to the gate of the ar base, I showed my travel orders and we were waved through. The terminal building was in plain view ahead of us. Behind it, on the massive system of runways, lined with all types of OD colored aircraft, was one large airplane that stood out from the rest. It was a shiny, white United Airlines Boeing 707—a "freedom bird" that was about to provide me with transportation out of the Nam and back to the world.

Randy pulled up in front of the terminal and shut off the engine. For a minute, the three of us just sat there, without saying a word or looking at each other. Mike broke the silence by saying, "If you want a window seat, you'd better get in there and check in."

"I don't plan to do much looking out the window," I replied. Randy then grabbed my duffle bag, and they walked me into the terminal. Once inside, it was back to military bullshit—lines, paperwork, and inspections. So it was time to say good-bye for the last time to two of the nicest guys that I had met in the Nam. We gave each other the handshake of brotherhood and then broke into real hugs. I promised I would keep in touch and asked them to do the same. "And remember…I want all the details on the aftermath of Article 138," I reminded them. Then I wished them good luck as I started walking backward toward the check-in area. "And don't take any shit from the lifers," I yelled to them. As they turned to leave, they both flipped me the peace sign. And then they walked out of my life forever.

BEHIND THE WIRE

When I got to the first processing station, I showed my orders and asked about the flight's itinerary. I was told we were headed to Osaka, Japan, where we would refuel. From there it was non-stop over the Arctic Circle to Travis Air Force Base in Oakland, California. They then stamped my orders and gave me my boarding pass, and I moved on to the next station. This is when I started getting tense. They were going through everyone's bags, looking for weapons and any kind of contraband. Of course, I wasn't carrying any weapons or ammunition, not being into that kind of war souvenir. I did, though, ship back a long, curved knife pounded out of metal that was so crude that it was already covered with rust spots. I obtained it from the Montagnard when I visited their village. It came in a hand-carved wooden sheath, and I considered it more of an artifact than a weapon. But a lot of guys did ship back (or smuggle) weapons and ammunition, especially AK-47s that they either took right from the enemy (killed or captured) or from uncovered weapons caches. The lifers were into acquiring weapons as war souvenirs a lot more than the average soldier, with the AK-47 being the real Nam war trophy. In the early years of the war, some of these war trophies, like AK-47s, could actually be shipped home legitimately. But they eventually cracked down on this practice when it got out of control, and thus the art of smuggling these weapons out of country began. Some guys actually disassembled their M-16s or 45-caliber hand guns and shipped them home in pieces, reassembling them when they returned.

But no, getting caught with a souvenir weapon wasn't what I was worried about. If they caught you with a weapon, they merely confiscated it and let you move on without further question. My worry was my scrapbook, which contained, in my estimation, the quintessential souvenir of Vietnam and, to a lesser extent, the Valium tablets I had in a plastic bag in my pocket. If they found the Valium, I'd merely say it was prescribed to me by the company doc and let them take it from me without an argument if it came to that. But discovering the pot in my scrapbook, on the other hand, could get me into real trouble, not to mention losing all the mementos and pictures from my year in the Nam that were contained in the pages of that scrapbook.

I found the whole thing quite peculiar, if not unsettling. If you were caught with a weapon, they merely slapped your hand, if that, and let you move on. But if you were caught with a little pot for personal use, it could land you in the stockade. Something just didn't add up there. Yea, I knew I was doing something that wasn't permitted and was illegal. But if the lifers could ship back AK-47s and other weapons as souvenirs of the war (not to mention heroin in hollowed out stereo speakers), then why couldn't I bring back my version of a war souvenir? I mean, the pot that made it home with the GIs only got a few people a little high. The weapons, on the other hand, were occasionally used as instruments of crime—even murder.

As soon as I saw what they were doing with the baggage, I began to panic. I could feel my armpits starting to drip, although I did my best to not appear nervous. There was still time to ditch the scrapbook into one of the nearby trash receptacles, but even making that move in the crowded terminal seemed risky. So I decided to go for it and got into the personal effects inspection line. While waiting in line, with my paranoia increasing, I remembered hearing that they were starting to use pot-sniffing dogs as part of the crackdown on drugs. My head started turning from side to side, with my eyes searching to see if there were any dogs in the terminal. There were none in sight.

Finally, it was my turn to approach one of the three tables that were set up to inspect baggage. The inspector had me open my duffle bag and empty its contents onto the table. I did so in a modified dumping fashion, so my scrapbook, which was on top, would be at the bottom of the pile, with all my clothes on top of it. I also had a poncho liner in my bag, which technically was classified as military property, and should have been turned in before leaving my unit. I quickly decided to make an issue out of trying to depart with the poncho liner, hoping it would distract him from looking too closely at my scrapbook. I told him how much I loved the thing and how it had been my only constant companion during my year in the Nam (kind of like my "blanky," which I didn't say to him, by the way). The tactic apparently worked, as he half laughed at my "confession" and told me to keep the thing. "A lot of guys try to leave here with a lot worse," he told me, as he stuffed my clothing and personal effects back into my duffle bag. The last item he put in was my scrapbook, not even bothering to open it. With a great (internal) sigh of relief, I closed the bag, thanked him, and moved on to the last station.

The only thing I had to do at the last station was fill out one last form, have my orders reviewed one last time, and get my bag tagged. They then put my bag onto a cart to be loaded onto the aircraft and that was it. By this time, my hands were shaking from the experience. I'm the kind of person who always imagines the worst. And in this case, the worst was having my travel orders frozen and getting busted for drugs. It suddenly hit me that trying to smuggle pot out of the country was a really stupid idea, especially when I had come this far without incident—a whole fucking year in the Nam to be exact—and considering what was at stake if I didn't make it home on time. But I had made it through and decided to put the experience behind me and try to relax. It was time to focus on the fact that I was getting the hell out of the Nam and to try to enjoy the long journey home that I had ahead of me.

I had no sooner bought a cold Pepsi and found a place to sit than an announcement came over the PA system informing us that MAC Flight #342 would be boarding in ten minutes. As I sat there, I looked around the terminal…at the faces of the hundreds of GIs who would be my traveling companions. They were hanging around in small groups, or like me, were off by themselves. The noise level was that of a low murmur, as opposed to the sounds of laughter and shouts of excitement that one might expect to be filling the air. There was also a sense of tension…of anticipation…in the air that was so thick you could almost cut it with a knife. It was as if we were all thinking to ourselves, "We're so damn close to getting out of here that we can't jinx it by getting too excited and starting to celebrate."

As soon as the boarding announcement was made, a group of lifers came scurrying out of the woodwork to herd us toward the doors leading to the tarmac. Once outside, we were divided into two lines, and then we proceeded in single file toward the aircraft, which was being boarded from both ends. And there it was, in front of me, my freedom bird. It was a beautiful sight. I had waited one long year for this moment…and it had finally arrived.

Except for a few lifers in summer khakis, we were all wearing faded and well-worn jungle fatigues, presumably for the last time (there were no turtles among this group of seasoned vets). As we walked toward the aircraft, the heat of the day struck me, as if for the first time. But like a now-familiar friend, I instinctively turned my face up toward the sun, absorbing its power one last time. As I did this, an adrenaline rush came over me, and my senses came alive. As I started to ascend the stairway I paused, closed my eyes, and flashed back to the first sensation I had when I stepped into the Vietnam atmosphere for the first time—almost a year ago to the minute—recalling the blast of heat and the pungent smells that first greeted me. My reverie was broken by the guy behind me on the steps, nudging me forward.

It didn't take long to fill the aircraft, as we took seats in boarding order, from front to back and back to front. I had a center seat for the first leg of the journey, which didn't bother me in the least. Any seat on a plane leaving the Nam suited me just fine. I said a quick hello to the guys on either side of me, but other than that, we all just sat there and didn't say a word. In fact, the plane was so quiet that it was almost eerie. And it was hot. Sweat beads started to form on our foreheads as we waited in nervous anticipation for the engines to start. In true army "hurry up and wait" fashion, they had rushed us on board before our baggage was fully loaded and ready to go. And, of course, it was taking them three times as long to load our gear than it took to load us. We did, however, have the pleasant distraction of the five stewardesses, who on this flight were a lot younger and more attractive than those on the flight over.

Finally, after about twenty agonizing minutes, we were loaded. The doors were closed, the stairways rolled back, and the engines started to crank. After a minute or so, they mercifully turned on the air, which blew across our faces with a freshness that smelled like civilization. As we taxied to the end of the runway, you could feel the tension in the air. The silence continued to be deafening. The flight attendants were doing their safety thing, but no one was paying attention. We were all either looking out the window or staring straight ahead, each of us dealing with saying good-bye to the Nam in our own way. And then, suddenly, with a force that was as powerful as the experience we had just been through, our freedom bird roared down the runway and tilted up toward the Vietnam sun.

As soon as the wheels lifted off the ground, all hell broke loose. There were cheers, screams, and whistles, as well as thunderous applause, as each and every guy on that plane let out his own cry of relief. A year's worth of anticipation, frustration, and for many, agony and grief, had come to an end. Now it was time to sort it all out…to reflect on the bizarre experiences that each of us had been through. And then, just as quickly as the outburst of emotion had started, it ended, and the plane fell back into an unnatural silence. It remained that way for most of the flight back to the world.

They served us lunch on the three-hour flight to Japan, but otherwise, the trip was uneventful. I shut my eyes a few times, but I didn't really sleep. I couldn't. My adrenalin was still pumping, and my mind was racing in an unconscious effort to put the past year behind me and prepare me for the days ahead. At one point, I got up to go to the head. As I walked toward the rear of the aircraft, I looked at the faces of the GIs who had just spent a year in the Nam. Some were sleeping peacefully; others were staring straight ahead. Some guys were sweating profusely—and shaking. When I got back to my seat, I noticed that one of the guys in the aisle across from me was really suffering. These were the guys who had become addicted to heroin during their tour—soldiers who were trying to shake the habit before returning home. I had spent some evenings back in Bien Hoa with guys like this, watching them suffer through an excruciating withdrawal. Some of them would make it, but many of them would not. Many of them would end up on the street, doing whatever it took to feed their habits. It was certainly one of the uglier legacies of the war, and I wished them luck.

We had a ninety-minute layover in Osaka, just enough time to browse in the gift shops and grab a bite to eat. I would have loved to have seen some of Japan, but a ninety-minute layover at the airport wouldn't allow it. It was going to be one of these situations in the future where, if someone asked if you've ever been to Japan, you would respond, "Yes…well…no, not really. But I spent some time in Tokyo at the airport on my way back from the Nam."

Since we didn't have assigned seats, when it was time to reboard the aircraft, we got in line and did the loading from the front to the back thing. But this time I got a window seat, which would make the ten-hour flight to California a lot more bearable. And again, you could almost feel the tension in the air as we took off. But this time, there were no cheers of joy, no applause, and no whistles…just a plane filled with silent anticipation of making it home.

Not long after take-off, they fed us dinner. At the end of the meal, before they cleared my tray, I reached into my trouser pocket and pulled out the plastic bag containing the Valium tablets. There were six of them, and I took four. I was going to offer the other two to the guy sitting next to me, but he was already sleeping, so I shoved them back into my pocket. Then I remember looking out the window at the vastness of the Pacific Ocean and watching the sun starting to set. But that's all that I remember about the flight to Travis Air Force Base.

I was awakened by the guy sitting next to me, who gently shook my shoulder to bring me back to consciousness. He did so as the pilot was announcing our descent and arrival back to the United States of America. I looked at my watch and realized that I had been asleep for almost nine hours. I also realized that it was still May 12, 1971, (as we had crossed the international dateline and gained a day) a year to the day that I had left the United States. My year in the Nam had officially come to an end.

As the California coastline came into sight, the passengers again erupted into cheers. Only this time, the chatter and levity continued until long after we landed, as if we were returning from a month-long vacation in Hawaii. As the plane touched the ground, the reaction was deafening. Fists flew into the air, and tears of joy streamed down the faces of even the most hardened of combat veterans. Hugs and handshakes of brotherhood abounded. Truly, it was one of the most emotional moments of my life, and one that I will never forget.

We were greeted by a contingent of army personnel in stateside uniforms and five OD buses that would carry us to the processing station at the other end of Travis Air Force Base. Once inside, it appeared that it was back to life in the stateside military, as we were directed to stand in various lines in order to be "in-country" processed. Only this time, there was no screaming and verbal abuse. Instead, we were treated with kindness and respect, as if they actually appreciated what we had just been through.

This time, there was no paperwork to fill out. They merely verified our orders and issued us airline tickets to our final destination. And then, those of us who weren't ETS status were sent to an adjoining building to be fitted with stateside uniforms. We were given one pair each of black shoes and boots, one dress green uniform, two pairs of summer khakis, and the miscellaneous accessories that went with the uniforms. They let us keep our jungle fatigues and combat boots, but we were required to wear dress greens when leaving the base. And that's all there was to in-country processing. So with a duffle bag in each hand—one filled with Vietnam stuff, the other with newly acquired stateside uniforms—I headed for the base reception area, where I was to meet cousins from Sacramento who I had arranged to come and pick me up.

Since I had never been to California, they drove me to San Francisco so I could see the city and then I went to their home in Sacramento to spend the night. The next morning, they put me on a flight to Los Angeles, where I had been ticketed by the army for my return to Philadelphia. I had cousins there as well and got a blitz tour of LA and Hollywood before spending my last night before going home. That night, I had a very intense and vivid dream about my year in the Nam. Only, as dreams have a way of doing, the experience was even more bizarre than it actually had been—if that was even possible—even in a dream. It concluded with my orders being cancelled, and my being thrown into the stockade, with every nasty lifer I'd met in the Nam peering in at me. As the dream ended, I sat up in bed with a bolt. Sun was pouring in the window, and the room was hot and still. I noticed that the sheets were drenched, and that sweat was pouring down my forehead. I guess I had just been through my first flashback (or nightmare) of my year in the Nam.

My cousins dropped me off at LAX later that morning, about an hour before my plane was due to depart. I thanked them for the quickie tour and made my way into the terminal. I was feeling pretty good, thinking about Paula, who was waiting for me on the other side of the country. But then, as I started walking through the terminal, I began to notice that people were staring at me. At first, I thought it was just my imagination or post-traumatic stress or culture shock or jet lag or perhaps just coincidence. But when it continued, I started to become paranoid. I couldn't figure out why people were looking at me. And then it hit me. It suddenly dawned on me how unpopular the war was, especially in urban areas of the states, and how dominant the anti-war movement had become. I started feeling guilt by association, becoming very aware that I was wearing an army uniform that was lined with Vietnam service ribbons, not to mention a big "1st Cav" patch on my shoulder, and that I was a soldier and a Vietnam veteran who wasn't thought of very highly by my fellow countrymen. I wanted to shout out, "But I'm not one of them." But then it hit me…I was.

Instead of being welcomed back with open arms, with brass bands and banners, I was being stared at. I started feeling guilty about what I had done, or participated in, even though I really hadn't done anything other than serving my country. But people apparently didn't understand that…or care.

People weren't coming up to me, saying, "Welcome back," or "Thank you for your service." No, I was either being ignored or looked at with distain. It was a very strange and discomforting feeling. All I wanted to do was get home…and get out of this uniform.

Epilogue

Paula and I were married on May 29, 1971. After a week-long honeymoon, and nearing the end of my thirty-day leave after returning from Vietnam, we packed a U-Haul trailer with our few belongings, pulled it behind her 1965 navy blue Pontiac Lemans convertible, and headed to Columbia, South Carolina, home to the army's Fort Jackson Training Base.

The day we arrived, we found a nice apartment complex just outside one of the side entrances to the base (since I was an E-5 and married, I didn't have to live in military housing on the reservation). It was a little nicer and a little more expensive than most off-base apartment housing used by army personnel. But we didn't care. The way we figured it, we'd just rent furniture and play house until I got out of the army.

As it turned out, the apartment complex was occupied primarily by officers and high-ranking NCOs. When they discovered that a lowly enlisted man was living in their ranks, so to speak, they didn't like it one bit. We could tell by the looks we got, not to mention the cold shoulder. Paula said all the officers' wives ignored her at the pool. So I guess it was back to the caste structure of the military. But I was an E-5, even if lowly, and there was nothing they could do about it. And besides, we didn't give a shit. In fact, we kind of enjoyed flaunting our non-status status.

Two days after we arrived, on the date specified in my orders, I reported for duty. In short order, my paperwork was processed, and I was assigned to the post public information office. But before leaving the reception station, I was told to report to the post housing officer. He asked me if I needed assistance finding housing, and I said, "No, sir, I've already moved into the Lakeshore Apartments." When I said this, he just looked at me for a moment, then he said, "Can you afford that kind of housing on your pay, specialist? We normally refer officers and high-ranking NCOs to that unit."

"I wouldn't be there if I couldn't afford it, sir," I responded. "Is there a problem with that, sir?" I asked. He didn't respond, but just scribbled something as he looked down at my paperwork that was on his desk. So I saluted, did an about face, and left for the information office.

The PIO was in an older building in the middle of the headquarters and administrative section of the base. It was surrounded by large white pine trees—with pine needles and large pine cones strewn all over the ground—a very common feature of the South Carolina landscape. My boss was a civilian woman, Mrs. Lois Prince, an extremely nice lady who would make my assignment at Fort Jackson as pleasant as it possibly could be. She was a civil servant who reported to the base public information officer. She was also an experienced journalist who really knew her stuff and acted more like our den-mother than a boss—a very sweet person. Mrs. Prince started me as a reporter, but within three months, due to rotations and ETSs, I was named editor of the post newspaper, the *Fort Jackson Leader*.

I met a lot of nice guys—and a few characters—while working on the post newspaper. Most were remnants of the draft, so many of the guys I worked with were college educated. For example, one of the writers' (a polite and charming Georgia boy) father was a Georgia state trooper, so we occasionally got to share some of the moonshine that his dad had confiscated from raids on stills. Another writer was an educated hillbilly from West Virginia, who constantly entertained us with his accent and hilarious colloquialisms. But none of them had been to the Nam. So even though we had a lot of fun working together and became drinking (or even "smoking") buddies and occasionally also socialized with our wives or friends, it just wasn't the same as it was in the Nam. It was more like having normal at work relationships than sharing that special, intense camaraderie that existed in Vietnam. It's hard to explain...You had to be there to truly understand.

My life at Fort Jackson became routine pretty quickly, and it was a stark contrast to my all-encompassing life in the Nam. But it didn't take long to get used to and enjoy the differences. Of course, I still had to wear a uniform to work. But other than that, it was pretty much like having a civilian job. I reported to work at 0800 hours, got an hour off for lunch, and then drove home from work at 1700 hours. I mostly wrote feature stories and covered post events, like accompanying Senator Strom Thurmond on his annual Thanksgiving visit with the troops. I remember that one in particular, as he was a long-serving United States senator, and because he kept called me "sarge" as I followed him around the mess hall, listening to him babble at the troops as they tried to eat their army version of a Thanksgiving dinner.

About three weeks into my routine, Paula had something to give me when I returned home from work. It was a letter from the Nam...from Mike. I had been waiting for a letter from him, as I was dying to find out what happened with the Article 138 case after I left. I practically ripped the letter in half as I hurriedly pulled it out of the envelope. Paula just sat there watching me as I started reading the letter.

A big smile came over my face as I read out loud:

> We sure miss you around here. The place just hasn't been the same. But I thought you'd like to know the fallout from the Article 138 case. We didn't hear much of anything for a week or so after you left. The food did, however, continue to get better. And we even have a few toilets that actually flush...and "warm" water. But then, on May 29, word made it down from brigade HQ of the action General Zink had taken. LTC Wise received an official reprimand, and Captain Stein was relieved of his command. We got a new company commander the next day, a Captain Tom Plank, and he's actually a nice guy...

I couldn't believe the news…What a wedding present (it happened on May 29, my wedding day). General Zink had actually followed through. But then again, I guess we didn't give him much choice, since by law he had to file a report with the Secretary of the Army. I was elated and couldn't contain my excitement. From what I had told her of the case, she could see why I was happy, but she didn't fully understand why I was so excited. So I explained the meaning of the actions taken by General Zink. I told her that an official reprimand on LTC Wise's record was a serious black mark that could prevent him from getting a future promotion or high-ranking position. And as for Captain Stein, being relieved of his command, especially in a combat zone, essentially ruined any chances he had of advancing in the military. We had succeeded in getting back at those bastards, and I couldn't have been happier. I immediately wrote a letter back to the guys congratulating them and wishing them all well in their final days in the Nam (if the letter would even get to them before they left).

The only other follow-up I got regarding the Article 138 case was a letter from Congressman H. Edward Herbert, of Louisiana, the chairman of the House Armed Services Committee. I got a letter from him (that had been sent to my last Vietnam address and was forwarded to me in a package along with all the other mail that I received after I had left), acknowledging receipt of the copy of the Article 138 document. In true bureaucratic style, he said his committee would look into the matter and issue a report of its findings. I never heard back from him, or anyone else, on the matter.

It was now February of 1972, and Paula and I were enjoying a relatively mild South Carolina winter, especially by Pennsylvania standards. She had gotten a job at one of the local TV stations as a copywriter and was actually getting into her new career in television. I was fairly settled as well, enjoying the easy life of an information specialist at an army training base. But when I arrived at work one Monday morning early that month, I got some news that was about to change all of that.

Mrs. Prince called me into her office and said she had some good news for me and that she had mixed emotions about it. I wasn't expecting a promotion or an assignment transfer, so I couldn't figure out what it was. But when she finally told me, I actually wasn't surprised.

Even though the U.S. military continued to withdraw its troops from Vietnam at an accelerated pace, it still wasn't meeting the troop reduction numbers recently mandated by Congress. And it wasn't just a Vietnam War issue anymore, but also one of dollars and cents. The war had not only drained the life out of the country, it had drained the federal budget as well. So the Pentagon had to make deeper cuts in troop levels beyond those being withdrawn from Vietnam, and that's where I came in. Mrs. Prince informed me that she had just received word that I was getting a six-month early out. So instead of serving three years in the army, my sentence had been reduced to thirty months. I was elated.

I spent my last thirty days at Fort Jackson showing up for work, finishing my writing assignments, and applying for jobs with newspapers and magazines around the country, like the *New York Times, The Washington Post,* and *Newsweek*. I was lucky if I even got rejection letters. So at the end of March 1972, Paula and I packed up a U-Haul and made our way back to Lancaster, Pennsylvania. I accepted a job as a writer in the Advertising and Marketing Services Department of the Armstrong Cork Company (now Armstrong World Industries) and began my corporate career. Paula got a good position at a local university (she had taught high school English for two years before we got married).

By mid-1974, the last U.S. troops left Vietnam, and the Army of the Republic of South Vietnam took over total control of the war. And then, on April 30, 1975, North Vietnamese troops, who had been moving in on the city for weeks, stormed into Saigon. With little opposition, they made their way to the American embassy, which was madly evacuating the last of its personnel and whatever local staff they could cram onto the final helicopters out. And the rest is history.

The United States of America, along with its corrupt ally, the Republic of South Vietnam, had lost the war. There are some who still believe that our sacrifice in Vietnam was worth the effort…that we were part of an essential international effort that was needed to stop the spread of communism. They point to the fall of the Soviet Union and what happened in Eastern Europe as a testament to this. But the Socialist Republic of Vietnam remains in power to this day, ruling with a benevolent hand, I might add. They have a booming tourist industry, a booming manufacturing sector, and they've become a growing trading partner with the United States. And then there's China, another communist country that's a huge trading partner with the U.S. It appears having a relationship with a communist country, based on mutual interests, isn't so bad after all. The trumped up "Gulf of Tonkin Resolution," coupled with a lack of righteous cause and moral purpose that most Americans came to believe was missing from this war, fulfilled its own destiny. And in the aftermath, more than *58,000* American lives were lost, and countless others were wounded both physically and psychologically. In fact, the whole country suffered incalculable damage from the Vietnam War—damage that we are still recovering from to this day. And when you add to that the incredible loss of life and suffering that was inflicted on the Vietnamese people, reflecting on the experience becomes even more painful…and important.

The United States learned a very costly lesson in Vietnam. You would think that this country would have learned from that experience. But sadly, in recent years, it again entered a war illegally, using pretenses that were later determined to be lies. And again, it cost the country dearly in life, limb, and financial burden. And isn't it ironic that those who led us into the war in Iraq - President George W. Bush and Vice President Dick Cheney - were the same two characters that I mentioned at the beginning of this story…the same two who had dodged service in Vietnam.

I returned to Vietnam as a tourist in April of 2007 with my two best friends as part of a small tour group. We landed in Hanoi, and I couldn't believe that I was actually in the capital of the former North Vietnam—the mysterious and threatening north as I had envisioned it, so far away from where I had been stationed in the southern regions of the country. The now capital of the Socialist Republic of Vietnam was beautiful. We rode through the city in bicycle-driven rickshaws, watching people cook their meals on the street, with bustling commerce that was still primarily by foot, bicycle, or motor scooter. It reminded me of the Saigon I knew some thirty-seven years before. A tour guide took us by the lake in the center of the city where Senator John McCain's plane had been shot down, with a plaque on the shore commemorating the event. We rode past the "Hanoi Hilton" where our POWs were imprisoned.

We then traveled south, through the ancient imperial capital of Hue, and drove past China Beach, and through Da Nang, where fierce and deadly battles had taken place between North Vietnam, the 1st Cav and other U.S. units. We went to Cu Chi, which was now a sprawling community, unrecognizable from the days when it was nothing more than a large army base camp, with a charming village nearby of the same name. We toured the now famous Cu Chi Tunnels (one of Vietnam's largest tourist attractions), over which I lived for five months on the base camp of the 25th Infantry Division, never knowing at the time that the tunnels existed. I crawled down into one of the tunnel complexes and had my picture taken with a one-armed former member of the Viet Cong— about my age—who was a tour guide wearing his VC uniform. And who knows, we could have laid eyes on each other when I was with the medics on that MEDCAP mission in Cu Chi village on that June day in 1970.

We went to Ho Chi Minh City, which was now a bustling metropolis of 7.4 million people. Except for the Caravelle Hotel (where we stayed, and I once stayed during one of my many trips to Saigon during my tour of duty), the Catholic Cathedral, and the Opera House in the city's main square, as well as Tu Do Street, the city was almost unrecognizable. We also toured the incredible Mekong Delta region—the lifeblood of Southeast Asia. The final night of our incredible guided tour of Vietnam featured a gala dinner with Vietnamese dancers in traditional garb, a seven-course meal of Vietnamese delicacies, all with an ambiance and charm reminiscent of old Vietnam. And believe it or not, the dinner was held in the former home of U.S. Ambassador to Vietnam, Henry Cabot Lodge. It was fucking surreal.

There were few, if any, visible scars from the war as I traveled throughout the country, visiting sites like the artist community of Hoi An, and even staying overnight on a Chinese junk floating through the spectacular and haunting beauty of the International Heritage Site of Halong Bay. The lush beauty of the countryside of Vietnam has been restored. The Vietnamese people remain simple and unaffected, radiating their beauty and charm. They welcomed us with open arms and couldn't have been friendlier. Even after all that we did to them and their country, they hold no grudge, nor showed no animosity toward America. They have proven, through their quiet dignity, that all they ever wanted was to be left alone, to be independent and not aligned with any nation, and to be able to lead productive lives. All they ever wanted was to be able to live in peace and to raise their families and enjoy the fruits of their labors… just like the rest of us.

ADDENDUM

Al Gore in Vietnam

Shortly before leaving Bien Hoa for the world, Captain Aulen asked me if I had heard that the son of the United States senator from Tennessee, Al Gore, Sr., was also an army journalist, stationed with the 20th Engineer Brigade in Long Binh, working as a writer for *The Castle Courier*, the brigade's newspaper. I replied, "No, I hadn't heard."

Yes, Al Gore, Jr., U.S. senator from Tennessee, vice-president of the United States for two terms, almost president of the United States, successful businessman, film producer and environmental champion, did the exact same job that I did, at the base next to me, in the very same place in Vietnam. His road to becoming an army journalist, however, was a lot easier than mine. To this day, I wonder if I ever, unknowingly, ran into him at one place or another in Long Binh, like at a USO show at the base EM Club.

A little background on Al Gore's military service, from Wikipedia:

> When Al Gore graduated in 1969, his student deferment ended and he immediately became eligible for the military draft. His father, a vocal anti-Vietnam War critic, was facing a reelection in 1970. Gore eventually decided that the best way he could contribute to the anti-war effort was to enlist in the Army, which would improve his father's reelection prospects. Although nearly all of his Harvard classmates avoided the draft and

service in Vietnam, Gore believed if he found a way around military service (like Bush, Cheney and Rumsfeld), he would be handing an issue to his father's Republican opponent. According to Gore's Senate biography, he appeared in uniform in his father's campaign commercials, one of which ended with his father advising: "Son, always love your country." Despite this, Al Senior lost the election.

Gore has said that his other reason for enlisting was that he did not want someone with fewer options than he to go in his place. Actor Tommy Lee Jones, a former college housemate, recalled Gore saying that "if he found a fancy way of not going, someone else would have to go in his place." His Harvard advisor, Richard Neustadt, also stated that Gore decided "that he would have to go as an enlisted man because, he said, 'In Tennessee, that's what most people have to do.'" In addition, Michael Roche, Gore's editor for *The Castle Courier*, stated that "anybody who knew Al Gore in Vietnam knows he could have sat on his butt and he didn't."

After enlisting in August 1969, Gore returned to the anti-war Harvard campus in his military uniform to say goodbye to his adviser and was "jeered" at by students. He later said he was astonished by the "emotional field of negativity and disapproval and piercing glances that… certainly felt like real hatred."

Gore did his basic training at Fort Dix from August to October of 1969 [I did my basic there from September through November of that year, another "at the same place at the same time" coincidence], after which he was assigned to be a journalist at Fort Rucker, Alabama. In April 1970, he was "Soldier of the Month."

His orders to be sent to Vietnam were held up for some time, and he suspected that this was due to a fear by the Nixon administration that if something happened to him his father would gain sympathy votes. He was finally shipped to Vietnam on January 2, 1971, after his father had lost his seat in the Senate during the 1970 Senate election, becoming one of only about a dozen of the 1,115 Harvard graduates in the Class of '69 who went to Vietnam. Gore was stationed with the Twentieth Engineer Brigade in Bien Hoa and was a journalist with The Castle Courier. He received an honorable discharge from the Army in May 1971.

Of his time in the Army, Gore later stated, "I didn't do the most, or run the gravest danger. But I was proud to wear my country's uniform." He also later stated that his experience in Vietnam "didn't change my conclusions about the war being a terrible mistake, but it struck me that opponents to the war, including myself, really did not take into account the fact that there were an awful lot of South Vietnamese who desperately wanted to hang on to what they called freedom. Coming face to face with those sentiments expressed by people who did the laundry and ran the restaurants and worked in the fields was something I was naively unprepared for."

Gore was "dispirited" after his return from Vietnam. The Nashville Post noted that, "his father's defeat made service in a conflict he deeply opposed even more abhorrent to Gore. His experiences in the war zone don't seem to have been deeply traumatic in themselves; although the engineers were sometimes fired upon, Gore has said he didn't see full-scale combat. Still, he felt that his participation in the war was wrong."

About the Author

Jim Stoup has wanted to tell his amazing Vietnam story ever since returning from his tour of duty in 1971, and even though "life got in the way," as he puts it, he was always planning and writing the project in his head. In 1994, he finally completed a first draft of the book, but the demands of his career and a lack of interest in Vietnam stories at the time prompted him to shelve the project. Some twenty years later, he decided the time was right and did a complete re-write. The result is his non-fiction novel, *Behind the Wire*.

After his military service as an Army journalist ended in 1972, Jim pursued a career in corporate and marketing communications, eventually transitioning into writing and producing video and film presentations, and corporate events production management. In the latter phase of his career, he circled the globe as a consultant to some of the world's largest multi-national corporations. Now retired, he is currently working on his second non-fiction novel, traveling when he can for adventure and to visit family, friends, and his two granddaughters, and enjoying life in south Florida with his partner.

CPSIA information can be obtained at www.ICGtesting.com
Printed in the USA
BVOW11s0920211115

428024BV00008B/77/P